The
Eisenhower
Administration
and
Black
Civil Rights

Twentieth-Century America Series

The Eisenhower Administration and Black Civil Rights

Robert Fredrick Burk

THE UNIVERSITY OF TENNESSEE PRESS/KNOXVILLE

ᔰ Twentieth-Century America Series

DEWEY W. GRANTHAM, GENERAL EDITOR

Frontispiece:
National Park Service/Dwight D. Eisenhower Library
Eisenhower's only White House meeting with black civil rights
leaders during his administration, June 23, 1958. *From left to right:*
Lester Granger, Martin Luther King, Jr., E. Frederic Morrow, President Eisenhower, A. Philip Randolph, Attorney General William
Rogers, White House aide Rocco Siciliano, and Roy Wilkins.

Library of Congress Cataloging in Publication Data

Burk, Robert Frederick, 1955-
    The Eisenhower administration and Black civil rights.

    (Twentieth-century America series)
    Bibliography: p.
    Includes index.
    1. Afro-Americans—Civil rights. 2. United States—
Politics and government—1953-1961. 3. Eisenhower,
Dwight D. (Dwight David), 1890-1969. I. Title.
II. Series.
E185.61.B955   1984   353.0081'496073   84-2312
ISBN 0-87049-431-7 (cloth)
ISBN 0-87049-493-7 (paper)

Preface

The late 1970s and the early 1980s have witnessed a new phenomenon in the historiography of postwar American politics—the flowering of "Eisenhower revisionism." Upon reexamining the record of the Eisenhower administration, a variety of scholars have concluded that neither the period nor the White House occupant merited the scorn heaped upon them during the previous fifteen years. The image of Dwight D. Eisenhower as a fumbling, albeit well-intentioned, political novice has been challenged by one of a calculating, manipulative executive with a clear guiding vision of the nation's future. The 1950s likewise have been found to be a more agreeable decade than imagined earlier, with the revised portrait aided by its comparison with the political and military traumas of the 1960s and early 1970s.

Much of the contemporary enthusiasm for the Eisenhower years stems from an understandable desire to duplicate the relative peace and prosperity of that decade. This nostalgia for the 1950s also has contributed to a growing association by scholars of the "success" of the decade with Eisenhower's less public, "hidden-hand" leadership style in the White House. Given the foreign policy nightmare of the Vietnam War and the power-hungry machinations of Watergate, disillusionment with activist, power-seeking presidents is an understandable reaction. Yet much of the recent writing on presidential power and postwar American politics has tended only to condemn the excesses of activist presidential leadership, without considering at the same time the limitations of a narrowly defined conception of presidential power or asking whether an assertive presidency really requires unconstitutional actions in order to be effective.

Eisenhower revisionism has altered our perception of the basic intelligence of Dwight D. Eisenhower and his involvement in policy questions. For the most part, however, this scholarship has dwelt more upon the favorable effects of his restrained leadership, particularly in the realm of foreign policy, than upon the limitations of his leadership in important domestic policy areas. For this reason, an examination of the Eisenhower administration's response to the issues of black equality in the 1950s is particularly timely. The Eisenhower administration, presiding as it did over eight crucial early years of the Second Reconstruction, helped institutionalize an official definition of racial inequality, a pattern of federal response, and a public expectation of civil rights advance within a framework of political moderation and consensus that contributed both to the progress in civil rights in the 1960s and to the serious limitations and disillusionment that accompanied it. Whether one points to the enactment of voting-rights legislation, the disputation over racial integration, or the continuing deprivations of urban ghetto life, the Eisenhower presidency in important ways helped mold the contemporary racial agenda and the social realities that black Americans face today.

The Eisenhower Administration and Black Civil Rights is an account of the racial policies of the Eisenhower administration and an effort to explain why particular approaches were adopted by the executive branch in the 1950s and others were not. It does not pretend to exhaust the general subject of civil rights activism in the 1950s. It is neither a thorough treatment of the activities of civil rights organizations in the period nor an analysis of the internal dynamics of congressional or judicial consideration of racial issues. For these reasons, this book falls within a general category of works described by historian C. Vann Woodward in which Afro-Americans are more often the "object" that the "subject" of study. This should not be interpreted to mean that blacks themselves played an insignificant role in exerting pressure on federal officials to respond to racial issues. Rather, it is a personal plea for additional studies detailing the role and effectiveness of grass-roots black mobilization and civil rights lobbying activity in the 1950s.

In the course of my study I accumulated a great many obligations. The staffs of both the Dwight D. Eisenhower Library in Abilene, Kansas, and the State Historical Society of Wisconsin were models of professionalism and friendly assistance. To my graduate colleagues at the University of Wisconsin, my appreciation is great both for the rigorous criticism and for the camaraderie they have offered. Special thanks go to Bill Trollinger, whose infinite good sense has helped me more times than he knows. Professors Allan G. Bogue, Stanley Schultz, Leon Epstein, and Tom Shick of the University of Wisconsin, Dewey W. Grantham of Vanderbilt University, and Gary W. Reichard of the University of Delaware also deserve much appreciation for wading through the manuscript and offering cogent criticisms; if I have been too stubborn always to listen, it is not their fault. Mavis Bryant of the University of Tennessee Press proved an unwavering source of encouragement and help at various stages of the book's preparation. To my adviser and friend John M. Cooper I can only offer my deepest thanks for many kindnesses, not the least of which has been extending me the freedom to follow my own intellectual convictions without fear of reproach. Finally, to Patricia Geschwent, my gratitude and love for her patience and partnership in work and at home, without which all this would be unimportant.

Contents

Illustrations

Prologue

1.

Civil Rights
and Republican Resurgence

The difficulty of black Americans in securing the legal guarantees and the practical benefits of equal opportunity continues to call into grave doubt the depth of the nation's public commitment to democratic principles. When defining the current problems of racial inequality and formulating responses, Americans today instinctively employ the all-encompassing label inseparable from the field of race relations—civil rights. The term *civil rights* has assumed such an unquestioned place in the national political dialogue that its importance in defining the limits of official racial policies generally has been overlooked. Drawing upon the heritage of Reconstruction era protections of citizenship rights and voting contained in the Fourteenth and Fifteenth amendments, the modern civil rights movement has focused upon the role of legal and governmental barriers to equal opportunity as primary obstacles to racial equality. The postwar history of the "Second Reconstruction" still evokes for Americans vivid images of the struggle of blacks in the Jim Crow South to obtain the legal protections long taken for granted by white citizens. Central to the adoption of the civil rights perspec-

3

tive by national policy makers has been the assumption that an image of racial democracy projected through laws and official actions will function as a compelling moral example for private citizens to follow in their everyday lives.

In the four decades since World War II, the federal government has measured black progress by the steps it has taken to guarantee a set of legal standards of equal citizenship. This definition of racial advance has provided the sense of direction necessary for a number of achievements, including the extension of black voting rights throughout the nation and increased access to integrated public accommodations and educational opportunities. In addition, federal antidiscrimination policies have helped project a symbolic image of American racial democracy to observers both at home and abroad. However, fundamental problems largely have remained unaddressed despite the official attention given to legal protections of equal citizenship. Structural economic discrimination, the expansion of the white-collar suburban economy, inadequate supplies of affordable housing, and the perpetuating material and emotional miseries of the ghetto have left a substantial proportion of the black population without the access to material resources that enables the practical utilization of legal guarantees of equal opportunity.[1]

Because the civil rights perspective so dominates the contemporary public outlook on racial problems, we often forget that its reemergence is a relatively recent phenomenon. By the end of the nineteenth century, politicians of both major parties had emasculated Reconstruction statutes designed to protect the political rights of the black freedmen, and the promise of Negro legal equality had been forfeited in favor of Jim Crow caste systems and judicial retrenchment. At the beginning of the twentieth century, most prominent American politicians, including avowed progressives, were either indifferent to black difficulties or displayed open racism. Theodore Roosevelt received Booker T. Washington at the White House, but the Progressive party refused to seat Southern black delegates at its 1912 convention. Woodrow Wilson told "darky" stories to his cabinet and did nothing to restrict segregation in federal departments. Even in the midst of the Great Depression of the 1930s, Franklin D. Roosevelt generally ignored

1. For valuable insights on the symbolic value of American racial policies and their practical deficiencies, see Murray Edelman, *Politics as Symbolic Action* (Chicago, 1971), and *The Symbolic Uses of Politics* (Urbana, Ill., 1964); Thomas R. Dye, *The Politics of Equality* (Indianapolis, 1971); and Edwin Dorn, *Rules and Racial Equality* (New Haven, 1979).

racial discrimination, and the New Deal offered only limited economic and political patronage. Most politicians of both the Progressive era and the New Deal, except for small numbers who either viewed racial mistreatments as violations of civil liberties or saw Negroes as victims of a common class oppression, shared the general indifference to racism. Although New Deal officials occasionally ran into the reality of black material hardships in their implementation of relief policies, no major assault ensued on racial discrimination and segregation.[2]

The pattern of prewar indifference to black civil rights contrasted sharply with the passions displayed over racial issues in the decades after World War II. By the end of the 1940s, several states had enacted civil rights laws, hundreds of interracial committees had been formed, and the *New York Times Index* had given the topic "civil rights" a distinct listing for the first time. President Harry S Truman endorsed a civil rights program, began the integration of the armed forces, and reluctantly gambled his election prospects in 1948 on the inclusion of a strong civil rights platform plank. Under Dwight D. Eisenhower, the federal government would complete the Truman military desegregation program, begin the integration of public facilities in the District of Columbia and gain the passage of the first federal civil rights acts since Reconstruction. School desegregation suits, culminating in the *Brown* decision of 1954, brought renewed attention to the problem of officially sanctioned racial separation, and organizations and individuals dedicated to civil rights mounted increasingly successful challenges to the Jim Crow practices of the South. During the postwar years, white Americans acquired new perspectives on the nature, causes, and amelioration of racism that molded their reactions to specific racial issues. Spurred on by growing black legal and political activism, events provided the impetus for a gradual change in the publicly expressed racial values of national politicans and of official America.

The growing acknowledgment of the general principle of racial equality and the rise of postwar political interest in civil rights,

2. For a look at racial attitudes during the Pregressive Era and the New Deal, see Morton Sosna, "The South in the Saddle: Racial Policies during the Wilson Years," *Wisconsin Magazine of History* 54 (Autumn 1970): 30–49; Dewey W. Grantham, Jr., "The Progressive Movement and the Negro," *South Atlantic Quarterly* 54 (Oct. 1955): 461–77; Harvard Sitkoff, *A New Deal for Blacks* (New York, 1978); Raymond Wolters, *Negroes and the Great Depression* (Westport, Conn., 1970); and John B. Kirby, "The Roosevelt Administration and Blacks: An Ambivalent Legacy," in Barton J. Bernstein and Allen J. Matusow, eds., *Twentieth-Century America: Recent Interpretations* (New York, 1972), 265–88.

both important departures from the early twentieth century, occurred through a complex mixture of historical circumstances. The necessary conditions for renewed official interest in civil rights included the influences of America's confrontations with Nazi racism, Soviet expansionism, and Third World nationalism; the growth, mobility, and uncertain loyalties of the black electorate; the increasing power and assertiveness of black organizations and their spokesmen; the declining political interest in aggregate economic issues in a revived America; and the fear of racial violence. The postwar national response to these developments focused on white prejudice as the immediate problem rather than on the persistence of black material hardships, and it stressed the importance of government in shaping popular attitudes rather than the role of cultural stereotypes, social customs, residential patterns, or market discrimination. As official concern over national economic prosperity and its equitable distribution faded, white politicians dedicated to preserving America's democratic image rejected overt racism as acceptable national policy. At the same time, however, they converted racism into an attitudinal abstraction for which the proposed remedy, the removal of official sanctions for discrimination, did not offer by itself direct and immediate relief for many black citizens.[3]

In laying the basis for renewed national political interest in civil rights, intensified postwar partisan competition played an important background role. The modern phenomenon of a solid black Democratic vote has concealed the extent of wavering in black support for the Democrats in the 1940s and 1950s, a vacillation part of a general fluidity in voter loyalties that followed the decline of New Deal economic activism. New Deal domestic reform had slowed to a crawl even before the onset of World War II, and during the war the Depression agenda further faded from view. Aided by these developments, the Republican party steadily gained strength until its narrow presidential defeat in 1948, in itself a major political upset. The 1946 elections produced a Republican Congress which, though short-lived, contributed to the buttressing of conservative alliances between Republicans and Southern Democrats. The death of Franklin D. Roosevelt in 1945 left liberal Democrats in turn with a leadership vacuum, and their

3. For an excellent analysis of the ideological roots of the postwar concern with civil rights, see Peter J. Kellogg, "Civil Rights Consciousness in the 1940's," *The Historian* 42 (Nov. 1979): 18–41. See also his longer "American Liberals and Black America: A History of White Attitudes, 1936–1952" (Ph. D. diss., Northwestern Univ., 1971).

desperate search for a substitute led to attempts to recruit Dwight D. Eisenhower as a presidential candidate in 1948. Within the Republican party the Northeastern wing, more receptive than the party as a whole to minority interests, controlled the presidential nomination process throughout the 1940s and 1950s. A number of Northeastern Republican politicians, including presidential candidates Wendell Willkie and Thomas E. Dewey, senators Henry Cabot Lodge of Massachusetts and Irving Ives of New York, and congressmen Jacob Javits of New York and Hugh Scott of Pennsylvania, were public supporters of civil rights measures.[4]

The unsettled nature of postwar politics assumed greater significance in encouraging the rise of civil rights because it coincided with renewed wartime migrations of Negroes to the cities and with dramatic increases in the membership, public visibility, and aggressiveness of black organizations. Membership of the National Association for the Advancement of Colored People (NAACP), the leading black organizational arm in the field of legal equality, mushroomed from approximately 50,000 in 1940 to 350,000 in 1945. The growth of the NAACP, the National Urban League, and other black interest groups enabled leaders to push racial questions more regularly into the mainstream of official discussion and decisions. By utilizing their newfound resources of membership and money to press legal challenges to discrimination, they gained greater public exposure for the cause of racial justice and created a ground swell of minority political pressure and legal momentum that eventually reached into the White House.[5]

Besides adding to the membership rolls and the financial coffers of civil rights bodies, Negro migration to Northern cities also significantly boosted the total black vote, since systematic official denials of electoral rights were not practiced in the North. With a growing black electorate concentrating in urban centers of key electoral states, its political choices were increasingly important in close presidential contests and congressional races. Aware of the new importance of black voters, both parties attempted to expand their appeals to Afro-Americans without provoking serious white voter backlash. Although the Democrats maintained consistent majorities among black voters after 1936, their margins

4. See Alonzo L. Hamby, *Beyond the New Deal: Harry S. Truman and American Liberalism* (New York, 1973), ch. 10; Henry Lee Moon, *Balance of Power: The Negro Vote* (Garden City, N.Y., 1948).
5. Donald R. McCoy and Richard T. Ruetten, *Quest and Response: Minority Rights and the Truman Administration* (Lawrence, Kan., 1973), 6–12.

of victory dropped in the 1940s. The wavering of black loyalties partly reflected the growth of an Afro-American middle class, for black income grew 80 percent faster than white from 1937 to 1952 and the black median family income rose from a pre-World War II level of 41 percent to 57 percent of that of white families. In order to reverse New Deal losses, the Northeastern wing of the Republican party made renewed efforts to win back blacks. Republican gestures included the adoption of a stronger civil rights plank than the Democrats in 1944 and Governor Dewey's endorsement of New York's pioneering fair employment commission bill in 1945. Even in 1948, presidential candidate Dewey received the endorsements of most black newspaper publishers, although he failed to pull large numbers of Negro voters away from Truman. Close local and national elections encouraged the Democrats likewise to step up their own recruitment of minority voters, and as a result both parties actively competed for Northern black electoral loyalties.[6]

At the same time that black voters were increasing in importance, the impressive growth of the American economy was contributing both to class stratification in the black community and to the weakening of the New Deal coalition. The immediate postwar concern over the possibility of a new depression and the accompanying demand for the creation of sixty million jobs soon evaporated in the face of impressive advances in gross national product and living standards after 1945. A symbolic indication of the change in popular expectations of the national economy's growth capacity was the shift from the usage of standard prewar measures of economic health—the volume of employment and industrial productivity—to new indices of the *rate* of economic growth. The new measures reflected underlying expectations of economic growth and job-creating capacity that dramatically separated the postwar years from the pessimistic Depression era assumption that the national economy had reached its limits. With Americans demonstrating renewed confidence in an expanding economy, New Deal issues pertaining to the fairer distribution of scarcity diminished in importance.[7]

If the fear of national economic scarcity eased because of wartime and postwar economic growth, the fear of racial violence did not. Public commentators openly fretted over the possibility of

6. John P. Davis, ed., *The American Negro Reference Book* (Englewood Cliffs, N.J., 1966), 220, 232, 235, 259; McCoy and Ruetten, *Quest and Response* chap. 7.
7. Hamby, *Beyond the New Deal*, 3–28, 293–310.

racial violence and its potential for undermining Cold War domestic unity. Terrible incidents of violence, including brutal attacks against black servicemen and the three-day Detroit race riot of 1943, had occurred during World War II, adding to the historical pattern of postwar racial tensions represented by the "Red Summer" of 1919. Escalating black demands for equal treatment at home produced fears of a new wave of racial unrest. A host of problems associated with reconversion contributed to the sense of alarm. Housing and recreational facilities were crowded, and severe job competition was expected to follow demobilization. These fears prompted intensified activity, led by the American Council on Race Relations, to counter the dangers of violence. Hundreds of interracial committees were organized from coast to coast during the immediate postwar period, with the major objective of promoting community cooperation with police departments to avoid major racial confrontations. The additional appointment of state and local race relations officials prompted the creation of the National Association of Intergroup Relations Officials, and the federal government followed by setting up its own network of race relations observers.[8]

The new receptivity of politicians to the consideration of civil rights as a distinct policy area, however, was not an inevitable reaction. Partisan competition and the fears of violence by themselves might have led only to traditional, localized responses, such as the "carrots" of limited black patronage and token economic benefits or the "stick" of police crackdowns on minority protest. Immediately after the Detroit riot of 1943, a Justice Department study actually advocated such a combination of rigid racial controls, including a limitation on black city migration, and small concessions of additional minority housing and social services. The Detroit recommendations represented continuity with New Deal urban policy, which had extended patronage to minorities but had displayed only minimal interest in limiting segregation or in calming the fears of white ethnic neighborhoods. Even the organized opposition to racial violence of the American Council on Race Relations did not represent civil rights advocacy, for such programs were directed primarily at developing channels of communication and upgrading police work rather than lobbying for a civil rights program. In a departure from the traditional

8. Kellogg, "Civil Rights Consciousness," pp. 26–30; John M. Blum, *V Was For Victory: Politics and American Culture During World War II* (New York, 1976), 199–207.

pattern, however, politicians moved in the 1940s to address the new national field of civil rights. Liberals in both parties advocated measures virtually unheard of in the 1930s, and other politicians less sympathetic to a reform agenda still felt compelled to respond at least in a symbolic fashion to the call for racial equality.

As the most committed white liberals proclaimed it, the distinguishing feature of the newfound concern with racial issues was that it focused upon white racism, particularly that racism which relied upon government sanction and enforcement. Since American officials consistently heralded the democratic character of their nation as the leader of the "free world," the problem of white official bigotry at home ultimately became a test of the moral integrity of all America. The brutal official racism of Hitler's Germany, dramatized by the extermination camps, had contributed a massive jolt to long-standing national complacency toward the most blatant forms of American racial prejudice. After seeing the ultimate horrors of an "Aryan supremacy" doctrine, few could still openly defend the American version by claiming for it a benevolent intent. Racism now stood exposed as an indefensible evil, and its continued, even sanctioned, existence in vast areas of the United States placed the nation's claim to democratic credentials in serious doubt. The preoccupation of civil rights supporters and politicians with the moral image of the nation as reflected in its official actions led to the twin conclusions that civil rights policy must focus upon the reformation of white racial attitudes and that such a reformation could be achieved most painlessly through the removal of discriminatory sanctions and the projection of an official image of racial equality.[9]

Civil rights advocates drew intellectual legitimacy and sustenance for their efforts to cleanse racism from the statute books from the writings of a burgeoning number of sociologists and race relations scholars. The work of the racial scholar-activists, who included Gordon Allport, Jacques Barzun, John Dollard, E. Franklin Frazier, Claude McKay, Gunnar Myrdal, Carey McWilliams, Father John La Farge, Charles S. Johnson, and St. Clair Drake, found its way into textbooks and professional journals and frequently was reviewed in liberal political journals. Southern critics of racial caste systems, including Wilbur J. Cash, Howard Odum, T.J. Woofter, and Rupert B. Vance, added to the literature their own critiques of Jim Crow as an outdated system

9. For a more detailed description of the white liberal crisis of conscience over racism, see Kellogg, "Civil Rights Consciousness," 30–31.

based upon faulty psychological assumptions and as a contributor to the region's economic backwardness. Many of the writers on race relations directly contributed their scholarship to civil rights organizations, including the NAACP and the American Council on Race Relations. Sympathetic religious groups, labor unions, and civil liberties organizations also incorporated the scholarly findings into their own cooperative lobbying efforts in behalf of civil rights proposals.[10]

The most famous of the studies of American race relations that emerged in the 1940s was Gunnar Myrdal's *An American Dilemma,* published in 1944 under the aegis of the Carnegie Corporation. Myrdal and his assistants made no attempt to conceal the deprivations of blacks in the American South, but *An American Dilemma* clearly displayed its authors' gradualist optimism. Although Myrdal abandoned Marxist analyses of racial injustice as unduly fatalistic and deterministic, his study betrayed its own brand of determinism in championing the ameliorating power of governments and laws to eliminate racial injustice by an indirect process of "cumulative causation." In Myrdal's view, the "American Creed" of democratic values was not merely one of a set of competing or contradictory public belief systems but was the national ethos, the measure by which all Americans gauged the morality of their actions. Alternative conceptions of a society rooted in equilibrium, in which egalitarian progress was preached but discrimination practiced with psychic impunity, were rejected. *An American Dilemma* presaged the concern of the coming generation with segregation as a special form of racial discrimination, and it dramatically described the effects of Jim Crow upon Southern society. But its chief message, suggested by its title, was that the "American dilemma" in race relations was primarily the failure of whites to live up to national ideals and its resulting damage to national morale and self-esteem.[11]

Not all American politicians and government officials, of course, were troubled personally at the moral gap between democratic ideals and official racial practice. Nevertheless, many of them were disturbed by the effect of overt discrimination at home upon the country's international image. Whether liberal or con-

10. See Sitkoff, *New Deal for Blacks,* ch. 8; Richard Kluger, *Simple Justice* (New York, 1975), 305–14.
11. Gunnar Myrdal, *An American Dilemma: The Negro Problem and Modern Democracy,* (2 vols. New York, 1944), lxix, lxxiii, 75–78. For critiques of Myrdal's approach, see Ralph Ellison, "An American Dilemma: A Review," in *Shadow and Act* (New York, 1953), 303–17; and Stanford M. Lyman, *The Black American in Sociological Thought* (New York, 1972), 107–18.

servative on other issues, a wide range of politicians in both parties recognized that foreign governments and peoples could be shocked and alienated by American official bigotry. Civil rights advocates, calling for a two-front war against foreign totalitarianism and domestic racism, openly played upon the fears of international backlash in pressing the cause of racial reform. In *A Rising Wind*, the NAACP's Walter White predicted a wholesale abandonment of the peoples of Asia into the Soviet orbit if America failed to measure up to the promise of equality. The official concern over international opinion intensified in the postwar period as many Third World peoples sought national recognition and the Cold War accelerated. As a consequence, by the late 1940s a degree of "consensus" was developing among racial activists, scholars, and politicians and government officials outside the South in support of limited antidiscrimination steps. Fueled by a mixture of moral conviction, the hope for partisan political gain, the aim of domestic racial peace, and Cold War propaganda needs, this emerging consensus viewpoint favored limited governmental reforms designed to cleanse the American democratic image of the stain of racism.[12]

Demonstrating the American national commitment to racial democracy required government action, but politicians of both parties also perceived the severe restrictions within which they had to operate. By the late 1940s, clear white popular support could be shown only for a few measures such as antilynching and anti-poll-tax legislation. Even in these instances, national white majorities concealed continuing regional divisions. Any legislative proposals in the civil rights field also faced the certain obstacle of Southern congressional opposition, a barrier made all the more formidable because of Southern control of the congressional committee structure. Political realities steered the proponents of civil rights measures away from any immediate prospect of extensive legislative actions and toward administrative and judicial remedies. Because of the greater hope for action through the executive branch and the courts, political constraints additionally served to focus racial activism even more sharply upon the seeking of legal protections against government-sanctioned forms of discrimination.[13]

Prompted by the combination of troubled consciences, concern

12. White quoted in Blum, *V Was For Victory*, 219.

13. Hamby, *Beyond the New Deal*, 344–46; George H. Gallup, ed., *The Gallup Poll: Public Opinion, 1935–1971* (3 vols. New York, 1972); see polls of Aug. 25, 1943, July 25, 1948, April 29, 1949, Jan. 8, 1950, and Aug. 16, 1952.

for the American national image, black pressure, and awareness of both the political importance and the potential dynamite of racial issues, politicians in the late 1940s delicately began to address civil rights issues. Responding to fears of racial unrest expressed by Walter White and other civil rights leaders, President Truman in 1946 promised to create a national committee to study racial problems. Instead of packing the committee with obstructionists, Truman appointed prominent men and women sympathetic to civil rights, a majority of whom were affiliated with the Americans for Democratic Action. Although Truman himself stressed the immediate need for black protection from violence, the committee interpreted its mandate more broadly, seeing violence as only the surface manifestation of a national pattern of discrimination. The committee's final recommendations marked a transitional position between earlier emphases on aggregate economic issues and the emerging preoccupation with equal citizenship rights, for they included the creation of a fair employment practices commission, an antilynching law, an anti-poll-tax measure, abolition of segregation in interstate transportation, and the end of discrimination and segregation in the military services and federal agencies. Southern members of the committee expressed serious reservations about an all-out attack on Jim Crow, and the final report, *To Secure These Rights*, did avoid the advocacy of public school desegregation. But the beginning could be seen of a shift away from the "separate but equal" standard of racial justice toward a rejection of segregation as a policy inevitably producing discrimination.[14]

Except in parts of the South, both the report and Truman's subsequent civil rights message of February 2, 1948, were well received in the press. Although Congress was not yet ready to override Southern filibusters and other delaying tactics to enact legislation, many members agreed on the necessity at least of giving lip service to race issues. An equally hesitant Truman also declined to use his powers immediately to end segregation in federal employment and the armed forces, although he did promise to issue executive orders in those areas. "The strategy," an aide to Truman later explained, "was to start with a bold measure and then temporize to pick up the right-wing forces." Truman eventually did order military desegregation, but only after the

14. See *To Secure These Rights: The Report of the President's Committee on Civil Rights* (New York, 1947); Barton J. Bernstein, "America in War and Peace: The Test of Liberalism," in Barton J. Bernstein, ed., *Towards a New Past: Dissenting Essays in American History* (New York, 1967), 305.

Dixiecrat walkout at the Democratic convention, strong pressure from A. Philip Randolph and Grant Reynolds of the Committee Against Jim Crow in Military Service and Training, and two years of political and military resistance.[15]

The platform fight over civil rights at the 1948 Democratic national convention gave an additional indication of the new political awareness of civil rights as a central issue. Although Truman initially sought to ease Southern concerns by duplicating the party's mild 1944 racial plank, both urban bosses and liberals demanded a stronger statement. Liberals recognized that civil rights was a potent moral issue that separated them from Southern conservatives in an advantageous manner and provided them a forum for demonstrating their democratic racial principles. The ultimate adoption by the convention of a stronger civil rights plank did not constitute an unqualified triumph for racial justice, however, for the plank still failed to pledge genuine social equality for blacks. By promising a vague equality when many whites, especially in the South, still regarded equality as compatible with segregation, the platform did not match Minneapolis mayor Hubert H. Humphrey's call to "walk forthrightly into the bright sunshine of human rights."[16]

Following the creation of the States' Rights party by dissident Southern Democrats, Truman issued the delayed executive orders that established a federal antidiscrimination board, declared a policy of equal opportunity in the military services, and created a committee to end military discrimination and segregation. Through his release of the orders Truman openly cultivated black voters, and he succeeded in halting the plans of A. Philip Randolph to lead a black revolt against the draft in the event of presidential inaction. The Randolph threat represented a brief revival of the concept of mass black popular protest, used previously in the March on Washington movement of 1941 in behalf of the creation of a fair employment practices commission. In general, however, black organizations and spokesmen, led by the NAACP, continued to place greater confidence in the tools of legal action and lobbying activity than those of mass protest.

The Truman administration left a mixed civil rights legacy, but its actions suggested the likely direction of civil rights policies in

15. Bernstein, *Towards a New Past*, 305–6; Richard M. Dalfiume, *Desegregation of the U.S. Armed Forces: Fighting on Two Fronts, 1939–1953* (Columbia, Mo., 1969).

16. Bernstein, *Towards a New Past*, 306; McCoy and Ruetten, *Quest and Response*, 123–26.

the 1950s. Although Truman was unable to secure his civil rights legislative program in the face of Southern and partisan opposition, he set in motion an official pattern of seeking the alleviation of white racism through increased protection of black citizenship rights. The political interest in the economic justice aspects of racial reform continued to fade, interrupted only briefly by the creation of a temporary fair employment practices commission during the Korean War. The Federal Housing Authority upheld federally assisted mortgages on property under restrictive covenants, and housing policies continued to protect residential segregation. However, in policy areas that more clearly reflected the new official concern with the effects of overt official discrimination on the American national image abroad, bolder initiatives followed. Truman's special committee quietly began the integration of the armed forces, and the army abolished racial quotas following presidential reassurances to restore them if racial imbalances became acute. The Justice Department made its initial foray against Jim Crow, entering cases as amicus curiae in opposition to restrictive covenant enforcement, segregated facilities requirements in interstate transportation, and segregation in higher education. In the summer of 1952, the Justice Department also won administration approval for a brief challenging enforced segregated primary education.

Despite the initial steps taken for increased federal action in the civil rights field, however, both the Democrats and the Republicans paid greatest attention to other issues in 1952. Northern Democrats and their candidate, Adlai E. Stevenson, sought reconciliation with the white South and suspended extensive debate on civil rights. The Republican campaign's own emphasis on the "K_1C_2" (Korea, corruption, and communism) formula also left little room for extensive discussion of racial issues and encouraged conservative positions on domestic issues, as did the primary fight between Dwight D. Eisenhower and Senator Robert A. Taft. Still, neither party could completely ignore the growing number of black registered voters and the public proddings by black spokesmen. On June 5, in one of the few statements on the subject of civil rights in the Republican primary campaign, candidate Eisenhower pledged his general support for racial equality and continued armed forces desegregation, but he noted his preference for state antidiscrimination laws rather than a federal fair employment practices commission. Although he acknowledged, "We can no longer afford to hold on to the anachronistic principles of race segregation in the armed service organizations," the general disavowed an FEPC as a "Federally compulsory thing."[17]

Of the two principal Republican contenders for the presidency, civil rights supporters saw greater promise in Eisenhower, for he counted among his backers Eastern Republicans such as Governor Thomas E. Dewey and Herbert Brownell of New York, Senator James Duff and Congressman Hugh Scott of Pennsylvania, and Senator Henry Cabot Lodge, Jr., of Massachusetts. But although these leaders were sympathetic to civil rights proposals, their endorsement of Eisenhower was based primarily on their fear of Senator Taft's foreign policy unilateralism and their desire to halt the drift toward the "unbridled socialism" of the Fair Deal. The candidate's own racial attitudes, based largely upon his experiences in the segregated U.S. Army, generally were conservative. Although he professed his belief in black political and economic equality of opportunity, Eisenhower did not believe in "social mingling" or the idea that "a Negro should court my daughter." The general's racial opinions, when taken together with his adherence to an "anti-statist" program designed to maximize private freedom and voluntary cooperation, suggested that he would support only executive actions in civil rights consistent with the goal of limiting federal power.[18]

Eisenhower's support for the removal of official segregation mandates in the military services and in the District of Columbia signaled his approval of limited steps to promote a symbolic image of racial democracy while reducing government "paternalism." His opposition to an FEPC, on the other hand, reflected his equally strong aversion to the use of federal power as a coercive instrument that might threaten social harmony and weaken local authority. Many black Republicans understandably wanted the candidate to go further in behalf of civil rights. At the Republican convention, two Negro delegates shifted briefly to the "more responsive" Taft, only to return to the fold after being pressured by other members of the New York delegation. The GOP platform, however, mirrored Eisenhower's reluctance to assert federal power while it sounded general claims of support for civil rights and racial equality. The platform gave the states primary

17. William C. Berman, *The Politics of Civil Rights in the Truman Administration* (Columbus, Ohio, 1970), 204–208; National Jewish Congress and the NAACP, *Civil Rights in the United States, 1952*, 19.

18. Dwight D. Eisenhower, *The White House Years: Mandate for Change, 1953–1956* (Garden City, N.Y., 1963), 51, 234, 442; Sherman Adams, *Firsthand Report* (New York, 1961), 333; Arthur Larson, *Eisenhower: The President Nobody Knew*, (New York, 1968), 126.

responsibility for "domestic institutions," but at the same time told the federal government to "take supplemental action within its constitutional jurisdiction to oppose discrimination against race, religion, or national origin." Singled out as appropriate avenues for federal action were antilynching and anti-poll-tax legislation and the desegregation of public facilities in the District of Columbia. The Republicans gingerly sidestepped the issue of hiring discrimination by calling for legislation that "should not duplicate state efforts to end such practices" and "should not set up another huge bureaucracy."[19]

Having secured his party's presidential nomination, Eisenhower set out on the fall campaign with a major political objective of cultivating white Southern voters, particularly those in the upper South and border states. The campaign itinerary included an early fall swing through the region, and Eisenhower's support for the tidelands oil claims of Texas, Louisiana, and California brought him the endorsements of Democratic governors Allan Shivers of Texas and Robert Kennon of Louisiana. Eisenhower's refusal to endorse a federal FEPC, paired with Democrat Stevenson's grudging support of the agency, won the Republican ticket the additional support of South Carolina Governor James F. Byrnes and Senator Harry F. Byrd of Virginia. While on his Southern tour in Columbia, South Carolina, the candidate joined Byrnes at a rally and joined supporters standing and clapping to the playing of "Dixie." Only upon his arrival in Wheeling, West Virginia, did Eisenhower address civil rights issues. At that time he advocated the end of segregation in the armed forces and the District of Columbia and urged the lifting of black voting restrictions. Eisenhower declared, "We seek in America a true equality of opportunity for all men. I have no patience with the idea of second-class citizenship. For many years the administration has been pointing to a promised land where no American could be subjected to the indignities of discrimination. But their promised land has always proved to be a political mirage."[20]

Black spokesmen and newspaper columnists were hardly enthralled by Eisenhower's open courtship of Southern white voters, even though it was followed by verbal support of the principle of equal opportunity. After a meeting with Eisenhower

19. Berman, *The Politics of Civil Rights*, 208; Herbert S. Parmet, *Eisenhower and the American Crusades* (New York, 1972), 98; Congressional Quarterly, Inc., *National Party Conventions, 1831–1972* (Washington, D.C., 1976), 74.
20. *New York Times*, Oct. 16, 1952; Parmet, *Eisenhower*, 108; Berman, *The Politics of Civil Rights*, 222–224.

on August 26 in which the candidate reaffirmed his opposition to an FEPC and declared his inability to change Senate filibuster rules, the NAACP's Roy Wilkins responded: "General Eisenhower is friendly and gracious. He appears honest and sincere in his declared opposition to discrimination, but he speaks always in general terms. He sees nothing inconsistent, apparently, in his opposition to a federal FEPC and the sponsorship of such a bill by leading Republican Senators, including Senator Ives of the key state of New York. Eisenhower wants merely to survey discrimination in employment, not enact a law to correct the condition." After examining Eisenhower's civil rights positions, the Kansas City *Call* concluded, "If there is going to be a wholesale swing of colored votes to the Republican column this year, it will go down as the best kept secret of the century." C.A. Franklin of the *Call* scornfully labeled the general a "changeling" who bounced between courtship of Northern blacks and Southern segregationists such as Byrnes. The *Afro-American* proclaimed that its friends were not "the Dixiecrats whom Ike loves," and the *Amsterdam News* refused to support Eisenhower because of his Southern forays. By election day, virtually all of the black press had endorsed the Stevenson ticket, a sharp reversal of the partisan preferences of the black press from 1948.[21]

Black criticism of Eisenhower's weak commitment to federal action in behalf of civil rights was followed by blasts from lame-duck President Truman, who chastised the Republican candidate for claiming to have supported military desegregation while in the army. In response to Truman's attacks, Eisenhower countered by charging the incumbent with voting in 1942 against waiving state poll-tax requirements for members of the armed forces, and he added his own pledge to support the creation of FEPCs in each of the forty-eight states. Following continued sniping from Truman in behalf of the Stevenson ticket, during a rally in Harlem Eisenhower repeated his earlier promise to desegregate the District of Columbia. Attacking the Democratic record on civil rights, he proclaimed, "If you want to put this crusade at the helm of your government . . . based upon merit and without respect to color or creed; if you want to have a government of that kind, then you belong in this campaign."[22]

The Harlem speech was Eisenhower's last major civil rights

21. Berman, *The Politics of Civil Rights*, 220–22; McCoy and Ruetten, *Quest and Response*, 327–39.
22. Dalfiume, *Desegregation of the U.S. Armed Forces*, 218–19; Berman, *The Politics of Civil Rights*, 226–28.

Chicago *Daily Defender*
"Ike At The Dike" by commodore. Eisenhower's courtship of white Southern politicians during the 1952 campaign brought sharp comment from the black press, as this cartoon indicates.

statement of the campaign. Despite Stevenson's hesitant stance, Truman's late activity and Eisenhower's assiduous courtship of the white South and border states ensured that black voters stayed with the Democrats by a wide margin. Stevenson received approximately three out of every four black votes, equaling and perhaps bettering Truman's percentages of four years earlier. Confidence in the Eisenhower camp over the electoral outcome, based partly upon the candidate's inroads in the white South, ruled out any last-minute Republican overtures to black voters. On the Monday before the election an unidentified group showered antiblack leaflets from airplanes in Southern cities, but attempts by the NAACP's Walter White to get a public condemnation of the incident from the Republican candidate fell on deaf ears. Campaign aide Sherman Adams only transmitted a disavowal letter to White marked "personal and confidential" and delivered copies of past Eisenhower speeches as "sufficient answer."[23]

Despite the low-key manner in which both parties had addressed civil rights in the campaign, and despite the minimal contribution of black votes to the Eisenhower victory, civil rights spokesmen remained optimistic that the momentum generated during the Truman administration for civil rights progress would continue. The NAACP insisted that the new Republican administration would be compelled by the pressures of politics and conscience to produce additional results, and its spokesmen immediately called for presidential cooperation in attacking Senate filibuster Rule 22. Noting the impressive margin of the Eisenhower victory, the Kansas City *Call* urged the nation to close ranks behind the new president.[24] Civil rights advocates clearly expected continued involvement by the federal executive in the civil rights field, but much would depend upon the personal commitment and the political philosophy of the new Republican administration and its leader.

23. According to black election figures from Henry Lee Moon, "Election Post-Mortem," *Crisis* 57 (Dec. 1952): 616–17, Stevenson received 73 percent of black votes, a 4 percent improvement over Truman in 1948. According to American Institute of Public Opinion surveys for the two elections, Stevenson received 76 percent in 1952, 1 percent *less* than Truman four years earlier. See also Everett Carll Ladd, Jr. and Charles D. Hadley, *Transformations of the American Party System: Political Coalitions from the New Deal to the 1970s* (New York, 1975), 112; Numan V. Bartley, *The Rise of Massive Resistance* (Baton Rouge, La. 1969), 47–51; Berman, *The Politics of Civil Rights* 231.

24. Berman, *The Politics of Civil Rights*, 224–25; McCoy and Ruetten, *Quest and Response*, 331.

Official
Crusades
and
Lost
Opportunities

2.

Soldiers of Freedom

In his initial State of the Union address, February 2, 1953, President-elect Eisenhower briefly outlined the basic tenets of his civil rights philosophy. Observing that "discrimination against minorities exists despite our allegiance" to the ideal of equal opportunity, he added, "Much of the answer lies in the power of fact, fully publicized; of persuasion, honestly pressed; and of conscience, justly aroused." But the new President did not intend such education to extend to his own use of the presidency as a "bully pulpit." Eisenhower disliked speech making, and he particularly felt uncomfortable in using the words "discrimination" and "racial" in addresses. Because of his unease with racial matters, he insisted that civil rights issues be handled at the cabinet or subcabinet level. Acutely aware of the political risks inherent in a public leadership role in civil rights, he preferred to limit his involvement in racial questions to the occasional assertion of general democratic principles. At the same time, the President carefully circumscribed his subordinates' activities to areas of clear federal jurisdiction, greatest international propaganda value, and minimum risk of political fallout or domestic unrest.[1]

The military services of the United States offered a logical starting point for the application of the President's precepts for promoting a national image of racial democracy. The armed forces comprised an area of clear federal jurisdiction; and the Truman administration's initial implementation of racial non-discrimination in the military had reduced the political risk for the incoming Republicans in continuing anti-discrimination policy. The pursuit of military nondiscrimination also provided the new administration an early forum for highly visible progress in race relations, symbolizing the American commitment to democratic principles at home and abroad and projecting an image of American servicemen as embodiments of "soldiers of freedom."

Many military officials privately expressed reservations about presidentially sponsored integration and nondiscrimination plans, for they feared that the attempt to renovate service racial policies would make the military a "sociological laboratory" and thereby lessen the readiness of American forces. As implemented by the Eisenhower administration, however, nondiscrimination never demonstrated the thoroughness or the attention to detail of the scientific laboratory. Instead, administration nondiscrimination plans for the military resembled more closely the scripting of a modern morality play, staged for the benefit of foreign and domestic observers rather than benefiting the black serviceman himself.

American strategic planners were keenly aware of the diplomatic and military importance of a racially "clean" image in the postwar ideological competition with the Soviet Union. United Nations ambassador Henry Cabot Lodge maintained that continuing racial discrimination was the "Achilles heel" of American foreign policy. William H. Jackson, heading a special committee appointed by Eisenhower to study means of combatting Communist propaganda, cited the importance of military racial improvement for American success in the Third World, noting, "It puts us on their side in their drive for national identity." The most optimistic observers of racial policies within the military services also hoped that integration of units and adoption of nondiscriminatory practices would have a "trickle-down" effect upon the home front. Major General Charles S. Carpenter, chief of air force chaplains, claimed in 1954: "You can't turn a million guys into the military this year, and have them live and work together without

1. Eisenhower, *Mandate for Change* 235; Larson, *Eisenhower*, 126.

segregation, without some impression when they return to their own communities. Integration is already having an impact, though not out in the open. It's working like yeast, quietly."[2]

The initial steps converting official military policy from enforced segregation to nondiscrimination and desegregation had proceeded slowly and clumsily. The Selective Service and Training Act of 1940 had been interpreted by federal authorities to call for "separate but equal" racial facilities, and although Walter White of the NAACP and A. Philip Randolph of the Brotherhood of Sleeping Car Porters urged President Roosevelt to require integration, military commanders rejected even mild prodding as "destructive to morale." But the pressures exerted by black servicemen and leaders, the moral demands of the war effort against the Axis, and the demand for additional manpower encouraged a thorough reevaluation of service racial policies. In 1945, a three-man board studying the future utilization of black manpower, headed by Lieutenant General A.C. Gillem, recommended the eventual abolition of all-black divisions. Widespread patterns of discrimination in assignments, transfers, promotions, housing, and education remained entrenched, however. By July 1949, no black officers served in the navy or marines, and only 1.8 percent of army and 0.6 percent of air force officers were black. In mid-1950, 385 all-black units remained within the services.[3]

Greater progress clearly required additional executive pressure mandating an overall nondiscrimination policy for the military services. Concerted presidential action began in 1949 with President Truman's executive order calling for an end to discriminatory practices, followed by the formation of a seven-member advisory committee on military desegregation headed by former solicitor general Charles Fahy. The final report of the Fahy Committee, issued in 1950, established a target date of summer 1954 for the abolition of all-black military units. Spurred by Truman's executive order and the Fahy report, the armed forces made considerable advances. By August 1953 only eighty-eight all-black units remained, and by September the army reported that 95 percent of its black troops were in desegregated units. The air force and the marine corps, with much smaller numbers of black servicemen, were able to desegregate even more rapidly, finishing their programs by late 1952. The U.S. Army-European Theater (USAEUR), aiming at a target date of the middle of 1954, initiated

2. *New York Times*, March 11, 1954; Lee Nichols, *Breakthrough on the Color Front* (New York, 1954), 167, 177–78.
3. Jack Greenberg, *Race Relations and American Law* (New York, 1959), 356.

its own desegregation program in 1952, setting a 10 percent maximum figure for blacks within its units (a figure subsequently expanded). By April 1953, USAEUR claimed that its desegregation plan was 98 percent complete, although thirty-eight all-black units remained.[4]

During the implementation of its desegregation programs, the army commissioned tests to examine the attitudes of servicemen and to warn authorities of potential trouble spots. "Project Clear," a study undertaken by staff members of three universities and civilian agencies under contract to the army, indicated encouraging changes in the attitudes of white soldiers. The good news contained in the committee's report, however, was kept secret in order to avoid the political wrath of congressional armed services chairmen Carl Vinson and Richard B. Russell of Georgia. The army study did find that most GIs surveyed found the performance of their integrated units equal to that of segregated ones, and white soldiers' assessments of black performance rose with actual biracial experience. Seventy-three percent of more than 4,000 Northern whites interviewed, as well as 65 percent of more than 500 Southern whites, claimed to have black friends, although only 19 percent said they spent off-duty time with them. A large majority of interviewees in Korea also favored sharing post exchanges with black soldiers, and a smaller majority favored sharing rest areas.[5]

If the overall process of desegregating military units had proceeded with encouraging results, however, discrimination in a wide range of procedures and military acquiescence in civilian customs of segregation remained deeply rooted. Blacks continued to face unfair obstacles in promotions and transfers; service forms and designations still contained racial labels; housing, whether because of adherence to local custom or seniority, remained segregated and unequal; and educational facilities for servicemen and their dependents continued to be subject to the Jim Crow practices of local communities. Local segregation policies also carried over to the treatment of civilians employed on federal military property. The unwillingness of the service branches to

4. Headquarters, U.S. Army, Europe, Historical Division, "Integration of Negro and White Troops in the U.S. Army, Europe, 1952–1954," in Morris J. MacGregor and Bernard C. Nalty, *Blacks in the Armed Forces: Basic Documents, Vol. 12 — Integration* (Wilmington, Del., 1977) 265–75; Jack D. Foner, *Blacks and the Military in U.S. History* (New York, 1974), 193. For an overview of Truman's military desegregation program, see Richard M. Dalfiume, *Desegregation of the U.S. Armed Forces.*

5. William Peters, *The Southern Temper* (Garden City, N.Y., 1959), 139–40.

challenge local customs of segregation, particularly in the South, received endorsement in an internal navy memorandum of January 1952 that sanctioned segregated base facilities for civilian workers if consistent with local custom.[6]

During the 1952 campaign, Eisenhower and the Republican national committee had blasted the Truman administration's policies as ineffectual "tokenism" and had promised greater success with a Republican and former military man as president. "Segregation in all installations where federal money was spent should become a thing of the past," the candidate insisted, and in his initial State of the Union message he repeated his promise to use presidential authority to end discriminatory racial practices in the armed forces. Despite Eisenhower's pronouncements, his military career revealed little personal willingness to take the lead in fighting for racial equality. During his stays on bases in the South, Panama, and the Philippines, he had never demonstrated discomfort with racial caste systems, and his main exposure to black soldiers had been in their role as servants. A brief early encounter as a drill instructor with black Illinois National Guardsmen who "just couldn't do anything" had only reinforced his doubts about the motivation and capabilities of black soldiers.[7]

When confronted as supreme commander in Europe during World War II with manpower shortages aggravated by racial segregation, Eisenhower had demonstrated a limited willingness to bend rules for the sake of larger strategic objectives. During preparations in England for the Normandy invasion, he had resisted attempts to curtail soldiers' interracial contacts with the British population, and he had ordered the desegregation of overseas Red Cross clubs. When pressed to provide riflemen for the Ardennes counterattack of early 1945, he had temporarily ordered the use of blacks from the supply services to fill depleted white front-line units. After protests from General Walter Bedell Smith that his action violated War Department policy and was "most dangerous . . . in regard to Negro relations," Eisenhower had agreed not to "run counter to regulations in a time like this" and countermanded his order.[8]

6. Nichols, *Breakthrough on the Color Front*, 212.

7. Eisenhower, *Mandate for Change*, 234–35; Berman, *The Politics of Civil Rights*, 204–5; Larson, *Eisenhower*, 149; E. Frederic Morrow Oral History, Dwight D. Eisenhower Presidential Library 1977, [hereinafter noted as Morrow OH, 1977, DDEL], 20.

8. John Gunther, *Eisenhower* (New York, 1951), 56; Kay Summersby, *Eisenhower Was My Boss* (New York, 1948), 291; Elmo Richardson, *The Presidency of Dwight D. Eisenhower* (Lawrence, Kan., 1979), 105.

Once the emergencies of wartime had passed, however, the general had refused to endorse any additional military desegregation measures. In 1947 the Army General Staff, without objection by Eisenhower, agreed to withhold federal recognition from National Guard units that integrated in opposition to army practices. Testifying before a congressional committee in 1948, Eisenhower stated his personal opposition to desegregation below platoon level. Citing the difficulties for black promotion that integration would create, the general volunteered the opinion that "if we attempt merely by passing a lot of laws to force someone to like someone else, we are just going to get into trouble." After meeting candidate Eisenhower in 1952, NAACP executive Roy Wilkins characterized his racial attitudes as "West Point" and "Old Guard." Not surprisingly, then, the new President was content to confine his administration's military desegregation activities to the quiet continuation of policies established by the Truman administration and the service branches, his campaign rhetoric notwithstanding. His decision mirrored the preference of many service officers on the race relations "firing line" for unobtrusive, gradual implementation of desegregation orders. As an example of the desire to avoid renewed public controversy over the details of carrying out desegregation, the USAEUR plan specifically recommended that military personnel avoid giving public references in *Stars and Stripes*, post newspapers, and the Armed Forces Network to desegregation timetables. At the same time the army issued assurances that it was not "concealing racial integration."[9]

The new administration's hopes of avoiding press scrutiny and public controversy over its method of military desegregation lasted only two months. The issue that broke the silence of administration officials was the persistence of segregation in educational facilities for military dependents. At a March 19, 1953 press conference, Alice Dunnegan of the Associated Negro Press queried the President on the continued existence of segregated schools on Army bases in Virginia, Oklahoma, and Texas. In response, the White House released a memorandum from Eisenhower to Secretary of Defense Charles E. Wilson that revealed that the army was "surveying" the willingness of states and local school boards to end post school segregation. "If such integration is not achieved," the memorandum concluded, "other

9. Parmet, *Eisenhower*, 438; Dalfiume, *Desegregation of the U.S. Armed Forces*, 76, 159, 167; "Integration of Negro and White Troops," in MacGregor and Nalty, *Blacks in the Armed Forces*, 276.

arrangements in these instances will be considered." White House press secretary James Hagerty indicated that these arrangements might include the expenditure of additional federal money to assume complete control of schools jointly operated by federal and local authorities, but he was privately warned by Army Secretary Robert T. Stevens that any such action could not prevent state attempts to block integration through denial of teacher accreditation. Six days after the press conference, the first formal presidential statement on post school segregation contained only an executive order banning segregation by September in post schools completely operated by the federal government. The declaration actually affected only one school, at Fort Benning, Georgia, for schools at five other bases already had begun to desegregate. Even this halting pronouncement, however, outraged Georgia's segregationist governor Herman Talmadge, who described the order as "a great mistake."[10]

On March 27, the dimensions of the administration's post school segregation problem became clearer. The Office of Education of the Department of Health, Education and Welfare identified twenty-one segregated schools on military bases left untouched by the President's action. Clarence Mitchell of the Washington Bureau of the NAACP, insisting that the President could end segregation by "calling the Pentagon on the telephone," protested the lack of administration action on the additional schools to HEW Secretary Oveta Culp Hobby. Mitchell received in response only a promise from the secretary to request an internal memorandum on the issue. Mrs. Hobby, publisher of the *Houston Post*, former head of the Women's Army Corps, and an Eisenhower Democrat in 1952, proceeded to demonstrate a sluggishness on desegregation matters that reflected both the prevailing attitudes of her state and the influences of her military background. On April 13, Hobby outlined to the President the problems posed by jointly operated base schools and off-base schools serving military dependents, and she requested a delay in federal action on the twenty-one base schools pending an expected Supreme Court ruling on school segregation at the end of the year and the fate of HEW legislation in the Congress.[11]

10. Eisenhower, *Mandate for Change*, 235; Parmet, *Eisenhower*, 419; Nichols, *Breakthrough on the Color Front*, 198; "Memorandum, Secretary of Army Robert T. Stevens for James C. Hagerty, 20 March 1953," in MacGregor and Nalty, *Blacks in the Armed Forces*, 347–48; *New York Times*, March 26, 1953.

11. *New York Times*, March 20, 1953; Sec. of HEW Oveta Culp Hobby to Sec. of Defense Charles E. Wilson, 13 Apr. 1953, in MacGregor and Nalty, *Blacks in the Armed Forces*, 350–52.

Pressure from HEW on the White House to defer action, however, was countered by a "bombshell" telegram dropped by black congressman Adam Clayton Powell. Powell's letter to the President condemning administration inaction, only the first in a series of embarrassing revelations by the Harlem Democrat, reached the Washington, D.C. press on June 3, and the *Washington Evening Star* blazoned the headline, "Hobby Flouts Seg Order, Powell Charges." White House correspondent Robert Donovan later noted, "No other newspaper story at the time ever caused such commotion in the White House so quickly." Powell charged deliberate noncompliance with administration antidiscrimination pronouncements by the Defense Department, the Veterans Administration, and HEW and claimed that Secretary Hobby had "virtually countermanded" Eisenhower's policy regarding base schools. Eisenhower's ire at the charges was far overshadowed by his personal indignation with Powell for having made the telegram public knowledge without White House consent. Although Eisenhower later learned from minorities adviser Maxwell Rabb that many of Powell's charges could be substantiated, the White House directed its initial response at containing embarrassing political fallout from the incident and denying partisan advantage to the Democrats. White House chief of staff Sherman Adams contacted Mrs. Hobby, Wilson, and VA medical official Joel T. Boone, and their aides drafted half-a-dozen reply letters to Powell, one of which accused the congressman of total fabrication. Mutual Security Director Harold Stassen, speaking to the NAACP's summer convention, appealed to its membership to counter popular "misconceptions" of American mistreatment of blacks.[12]

In addition to his aides' public relations actions, the President dispatched Rabb to meet Powell and obtain his cooperation in lessening the political damage of the telegram. At a meeting in which the political benefits of cooperation to both Powell and the administration were emphasized, Powell agreed to give the administration more time to carry out its desegregation program and to help dampen the controversy from his telegram. Rabb drafted for Eisenhower a conciliatory response to Powell's initial telegram stating, "I will carry out every pledge I made with regard to segregation" and adding that he had "made inquiries of the officials to whom you have referred." Releasing the President's letter

12. Parmet, *Eisenhower*, 419; Robert J. Donovan, *Eisenhower: The Inside Story* (New York, 1956), 155–56.

with his own reply on June 10, Powell publicly hailed the Eisenhower message as a "Magna Carta for minorities and a Second Emancipation Proclamation."[13]

Despite the White House's assurances, delays in the implementation of military integration pledges continued through the fall of 1953, fueled by disagreements between the departments of Defense and HEW over responsibility for integrating dependents' educational facilities. In December Clarence Mitchell again complained to Commissioner of Education Samuel Brownell, who assured the NAACP that the Defense Department would soon respond to the matter. On January 12, 1954, the Defense Department finally issued a formal policy statement on jointly operated post schools, setting a target date of September 1955 for complete desegregation and stating that resistance by local officials could be countered by tuition grants to military families or by provisions for desegregated base facilities through the office of the commissioner of education. Despite personal denials by Defense Secretary Wilson on February 2, press reports noted that a "high Defense Department" official had accused HEW Secretary Hobby of footdragging on the post schools question and suggested that the desegregation order had been obtained by the President over her objections. Hobby nevertheless could claim a partial victory, for a proposal to have the federal government's standard nondiscrimination clause inserted in all future education contracts with state agencies was shelved awaiting the Supreme Court's May decision on school integration.[14]

The announced intention of the Defense Department to achieve desegregation of all post schools by the autumn of 1955 met immediate resistance from Southern school boards. On March 25, 1954, the Norfolk, Virginia, school board issued a statement refusing to end racial separation, although Rear Admiral T.B. Brittain confidently predicted that base school desegregation would still occur on schedule. In April, a Dallas, Texas, school board also refused to assume operation of a newly integrated post school at Craig Air Force Base. The hesitancy of Defense Department and HEW officials to crack down on recalcitrant school

13. Parmet, *Eisenhower*, 419; Donovan, *Eisenhower*, 156–58; Eisenhower, *Mandate for Change*, 235; *New York Times*, June 11, 1953 and June 29, 1953.

14. Nichols, *Breakthrough on the Color Front*, 199; "Memorandum, Secretary of Defense Wilson for Secretary of the Army, *et. al.*, 12 Jan. 1954," and "Department of Defense, Office of Public Information, Press Release, 1 Feb. 1954," in MacGregor and Nalty, *Blacks in the Armed Forces*, 353–54; *New York Times*, Aug. 24, 1953, Nov. 16, 1953, Feb. 1, 1954, and Feb. 2, 1954.

boards added new delays in the implementation of the desegregation timetable. Deputy Defense Secretary Robert Anderson acknowledged in a memorandum to Wilson the department's instructions not to challenge the long-term leases of local operation of
segregated schools on four bases—Biggs Air Force Base, Texas;
Fort Meade, Maryland; Fort Bliss, Texas; and Pine Bluff Arsenal,
Arkansas. Plans for construction of an all-white school on property
of the Perrin (Texas) Air Force Base continued, and naval authorities in Bainbridge, Maryland signed agreements with Cecil
County school officials for the construction of a segregated school
on navy property. Further undermining the effectiveness of the
January 12 decree, HEW undersecretary Harold Hunt announced
that any withdrawal of federal grants to segregated base schools
could only follow a specific court determination of noncompliance with the *Brown* school desegregation decision of May 17,
1954.[15]

On August 21, 1955, Defense Secretary Wilson finally was able
to announce the beginning of desegregation at all base schools
save two, which received extensions from the deadline—Fort
Meade and Pine Bluff Arsenal. In seven instances, the Defense
Department assumed complete control of facilities following
refusals by local officials to oversee desegregation. In the two
exempted schools, "unbreakable" long-term leases blocked
immediate federal takeovers. The number of segregated schools
remaining on military bases soon increased to three, however,
when the navy leased on-base buildings in New Orleans for an
all-white school over the protests of the NAACP. Eliminating
segregation at the New Orleans facility, given Louisiana's role as a
leader of "massive resistance," became a time-consuming chore.
In the spring of 1956, the assistant secretary of the navy granted
extensions of the outstanding leases for a year in order to "give
school authorities time to construct necessary additional facilities." The deadline was pushed back to the summer of 1958 at the
request of local commanders, and extended yet again to the end of
1959 by Assistant Secretary of Defense Charles G. Finucane following a fire at a newly constructed off-base school in March 1958.
At Fort Meade, Maryland, Assistant Secretary of the Navy Hugh
M. Milton II declared in mid-1956 that "satisfactory" progress

15. *New York Times*, March 25, 1954 and Apr. 11, 1954; "Memorandum, Deputy
Secretary of Defense Robert B. Anderson for the Secretary of Defense, 7 June
1955," in MacGregor and Nalty, *Blacks in the Armed Forces*, 358; NAACP, *Annual
Report* (1955), 40.

was being achieved in Maryland, but after consultations with commanders and local authorities he revised his assessment, saying, "It is considered inadvisable to incorporate a non-segregation clause in the present lease." Defense Department officials did achieve a small measure of success in obtaining changes in the lease at Pine Bluff Arsenal from reluctant Arkansas officials.[16]

The conversion to desegregation in base schools did not by itself eliminate the possibility of a segregated education for military dependents. A continuing headache for the military was the educational segregation of dependents in schools outside base property. As late as August 1958, the air force announced its intention not to resist segregation practices at a federally assisted elementary school in Pulaski County, Arkansas, near the turbulent city of Little Rock. Influenced partly by the President's desire to avoid further turmoil in Arkansas over school desegregation, newly appointed HEW Secretary Arthur Flemming, after meeting with program officials, notified the White House in August 1958 that no HEW action would be taken on behalf of off-base air force dependents in the event local public schools closed to avoid integration. Exchanges between HEW and the air force throughout the remainder of 1958 over the Pulaski County situation illustrated the reluctance of both to assume school operations or to provide alternate means of integrated education.

An investigation of the Pulaski County problem by Defense Department representative Stephen S. Jackson led to the conclusion that a federal purchase of the elementary school's land and buildings provided the best available solution. Representatives of the Department of Justice concurred, and following Jackson's meetings with U.S. Attorney Osro Cobb and Little Rock business

16. Clarence Mitchell to Rear Admiral J.M. Will, Director of Personnel Policy, Office of the Assistant Secretary of Defense, 16 Nov. 1955; Will, "Memorandum for the Record, 19 Jan. 1956"; "Memorandum, Director of Personnel Policy, OASD for Stephen S. Jackson, OASD (Manpower and Personnel), 20 Jan. 1956"; "Memorandum, Assistant Secretary of Defense (Manpower, Personnel, and Reserves) for Assistant Secretary of the Navy (Personnel and Reserve Forces), 23 Jan. 1956"; "Memorandum, Assistant Secretary of the Navy (P&RF) for Assistant Secretary of Defense (M,P&R), 7 Apr. 1956"; "Memorandum, Deputy Comptroller, U.S. Navy, for Assistant Secretary of Defense (M,P&R), 5 July 1957"; "Memorandum, Assistant Secretary of the Navy Richard Jackson for Assistant Secretary of Defense (M,P&R), 6 Aug. 1958"; "Covering Brief, Director of Personnel Policy, U.S. Navy, to Assistant Secretary of Defense (M,P&R), 14 Aug. 1958"; and "Memorandum, Assistant Secretary of Defense (M,P&R) for Assistant Secretary of the Navy, 15 Aug. 1958," in MacGregor and Nalty, *Blacks in the Armed Forces*, 360–81.

leaders, Assistant Attorney General W. Wilson White agreed to attempt acquisition of the school by seizing the leasehold for one year through eminent domain. HEW in turn prepared to provide federal operating funds for the school. However, HEW and the air force continued their sparring over which office would actually initiate the request to obtain the leasehold. By January 1959, HEW officials had turned to a new strategy, proposing as part of the administration's 1959 legislative program on civil rights authorization for the commissioner of education to provide for the free public education of all dependents of military personnel if local officials refused. Desegregation of dependents in Pulaski County only occurred after two additional delays of thirty days each were granted to Assistant Attorney General White to pursue resolution of the dispute through voluntary agreement with local officials.[17]

Although the desegregation of schools attended by military dependents received greater public notoriety, the educational needs of servicemen themselves created additional difficulties in the Jim Crow South. Southern colleges and universities responded by devising various strategies to provide education for black servicemen while remaining in compliance with state segregation statutes. When massive resistance was forcefully imposed by a state's leadership, universities completely withdrew from on-post educational activity—the University of Georgia, for example, abandoned its on-post course offerings for black servicemen in June 1956. Many other states either complied with requests for serviceman education or worked out cooperative arrangements between white and black colleges. The University of North Carolina offered desegregated courses at Fort Bragg, and white Alabama State Teachers' College offered an on-base desegregated course with blacks receiving credit for their course work from a black teachers' college. Similar arrangements existed for troops at Fort Campbell, Kentucky, between the white Austin Peay State College and the black Agricultural and Industrial State University of Nashville. Despite the existence of such programs, military officials still were forced to make special arrangements for black servicemen in locations without ready access to on-base classes. The air force attempted to solve its problem by giving black soldiers the option of either going to all-black facilities or attending a desegregated school in another state.[18]

17. Greenberg, *Race Relations and American Law*, 367; "Memorandum, Assistant Secretary of Defense (M,P&R) for the Secretary of the Army *et al.*, 10 Oct. 1958," in MacGregor and Nalty, *Blacks in the Armed Forces*, 384–88.
18. Greenberg, *Race Relations and American Law*, 367.

Schools, of course, were by no means the only centers of segregation and discrimination on military bases. Especially within the shipyards and bases of the navy, an entire range of segregated accommodations existed that affected not only servicemen but civilian workers employed at the facilities. The pervasive patterns of segregation at navy yards in Norfolk, Virginia, and Charleston, South Carolina, created obvious eyesores both for black leaders and for administration officials concerned with promoting a clean racial image. Initial public accusations by Adam Clayton Powell and black newspaper correspondents had cited the existence of other segregated base accommodations at the same time that they had pointed out the segregation of educational opportunities. Following the March 1953 news conference at which military segregation policies first publicly surfaced in the Eisenhower administration, Navy Secretary Robert Anderson issued a directive on "equality of treatment and opportunity" pledging the navy's dedication to racial equality at its facilities.[19]

Despite Anderson's pronouncement, segregation practices in the shipyards continued unabated until the Powell disclosures of June 3, 1953. The congressman's list of charges included navy footdragging on removal of segregated accommodations for civilian workers at the shipyards, and Anderson's initial reply to Powell only confirmed the continuing navy practice of observing local segregation customs and laws. The NAACP already had assailed Anderson deputy Francis P. Whiteham for approving segregation at Norfolk and Charleston, and Powell answered the secretary's own reply by charging him with "insubordination" in not contesting conditions at the yards. As part of the administration's rapid reaction to the Powell controversy, Maxwell Rabb urged Anderson to correct the shipyards situation. In response, the secretary dispatched Undersecretary Charles S. Thomas to Norfolk and Rear Admiral George A. Holderness, Jr., chief of the Office of Industrial Relations, to Charleston to report on the feasibility of desegregation. Within a few days, Anderson was able to report to Rabb that segregation could be ended at the facilities.[20]

On August 20, 1953, Anderson issued a statement that noted the existence of segregation at about half of the navy's Southern bases and "requested" commanders to proceed "steadily and expeditiously" to end "all barriers to the free use of all facilities." Later the same day, however, the United Press quoted naval command-

19. Parmet, *Eisenhower*, 419; Nichols, *Breakthrough on the Color Front*, 212; "Secretary Navy Instruction 1000.2, 23 Mar. 1953," in MacGregor and Nalty, *Blacks in the Armed Forces*, 126.

20. Donovan, *Eisenhower*, 159; Nichols, *Breakthrough on the Color Front*, 213.

ers at the bases, including the Norfolk commander, that desegregation would not proceed without written *orders* from the secretary. After a day-long series of conferences within his department, Anderson issued new letters on August 21 that "directed," rather than "requested," the end of base segregation. In his directives, the secretary called for progress reports to the department every thirty days, with the first one due on November 1, 1953. Desegregation without public controversy was Anderson's aim, and commanders were advised to promote local cooperation by explaining the changes privately to civic leaders, local businessmen, and veterans' organizations. Seeking to reassure Urban League director and navy consultant Lester Granger, Anderson announced at a September 3 meeting his intention of achieving the "feather in my cap" of complete desegregation. In addition, Anderson conceded the insensitivity of his initial reply to Powell, attributing it to his lack of information on base conditions.[21]

Following Anderson's urgings for secrecy in the transition process, local commanders devised ingenious methods to achieve quiet desegregation. Buses with signs designating racial seating areas were removed for "maintenance" reasons and not replaced. Bathrooms were closed for "modernization," which actually consisted only of painting over racial designations above doorways. Lunchrooms were similarly adapted for integrated use. Trouble briefly surfaced at the Charleston yard on the first day of integration when local blacks scattered through the reopened cafeteria. Officials responded by closing the lunchroom again for three days, during which navy officials and Lester Granger urged local blacks to end all provocative gestures. When the cafeteria reopened, no further incidents were reported, but initially only about one-fifth of its former users returned. Nevertheless, at a November 11 press conference, the President declared his administration's desegregation policy "completely effective," and he released a navy report on the desegregation program along with his own "Statement on Elimination of Segregation in Civil Facilities at Naval Installations." By the end of November, fifty-nine of sixty naval bases and yards were desegregated, and Congressman Powell transmitted a personal apology to Secretary Anderson. Eisenhower, decidedly impressed by the secretary's skill in achieving the desegregation goals without incident or political embarrassment, later rewarded him with appointments as assis-

21. Parmet, *Eisenhower*, 420; Nichols, *Breakthrough on the Color Front*, 213–15.

tant secretary of defense and secretary of the treasury. Describing Anderson privately as the ablest member of the administration, in his diary the President expressed his personal wish for a 1956 Anderson vice-presidential candidacy, and urged him to consider a presidential race in 1960.[22]

Segregation of base facilities was far from the only blot on the record of the navy or the other service branches in their attempts to promote an egalitarian image to the outside world. The navy, and other branches, faced the frustrating problem of black concentration in menial job categories, illustrated most clearly in the navy's Stewards' Branch. To outsiders, the Stewards' Branch appeared to be little more than a sanctioned vestige of slavery. In a follow-up to his attacks of early June 1953, Adam Clayton Powell criticized the navy for assigning half of its black servicemen to mess duty. Powell denounced the service for perpetuating a "modernized, 20th century form of slavery," and added, "No one is interested in today's world in fighting communism with a frying pan or shoe polish." Defending the navy's record, Assistant Secretary John Floberg pointed out that enlistment in the Stewards' Branch was voluntary and that producing changes in black concentration was hindered by reenlistment rates of over 80 percent.[23]

Privately navy officials could not so easily dismiss the department's image problem in the Stewards' Branch. A research committee headed by Commander Durward W. Gilmore reported to Chief of Naval Personnel James L. Holloway, Jr., in late August: "We feel the Navy has made excellent progress in its continuing efforts to more efficiently utilize Negro personnel. Integration has been the means, and good public relations has been the result." Gilmore added the warning, however, that it would be "expedient to give particular attention to the Stewards' Branch. The segregation in that branch is a sore spot with the Negroes, and it is our weakest position from the standpoint of public relations." Before the September 3 meeting of Secretary Anderson with Lester Granger and navy officials, Holloway notified the secretary of the creation of an ad hoc committee to study the Stewards' Branch group ratings, manned by the deputy chief of naval personnel, other personnel officers, and officials of the Bureau of Supplies

22. Eisenhower, *Mandate for Change*, 235; Parmet, *Eisenhower*, 418, 420; Robert H. Ferrell, ed. *The Eisenhower Diaries* (New York, 1981), 308, 377.

23. Rep. Adam Clayton Powell, Jr., to Asst. Sec. of the Navy for Air John Floberg, 29 June 1953, and Floberg to Powell, 17 July 1953, in MacGregor and Nalty, *Blacks in the Armed Forces*, 301–2.

and Accounts. Talks with recruiting inspectors from New England and the mid-Atlantic region revealed resistance to schemes to recruit more whites into the Stewards' Branch and suggested that "integrated" recruiting areas such as Detroit, Los Angeles, and Buffalo offered the best hope for across-the-board recruiting of stewards.[24]

Separate recruitment of blacks into the Stewards' Branch finally ceased in March 1954, but whites were not reassigned to the service and black reenlistment rates remained high. With racial imbalances persisting, the ineffectiveness of navy action led in 1955 to Lester Granger's resignation as a race relations consultant to the Navy. In the same year, the American Civil Liberties Union reported the continuing deficiencies of navy policies designed to combat segregation and discrimination in the Stewards' Branch, the regular Reserve Officer Training Corps, and the officer corps. The navy could claim no black commanding officers and only about one hundred commissioned officers, and its promotional literature failed to highlight career possibilities for black recruits. Only two of forty-seven photographs in the navy's "Life in the United States Navy" pamphlet, for example, even showed a black seaman. The navy's intention of projecting a positive racial image was also poorly served by its failure to assign blacks to prominent guard duty at foreign embassies and missions. An update of the American Civil Liberties Union report sent in November 1957 to Navy Secretary Thomas S. Gates noted improvements in the Stewards' Branch but continuing shortcomings in other areas. Closer examination of navy personnel records revealed that even the small increases in the percentages of blacks in categories other than the Stewards' Branch owed more to serious declines in white reenlistment than to actual increases in black numbers.[25]

The armed forces were learning the hard way that mere declarations of policy eliminating official sanctions for segregated facilities and separate recruitment of Negroes into menial categories did not mean the end of racial discrimination in the armed forces. Blatant instances of segregation still persisted, eliciting cries of

24. Commander Durward Gilmore et al., to Chief of Bureau of Naval Personnel, Vice Admiral J.L. Holloway, 31 Aug. 1953, and "Memorandum, Chief of Naval Personnel for the Secretary of the Navy, 1 Sept. 1953," in MacGregor and Nalty, *Blacks in the Armed Forces*, 127–31.

25. NAACP, *Crisis* 62 (1955): 517; "Statement of American Civil Liberties Union Concerning Segregation and Discrimination in the U.S. Navy, June 1955," Patrick M. Malin (exec. dir., ACLU) to Sec. of the Navy Thomas S. Gates, Jr., 26 Nov. 1957; in MacGregor and Nalty, *Blacks in the Armed Forces*, 303–10.

outrage and belated corrective action. Following charges by Congressman Powell that the black 1802nd Special Regiment at West Point had been assigned to segregated barracks and confined to menial duties, Defense Secretary Wilson assured the congressman of prompt department action. Assistant Secretary of the Army James P. Mitchell ordered a survey of segregation on army bases similar to the one authorized by Navy Secretary Anderson, but he followed up only by encouraging the elimination of Jim Crow practices rather than requiring it. In 1956, Powell protested that daily report forms still contained racial designations, and the NAACP noted the continued use of racial identification tags at the 6th Army headquarters in San Francisco. The Defense Department responded by ordering the end of racial references in daily report forms, but promotions and reassignments continued to feature racial designations for months afterward. Two months after the issuance of a 1957 order banning racial identifications in reassignment orders after February 1, European orders included them. Personnel folders used by promotion boards still contained photographs, indicating race, and promotion boards themselves, being manned by personnel above the rank of colonel in the army and captain in the navy, reflected the absence of black officers. Black officer training and accreditation through Reserve Officer Training Corps programs effectively was blocked by Southern restrictions on admission to colleges offering ROTC training and by the lack of jurisdiction over educational matters provided to the Defense Department. Even at the three military service academies, black cadets numbered only twenty-one in a student body of about seven thousand.[26]

Blocked by discriminatory practices and regulations from advancement into higher classifications, officer training, and reassignment opportunities, black servicemen faced additional discrimination in seeking decent housing, medical care, and recreational opportunities. Even after the elimination of regulations requiring segregated base housing, assignments of housing based upon seniority or rank forced black servicemen to seek off-base accommodations, which heightened their chances of exposure to racism in transportation, education, and public facilities. In such circumstances, military jurisdiction to protect the serviceman was narrowly defined, and commanders' wishes to maintain

26. Richard J. Stillman II, *Integration of the Negro in the U.S. Armed Forces* (New York, 1968), 58; Greenberg, *Race Relations and American Law*, 361, 365–66; Herbert Aptheker, *Soul of the Republic: The Negro Today* (New York, 1964), 96.

good relations with local communities further restricted the reach of the military's protective hand. In one case, Lieutenant Thomas Williams of the air force was arrested in Crestview, Florida, in 1953 for refusing to take a Jim Crow bus seat. After being convicted by local authorities, he was reprimanded by his superior officers and dropped from the service later in an "economy move." NAACP appeals to air force secretary Harold E. Talbot produced a noncommital statement on the case by his staff assistant. In 1954, NAACP protests did force the Defense Department to give assurances that segregationist attempts to bar black soldiers from three Louisiana cities during "Operation Sagebrush" would not be honored. Although similar incidents commonly arose in the South, they were not confined to that region. In 1953, black airmen in Sault Sainte Marie, Michigan, were denied service by local businessmen, and despite NAACP complaints the air force rejected their transfer requests.[27]

Although black servicemen were entitled to the use of the medical facilities of the Veterans Administration, patterns of segregation and discrimination also pervaded the military health care system. Black pianist Hazel Scott, the wife of Adam Clayton Powell, relayed information to her husband on the persistence of VA segregation in Tennessee hospitals during a concert tour, and the congressman issued an angry public telegram on the subject on February 5, 1953. Powell's famous June 3 telegram also cited the discriminatory practices of Southern VA hospitals, but despite his protests, a survey in September 1953 indicated that 47 of 166 VA hospitals still followed segregation practices. Especially recalcitrant was the VA hospital in New Orleans, where segregation by wards persisted, dining areas were divided by race, and blacks were called by their first names. On February 4, 1954, the VA ordered the elimination of color designation forms, and in a report by Administrator Harvey Higley, the VA emphasized its commitment to ending segregation. But by February of 1955, the Department of HEW still continued to provide federal money to hospitals guilty of segregation practices. Even the attendance of black servicemen at sporting events involving the service academies did not escape the reach of discrimination. In 1954, the navy distributed 3,000 football tickets to whites for the Sugar Bowl Classic, only to be forced to reverse itself by order of Secretary Robert Anderson and repudiate the Jim Crow ticket distribution.

27. *New York Times*, Jan. 14, 1954, Aug. 30, 1953, and Sept. 2, 1953; NAACP, *Annual Reports* (1953), 51 and (1955), 45.

Navy policy, however, continued to permit spectator segregation at academy sporting events. When faced with the likelihood of segregated seating at the West Point-Tulane football game scheduled for New Orleans in 1957, the army transferred the game to West Point rather than refuse to play it.[28]

Discrimination against black servicemen in a variety of forms also extended to military posts abroad, a particularly serious problem given the administration's concern with foreign perceptions of American democratic practices. Even in the absence of Southern community pressures and customs of segregation and discrimination, the services' own heritage of racial discrimination carried over to foreign installations, frequently buttressed by host nations' own concepts of caste. Prompted by an air force reprint of a *Reader's Digest* article by Hanson W. Baldwin entitled "Our Fighting Men Have Gone Soft," Representative Charles C. Diggs of Michigan initiated a personal investigation of discriminatory practices on air force bases in the Pacific in 1960. In his account, Baldwin had blamed racial integration in part for reducing the quality of American troops abroad, but Diggs's own inspections of bases in Hawaii, Okinawa, Japan, and other Pacific islands, featuring interviews with black servicemen, pointed out the wide gap between air force antidiscrimination decrees and their realization. Diggs's report strongly argued that segregation, not integration, was contributing to low troop morale. Black servicemen's complaints included segregation of their housing and entertainments, unequal treatment of their dependents, and the perpetuation of symbols of racial prejudice, including displays of Confederate flags and a cross-burning.[29]

The continuation of discriminatory practices at military installations at home and abroad seriously weakened the administration's claims that the nation's military establishment exemplified equality of opportunity. Of all the racial shortcomings of the American military establishment, perhaps the most glaring failure involved the National Guard and the reserves, for many Americans the living embodiments of the revolutionary citizen-soldier ideal. In 1954, the army issued a directive ordering the omission of racial designations from the reassignments of reserve unit members. However, Representative Diggs pointed out in May 1955 the continued exclusion of blacks from the army and air National

28. Parmet, *Eisenhower*, 418–49; NAACP, *Annual Report* (1954), 42 and (1957), 39.

29. Rep. Charles C. Diggs, Jr., to Sec. of the Air Force Dudley C. Sharp, 7 July 1960, in MacGregor and Nalty, *Blacks in the Armed Forces*, 316–46.

Guard units in thirteen Southern states, despite subsidization by the federal government at $10 million a year. In early May, Adam Clayton Powell proposed an amendment to the National Reserve Training Program bill that would have prevented enlistments in, and transfers to, segregated units. Despite administration criticism, the Powell rider passed in the House of Representatives by a 126–87 vote, only to die with the entire bill on a later House vote.

In a message to House Armed Services Committee chairman Carl Vinson, Secretary of the Army Wilbur Brucker delivered the administration position, favoring a "continuance of the present policy which subjects National Guard units and personnel to all Federal regulations with respect to anti-discrimination and non-segregation" only "while they are in active Federal service." Following an Eisenhower press conference condemnation of the Powell amendment as "extraneous" on June 8, the House of Representatives defeated an amendment to a second bill denying draft immunity to National Guard volunteers in segregated units by a 105–156 vote on July 1, 1955. By 1960, the National Guard and Air National Guard remained segregated in sixteen states and the District of Columbia. As of late 1961, ten Southern states still excluded blacks from their National Guard and reserve units. Civil Defense and Civil Air Patrol programs remained virtually all white, and Southern cities maintained segregated fallout shelters.[30]

Although the major approach of military officials in racial policies throughout the Eisenhower administration remained the removal of official sanction for segregation, new issues emerged that demonstrated the adaptability of racial discrimination. Defense Department racial adviser James C. Evans indirectly referred to the new forms of racial inequality when he noted in a 1959 *Army Register* article that "segregation" or overt "discrimination" was giving way as his chief concern to the "refinement" of a more equitable distribution of blacks in the military ranks. "White flight" from reenlistment in lower ranks and a growth in minority enlistments contributed to the expansion of a black "underclass" within the armed services. The United States Army-European Theater cautioned that while its initial hopes of a 10 percent maximum black quota had been quickly dashed, its commanders still felt that an overabundance of blacks in particular units was "undesirable from the standpoint of operational efficiency." In

30. Donovan, *Eisenhower*, 161; Greenberg, *Race Relations and American Law*, 363; Ronald Alan Schlundt, "Civil Rights Policies in the Eisenhower Years" (Ph.D. diss., Rice University, 1973), 43–44.

many army stations, black limits of 12 percent for combat units and 18 percent for service units were exceeded. In other instances, however, rigid adherence to fixed limits on black percentages, defended by official assumptions of inferior black performance and the increasing complexity of military hardware, encouraged skewing of disciplinary actions against minority servicemen. USAEUR admitted withholding reenlistment from those "whose conduct has been prejudicial to the integration program in a disciplinary sense or those who had discredited the U.S. Army in the eyes of the European public," while conceding at the same time that a "large proportion" of those who had been dismissed were black.[31]

Racial discrimination based upon subjective measurements of mental aptitude rather than overt references to color continued to pervade the service branches long after the official adoption of a "nondiscriminatory" image. Demonstrating one officer's response to the "problem" of black mental inferiority, Lieutenant General Charles L. Bolte of USAEUR asserted, "I cannot permit the assignment of large numbers of unqualified personnel, regardless of race, to prejudice the operational readiness of our units in an effort to attain 100 percent racial integration, however desirable that goal may be." But acquiring the desired numbers of both skilled black enlisted men and noncommissioned officers required either a reassessment of army perceptions of the capabilities of black volunteers or the selective recruitment of better-educated blacks through an "affirmative action" program.[32]

The navy faced a similar dilemma in its own recruitment program. A January 1959 memorandum from the Bureau of Naval Personnel noted that the Defense Department had mandated quotas from four different "mental group" categories since 1952, aiming for a reduction in the number of recruits in the lowest, Group IV. Knowing that full implementation would mean fewer black recruits, the navy had joined the air force in requesting an abeyance of qualitative recruitment after recruiting few Group IV individuals in 1958. The navy's figures showed that almost 70 percent of all black recruits from 1953 to 1958 had fallen in the Group IV category, and 90 percent were in either Group III or IV. For black recruits accepted in these categories, their classification ensured continuing concentration in menial job categories, including the Stewards' Branch. Admitting that mental group classi-

---

31. Stillman, *Integration of the Negro* 63; "Integration of Negro and White Troops" in MacGregor and Nalty, *Blacks in the Armed Forces*, 270.

32. "Integration of Negro and White Troops" in MacGregor and Nalty, 270.

fication opened the way for accusations of discrimination "should the recruitment of Negroes continue to be curtailed through the medium of qualitative recruiting," the report predicted: "The only alternative which would permit maintaining present Caucasian/Negro strength ratios would be to actively recruit Negroes in the higher mental groups. This solution would not be without pitfalls, as quotas would have to be established which might result in more accusations of discrimination."[33]

Officials of the Eisenhower administration had never seriously considered the possibility that the elimination of official buttresses of military segregation and discrimination would reveal more complex forms of discrimination. Serious consideration of the depth of racial inequality required more than pronouncements by administration spokesmen advocating an official end to discrimination in the services. Rather than designing a comprehensive strategy for racial equality, official calls for desegregation and nondiscrimination had cast American military personnel as the actors in a public display of symbolic allegiance to the ideal of racial equality. The military's mission, to reassure foreign and domestic observers of America's formal commitment to racial democracy, had not required the complete abolition of racial inequalities, but only the projection of a sought-after ideal. Political criticism, black organizational pressure, and press exposure, however, had chipped away at the facade of racial equality to reveal the limitations of a racial strategy based upon official pronouncement and symbolic action. All-black units were gone, but blacks remained concentrated in menial job categories, kept there by unequal educational opportunities, military seniority patterns, "white flight" from lower echelons, "qualitative recruitment" based upon pessimistic assumptions about black capabilities, and the increasing technological sophistication required of military service. Declarations of nondiscrimination had been followed by new devices of delay and frustration. Progress had been made, but the American military remained less a model of American democracy in action than a mirror of its racial shortcomings.

33. Bureau of Naval Personnel, "Memorandum on Discrimination of the Negro, 24 Jan. 1959," in MacGregor and Nalty, *Blacks in the Armed Forces*, 132–40.

3.

The Nation's Showplace

If the President and his subordinates intended the personnel of the military services to exemplify democratic idealism as "soldiers of freedom," their objectives for the renovation of the public image of the nation's capital were no less lofty. Washington, D.C. was for visitors and the official representatives of other nations the visible illustration of American democracy in action. But although billed as the "nation's showplace," the capital fell far short of the description in its treatment of black residents. The President's Committee on Civil Rights in 1947 had noted shameful patterns of officially sanctioned segregation and discrimination in Washington restaurants, theaters, public lodgings, housing, jobs, schools, recreational facilities, and the police and fire departments. Although the committee's findings were echoed the following year by the National Committee on Segregation in the Nation's Capital, responses to rectify the problems cited lagged badly. In the 1952 campaign, Dwight D. Eisenhower described District discrimination against nonwhite foreign visitors as "a humiliation to his nation," and added, "This is the kind of loss we can ill afford in today's world."[1]

Eisenhower would soon learn, as his predecessors had, that racial progress in the District was a goal easier stated than accomplished. Washington, D.C., remained a Southern town in many respects, although demographic change was leaving its mark upon the city. Wartime and postwar expansion of federal employment had encouraged additional black in-migration. By 1950 46,000 blacks worked for the federal government; another 2,000 were taxi drivers and chauffers, 2,500 cooked in District restaurants and clubs, and 8,000 served food and drink in city establishments. At the same time, owing to the presence of Howard University, the District's black professional elite numbered among the largest of any American city. However, by 1950 the average black family in Washington still earned only 63 percent of white family income; housing was increasingly segregated and dangerously overcrowded; crime and juvenile delinquency were rising to alarming levels; schools were old and deteriorating; and white migration was accelerating suburban residential segregation and central city decline. Expressions of concern by capital politicians about racial injustice made little apparent impact upon the racial customs of a community experiencing the pains of postwar migration and urban deterioration.[2]

The slowness of racial progress in the District sprang from many sources, including the lack of a central authority or electorate capable of demanding racial accountability and the influence exerted by congressional oversight committees dominated by Southerners. The President possessed the authority to appoint members to the city's Board of Commissioners, a three-person supervisory body composed of two civilians and a representative of the Army Corps of Engineers. However, Eisenhower's civilian appointments to the board—Samuel Spencer, a lawyer and Republican campaign contributor; Robert E. McLaughlin, an Eisenhower backer and former legislative director of the American Veterans' Service; David Karrick, president of Fidelity Stor-

1. Schlundt, "Civil Rights Policies," 22; Eisenhower, *Mandate for Change*, 234.
2. National Association of Intergroup Relations Officials, "Civil Rights in the Nation's Capital" (Washington, D.C., 1959), 1–2; Kluger, *Simple Justice*, 508–11. For an overview of the development of race relations in Washington, D.C., see Constance M. Green, *The Secret City: A History of Race Relations in the Nation's Capital* (Princeton, N.J., 1967).

age Company and a District real estate owner; and Mark Sullivan, an investment banker—followed the accustomed pattern of rewarding partisan loyalty rather than commitment to a cause. Although in the 1952 campaign Eisenhower had promised black supporter Bishop D. Ward Nichols of the African Methodist Episcopal Church to consider seriously a black candidate for the Board of Commissioners, his only major black city appointee was E.C. Hayes, named chairman of the District Public Utilities Commission. Even the selection of the more liberal Samuel Spencer to the Board of Commissioners in 1953 followed the ill-advised initial nomination of Walter Fowler, a former District budget director categorized as an integration opponent during his previous service on the Board of Recreation.[3]

The history of the Board of Commissioners revealed the importance of its third member, the engineer commissioner, as a "swing vote" on controversial city issues. Advocates of racial integration, however, took little comfort in the fact that the engineer commissioner's selection was dictated by the Corps of Engineers, whose funding priorities virtually mandated a cozy relationship with the congressional oversight committees and the city's conservative Board of Trade. The Board of Trade's own attitude toward "divisive" social issues such as racial integration was voiced by Vice President William H. Press: "Our job is to build a community here that is a prosperous community. Our principal interest is in the economics of the thing. The minute we get involved in these social problems we divide into different camps." The social camaraderie of Board of Trade members, reinforced by membership in exclusive private clubs such as the Chevy Chase Country Club and the Metropolitan Club, only added to their reluctance to risk personal antagonisms over District racial issues. A less exclusive civic organization, the Federal City Council, did appear in the fall of 1954, but it failed to maintain its initial commitment to the inclusion of women, labor, and minority representatives.[4]

In the absence of concerted business support for racial progress, the problem was left to community racial, religious, and civic groups, including the Urban League, the NAACP, the Council of Churches, the American Friends Service Committee, and the Federation of Civic Organizations. But the lack of black electoral

3. Schlundt, "Civil Rights Policies," 26; Martha Derthick, *City Politics in Washington, D.C.* (Cambridge, Mass., 1962), 58.
4. Derthick, *City Politics*, 41, 58, 61, 89–92.

leverage and the middle-class orientation of the advocacy groups themselves limited effective representation of the minority poor. As one black observer noted, "There is a fairly large segment of the Negro population which is, to put it gently, poor—laborers, dishwashers, and so on, who have borne the brunt of racial differences. They are unorganized with almost no political weight." The city's newspapers contributed little additional impetus for racial progress, with the Washington *Star* opposed to integration on procedural grounds and the chain newspapers—the *Times-Herald* and *News*—remaining silent. The city's "liberal" bloc— the Washington *Post*, the Central Labor Council, the Democratic Central Committee, the League of Women Voters, and the aforementioned racial and religious organizations—seldom could agree among themselves on the need for establishing racial progress as a top priority. Labor union support for integration, for example, was hampered by rank-and-file resistance, particularly within the building trades locals.[5]

Home rule, a legislative initiative with the potential for increasing minority influence in city affairs, received support in principle from President Eisenhower, but his own proposals were carefully restricted by partisan considerations. The President's support for District home rule in the 1952 campaign had covered only the election of local officials, and it failed to offer residents the national electoral rights or congressional voting representation of the states. Clearly aware of the political costs in the Congress of home rule endorsement, the administration plan only advocated the election of a mayor, city council, school board, and a nonvoting member of the House of Representatives. Eisenhower's support of any form of home rule actually reflected less his own commitment than the eagerness of some of his aides to advocate it in order to attract black voters.[6] District home rule attainments during the Eisenhower years, including the 1955 election law (authorizing the election of party officials and convention delegates) and the Twenty-third Amendment to the Constitution, approved by Congress in 1960, came without strong administration backing. The federal amendment itself was restricted to suffrage in national elections and limited the District to no more electoral votes than the least populous state in the Union.[7]

5. Ibid., 95–98, 102–17.
6. "Memorandum from Sturgis Warner, 8 Dec. 1953," White House Central Files, Subject Series, Box 23, DDEL.
7. D.C. Home Rule File, White House Staff Files, Gerald Morgan Records, Box 8, DDEL; Derthick, 73.

In addressing the District's racial problems, Eisenhower saw his primary duty not as the extension of capital home rule but rather the upgrading of the image of the "citadel of democracy" through unobtrusive executive actions. The removal of federal mandates authorizing discriminatory practices would demonstrate, in his view, the administration's commitment to the moral requirements of equal opportunity while limiting administration involvement to areas of clear federal jurisdiction. At a January 15, 1953, meeting with District committee chairmen Sid Simpson of Illinois and Francis Case of South Dakota the President received early, convincing proof of the reluctance of Congress itself to act against District segregation. Fearing inaction on any District legislative proposals, or even worse, Southern filibusters of administration legislation in other fields, Eisenhower directed his staff to develop a list of initiatives that would not require legislative fiat. A report delivered to the President on February 5 indicated that District desegregation in areas under his authority could require as many as eighty-four separate actions.[8] In his first State of the Union address, Eisenhower publicly pledged to "use whatever authority exists in the office of the President to end segregation in the District of Columbia." His actual legislative proposals to make the capital city "symbolic of the democracy of the Republic," however, were confined to limited home rule measures and the addition of two positions to the Board of Commissioners. Press observers concluded from the President's remarks that he had judged any compulsory civil rights program in the District or elsewhere to be "beyond the realm of practical possibility for a long time to come."[9]

The administration's first clear success in eliminating the blot of Jim Crow from the capital resulted not from legislation but from a court case involving segregated city restaurants. In the *District of Columbia* v. *John R. Thompson Co.*, the Federal Circuit Court of Appeals initially ruled on January 22, 1953, that the Reconstruction era "lost laws" passed by District legislative assemblies were invalid, thereby permitting continued racial exclusion by capital restaurants. At the urging of Interior Secretary Douglas McKay, the Justice Department filed a "friend of the court" brief before the Supreme Court on March 10 opposing the Court of Appeals

8. *New York Times*, Jan. 16, 1953; Dwight D. Eisenhower Diary, Jan. 15, 1953, Whitman File, Diary Series, Box 3, DDEL; Merlyn Pitzele to Eisenhower, Jan. 27, 1953, Thomas Stephens to Pitzele, Jan. 28, 1953, Official File, Box 282, DDEL.
9. *New York Times*, Feb. 3, 1953.

ruling. In openly contesting the decision, the Justice Department knowingly invited the wrath of District congressional committee members such as Representative James Davis of Georgia, who accused the administration of trying to "outdeal the New Deal." Despite the criticism, department spokesman Philip Elman, a Truman administration holdover, asserted that the District had been given powers to enact antidiscrimination laws similar to those of territories. Elman also urged the high court to rule quickly, given delays of home rule legislation in Congress awaiting the decision. On June 8, the Supreme Court sided with the administration by upholding the 1872 "lost law" barring racial exclusion from public restaurants.[10]

The *Thompson* decision furnished new muscle to the administration's behind-the-scenes attempts to persuade local businesses to discontinue segregated services. Eisenhower recognized the particular difficulty of persuading local proprietors to desegregate, given their control of "privately owned" enterprises "not subject to direct government control." After lengthy disputes two theaters did open their doors to blacks, as did three downtown movie houses. Selected hotels also allowed blacks to attend private functions, but not to use public dining areas. Stepping up his personal lobbying following the *Thompson* decision, Eisenhower directly courted the help of major Hollywood studio executives in exerting pressure on recalcitrant local movie house operators.[11] The administration's private campaigning bore fruit, for by the end of the year segregation officially had ceased in District hotels, motels, theaters, and restaurants. In addition, on November 25, 1953, Board of Commissioners president Samuel Spencer announced the official end of segregated facilities and personnel in departments within the board's direct authority. A proud Eisenhower wired Spencer, "Because the District is in an area of exclusive federal jurisdiction, I deem this progress to be of special significance."[12]

Although David A. Sawyer of the District Council on Human Relations later attributed the Board of Commissioners' November 25 action to White House pressure, outside black observers gave ultimate credit for the announcement to the importance placed

10. Ibid., Jan. 23, 1953, March 11, 1953, March 13, 1953, May 1, 1953, and May 2, 1953; Dwight D. Eisenhower, *The White House Years: Waging Peace, 1956–1961* (New York, 1963), 48.

11. *New York Times*, Jan. 23, 1953; Eisenhower, *Mandate for Change*, 236.

12. Adams, *Firsthand Report*, 334; Samuel Spencer to Eisenhower, Nov. 25, 1953, and Eisenhower to Spencer, Dec. 20, 1953, Official File, Box 282, DDEL.

National Park Service/Dwight D. Eisenhower Library
President Eisenhower outlines the administration's early accomplishments in desegregating the armed forces and the District of Columbia before the National Association for the Advancement of Colored People, March 10, 1954.

upon garnering favorable international opinion. Regardless of the reasons for his behind-the-scenes activity, Eisenhower received an outpouring of praise from civil rights advocates for his efforts in the District. The American Friends Service Committee saluted Eisenhower by noting, "We have been greatly aided by the President and his staff. It has been our hope that a general attitude and support for the President's pronouncement may be encouraged at all levels within the agencies of the federal government." In his radio report on the first year's achievements of his administration, Eisenhower claimed: "We have used the power of the Federal Government, wherever it clearly extends, to combat and erase racial discrimination and segregation—so that no man of any color or creed will be able to say, "This is not a free land' "[13]

Despite the President's optimistic assertions, much work remained unfinished in eradicating segregation from District facilities. Within the city's Welfare Department, the all-black Industrial Home School for Colored Children continued in existence until 1956, despite complaints of vandalism directed at overcrowded black juveniles at the home. The Home for the Aged and Infirm also remained segregated for two years after the Board of Commissioners' ban. Sections of the Department of Corrections, including the Jail Division, were not affected at all by the desegregation decree. Within the Department of Health, the Capital School of Nursing at the District of Columbia General Hospital stayed all white for three additional years, although the Health Department held its first desegregated mental health workshop for elementary schoolteachers in 1955. In July 1956, the American Veterans Council still reported the use of racial designations on rooming-house licenses. Seeking additional enforcement tools, the District Board of Commissioners on December 7, 1953 began new efforts to secure court rulings on the enforceability of the Act of 1872 and the ordinances of the Corporation of Washington of 1869 and 1870 prohibiting discrimination in public accommodations and entertainments. The President, however, denied any knowledge of the Commissioners' action, or cooperation in it, at a press conference the next day.[14]

13. Derthick, 121; Parmet, *Eisenhower*, 437; *Public Papers of the Presidents: Dwight D. Eisenhower, 1953–1961*, "Radio Report to the American People on the Achievements of the Administration and the 83rd Congress," 556.

14. Schlundt, "Civil Rights Policies," 28–29; Phineas Indritz (American Veterans' Council) to E. Frederic Morrow, July 14, 1956, White House Staff Files, E. Frederic Morrow Records, Box 10, DDEL; Jacob Javits, *Discrimination — USA* (New York, 1960), 222.

The most glaring deficiency of the District's new desegregation program was the continued segregation of facilities within the province of the District Board of Recreation, for many years a buttress of resistance to racial integration. In 1949, the board had turned aside proddings from the Interior Department to end separate facilities, and at the beginning of the Eisenhower administration, 100 out of 140 public recreation areas remained racially segregated. Although a majority of the members of the Recreation Board were appointed by the Board of Commissioners, it operated independently from the commissioners and was not subject to their segregation ban of November 25. The White House received a direct indication of the city's continuing segregation problem in 1954 when a Howard University choir scheduled to perform at official Lincoln's Birthday ceremonies refused to enter by a rear arena door and left the building. Eisenhower, one of the dignitaries present, learned of the incident only afterward from press secretary James Hagerty. Noting to the press his understanding that the choir's bus driver had refused to go around to the side door by which he himself had entered, Eisenhower jokingly added, "I hope there is no connection between these two facts." The President did state his intention to apologize to the choir if it felt it had been rudely treated, but declined to follow up the incident further. In April, the Recreation Board inched toward segregation's elimination by authorizing the Superintendent of Recreation to use his discretion in issuing permits for the unrestricted use of facilities. A comprehensive desegregation program, however, began only after the release of the U.S. Supreme Court school integration ruling in May. Responding to the *Brown* decision of May 17, 1954, White House aides relayed the President's wishes for prompt integration of recreational facilities to city officials, and the following day the Board of Recreation ordered the institution of a desegregation program in its facilities.[15]

The administration's ongoing efforts to eliminate official District segregation received renewed praise from local integration advocates. The Washington *Post*, in an April 22, 1955 editorial entitled "Discrimination on the Run," revised its initial skepticism toward administration desegregation policy: "We are now happy to acknowledge that it has been one of the strongest features of the Eisenhower Administration, and the community and

15. Schlundt, "Civil Rights Policies," 34; *New York Times*, Feb. 11, 1954; Adams, *Firsthand Report*, 334; Javits, *Discrimination — USA*, 218.

the country are healthier for it." In a backhanded compliment to the President, Representative Charles Diggs warned his Democratic colleagues that the Eisenhower ticket in 1956 would make serious inroads among black voters "unless the Democratic members of this body wake up and match the executive and judicial departments in civil rights accomplishments." Despite Eisenhower's efforts, however, the District remained far from a national showplace in the integration of public accommodations, entertainments, and recreational facilities. Country clubs still discriminated even against such highly placed black officials as White House aide E. Frederic Morrow. Bowling alleys and other public amusements continued to segregate, as did the police boys' clubs. As late as 1959, Virginia NAACP representatives still found it necessary to caution boosters of a world's fair in the District about the continuing segregation of the city's immediate surroundings.[16]

Although other vestiges of segregation lingered, after the *Brown* decision most official and popular attention shifted to the desegregation of the District's public school system. The task city school officials faced was enormous, for the system included over 100,000 students, 3,700 teachers, and nearly 160 buildings. Desegregation of this educational complex was further complicated by white movement to the suburbs, producing a white student decline from 50 percent of total school enrollment in 1950 to only 37 percent in 1955. In contrast, through the efforts of Archbishop Patrick A. O'Boyle, desegregation had already begun in the District's parochial schools. O'Boyle refrained from issuing a diocesewide integration decree, since five Maryland counties were included in his jurisdiction, but he promoted the development of a "smooth process" for desegregation that began in two high schools in 1950 and in the rest of the system the following year.[17]

Unfortunately, the District's own Board of Education, a nine-member body with three black members (appointed by the Federal District Court upon PTA recommendations), did not show equal initiative. In December 1952, the board did vote to invite community opinion on the integration issue, but public response

16. "Memorandum of E. Frederic Morrow," Oct. 26, 1959, White House Staff Files, Morrow Records, Box 10, DDEL; E. Frederic Morrow, *Black Man in the White House* (New York, 1963), 83–84; Donovan, *Eisenhower* 163; James L. Sundquist, *Politics and Policy: The Eisenhower, Kennedy, and Johnson Years* (Washington, D.C., 1968), 223.

17. "Civil Rights in the Nation's Capital," 5; Jeanne Rogers, "Nation's Showcase?," in Don Shoemaker, ed., *With All Deliberate Speed* (Westport, Conn., 1970), 147, 161.

was limited. Anticipating the phased elimination of mandated segregation, in 1953 the District did unify its separate boards of examiners, and joint examinations were prepared first in health, physical education, athletics, and safety in December. The following January, the board began to issue a single set of examinations for senior high school teachers' use in April and elementary and junior high schools in June. In addition, school administrators held seven conferences on intercultural relations, including the first interracial teachers' meeting in the District.[18]

Specific action by the Board of Education and the administration to eliminate mandated segregation, however, awaited the determination by the Supreme Court of the *Brown* suits, including the District of Columbia case of *Bolling* v. *Sharpe*. A previous circuit court ruling had maintained that two congressional laws of 1864 and 1874 on black school supervision and pupil assignment mandated racial segregation, and Attorney General Herbert Brownell reported deep splits within the Board of Education on challenging traditional school segregation. Brownell did note, however, the board's willingness to cooperate with the White House if it took the desegregation lead. Upon release of the Supreme Court's ruling on May 17, Eisenhower called a meeting with the city's Board of Commissioners the following day, and he urged their cooperation in making the city a model of peaceful desegregation. In addition, the White House requested that the District's Corporation Counsel prepare legislation designed to eliminate the city's dual school system.[19]

In its own response to the *Brown* decision, the Board of Education declared at its May 25 meeting: "We affirm our intention to secure the right of every child, within his own capacity, to the full, equal, and impartial use of all school facilities and the right of all qualified teachers to teach where needed within the school system." To meet the board's pledge, Superintendent of Schools Hobart M. Corning presented a five-point desegregation plan, including pupil and teacher assignments without regard to race; redrawing of District school boundaries for the 1955–56 term; a timetable for the integration of new students, transfers, and three thousand overcrowded blacks during 1954–55; and the desegregation of two teachers' colleges. Corning also privately relayed to Samuel Spencer his preference that new school district bound-

18. Derthick, *City Politics*, 214, 223.
19. Schlundt, "Civil Rights Policies," 30; Telephone call, Eisenhower to Att. Gen. Herbert Brownell, Nov. 5, 1953, Whitman File, Diary Series, Box 5, DDEL; *New York Times*, May 18, 1954 and May 19, 1954; Eisenhower, *Waging Peace*, 50.

aries take effect in the 1954–55 term to minimize the number of transfers involved in the desegregation process. Deferring action initially until June 2, the Board of Education then adopted the Corning plan and defeated a proposal for immediate integration in September by a 5 to 3 vote along racial lines.[20]

Despite criticism by the local NAACP chapter of the slowness of the desegregation program, the Board of Education backed down from part of its initial plan by reinstating a racial tally of pupil enrollment and teacher assignment for the fall term. Nevertheless, the anti-integration Federation of Citizens' Associations still attacked the revised District plan as too hasty, and hinted at a Supreme Court challenge. On September 4, the District began its transfer of three thousand black students and desegregated its kindergartens. According to Assistant Superintendent Norman J. Nelson, "not one single thing untoward" happened on the opening day of classes. The Federation of Citizens' Associations, however, pointed to the problems presented by "hardship cases" —children of one race isolated in schools of another. Seven elementary schools contained only one white child, and four other schools held fewer than twenty whites apiece. Four facilities contained only one black student, and fewer than twenty blacks attended each of twenty-three previously all-white schools.[21]

Encouraged at the absence of racial incidents, Superintendent Corning accelerated the desegregation calendar a week later by giving any desiring students the option of remaining in present facilities or of transferring immediately to the rezoned schools planned for the next school year. But one month after classes began, twenty-five hundred white students staged a four-day "strike" against desegregated classes at the Anacostia schools. Despite the pleas of Thurgood Marshall of the NAACP for direct White House intervention, school officials, armed with the threat of withholding picketers' school privileges, were able to quell the protests. Still criticized by the NAACP and the Americans for Democratic Action as too slow, the initial stages of the Corning plan proceeded without further incident. Genuine integration, however, remained a distant goal. Even after the 1954 start, 27 percent of District schools were totally segregated, another 37 percent were at least 98 percent of one race, another 18 percent

20. *New York Times*, May 26, 1954 and June 3, 1954; Spencer to Eisenhower, June 7, 1954, Official File, Box 282, DDEL; Rogers 147–49.

21. *New York Times*, July 14, 1954, Sept. 11, 1954, Sept. 14, 1954, and Sept. 16, 1954; Rogers, "Nation's Showcase," 149.

were at least 90 percent of one race, and only 18 percent were at least 10 percent mixed.[22]

In addition to transferring children to new schools, the District desegregation plan also phased out the system's dual administrative structure. Before the District had initiated its desegregation program, all six system-wide administrative positions had been held by white officials, with subordinate racial divisions staffed by dual sets of officials. After the beginning of desegregation, Superintendent Corning reshuffled his chief white lieutenants and created a position of deputy in charge of coordinated services for the former black division head. Separate slates of Board of Education candidates, another vestige of the dual system, merged into a single slate in the summer of 1954. Other duplicate positions disappeared through attrition, saving the District $90,000 but continuing white control of the subsequent administrative structure.[23]

During the tense first year of desegregation, Corning maintained that "the greatest of the education growing pains are yet to come." He added, "I held my breath and I'm still holding it — at the magnitude of the job." The "growing pains" Corning referred to centered upon the tensions produced in bringing together students with different racial, social, and economic backgrounds. Principal Charles E. Bish of McKinley High School, noting that "the cultures of the two races were not as near alike as many of us thought," advised black students to conform to white classroom guidelines on obscenity, weapon possession, and grooming habits. A teenage grievance committee was established to ease racial tensions, and the citywide association of student councils admitted black students into its membership. New programs in the desegregated schools included mixed "live history" assemblies, integrated athletic teams, and the desegregation of the high school cadet corps at the Tomb of the Unknown Soldier. Integrated dances were canceled the first year, but proms were scheduled for subsequent years. And grade school desegregation, less publicized than the movement of high school students, proceeded smoothly as white pupils gradually adjusted to the greater emphasis on discipline and formality in former all-black schools.[24]

With the transfer of twelve hundred high school students to

22. *New York Times*, Oct. 1, 1954, Oct. 5, 1954, and Oct. 8, 1954; Rogers, "Nation's Showcase," 149.
23. Rogers, "Nation's Showcase," 153.
24. Ibid., 148, 150–51.

neighborhood facilities in February 1955, the movement of pupils to new schools in the 1954–55 school year ended. On the first anniversary of the *Brown* decision, the American Friends Service Committee hailed the District's desegregation progress, but Superintendent Corning cautioned, "Desegregation, the mechanical mixing of people and things, virtually has been completed. But integration, the conversion of the two segments of the schools into a smooth running single system, still requires the work of all." Even by Corning's definition, desegregation actually had not been accomplished, for by the 1956 school year 25 out of 169 schools were still segregated, including 19 all-black schools. By the fall of 1956, more than 75,000 of the District's 108,000 students were black, the product of a white decline of more than 4,000 and a black increase of 5,000 within a single year. Overcrowded grade-school classes numbered from 36 to 48 pupils, and first-graders in some areas attended on a half-day basis because of shortages of administrators, teachers, and classroom space.[25]

White parents began to complain about a lowering of educational standards in the newly desegregated schools, and white administrators echoed their fears. One white grade-school principal claimed that declines in educational quality occurred "because so many Negro children come to Washington from an inferior school environment where they had, perhaps, not the same well-trained teachers." White fears of declining standards were not eased by the comments of a black principal who asserted the importance of "sacrificing standards to a reasonable limit to obtain the advantage of having both groups share the experience of living together." Citywide achievement tests given the first year of desegregation showed black students performing more poorly than whites, with overall District levels falling short of national averages in reading skills, spelling, arithmetic, and social studies. Eighteen hundred grade school pupils, predominantly black, were labeled "slow learners," and blacks constituted more than 3,000 of 3,899 students in "special classes." A 1955 request by school principals that the District investigate these problem cases overtaxed the resources of the board's research department. In addition, some principals accused their colleagues in formerly all-black schools of "dumping" their problem students on other institutions in order to increase their schools' academic honors and their own chances for career advancement. Charges of dump-

25. Ibid., 152–55.

ing were echoed by black Board of Education member Margaret Just Butcher, a faculty member at Howard University.[26]

Faced with growing accusations of declining educational quality, Superintendent Corning was forced to defend the District from charges by congressional committees that the desegregation program had left the schools "in a mess." At the instigation of subcommittee chairman James Davis of Georgia and Representative John Bell Williams of Mississippi, ten days of hearings were devoted to the District's school desegregation program in September 1956. Davis, an avowed segregationist, previously had accused Eisenhower of trying to make the capital "a second Harlem" and had ridiculed the President for sending his grandson to an all-white private school in Virginia. During Corning's opening testimony, Representative Williams attempted to force the superintendent to acknowledge White House pressure for integration, but Corning replied, "This is not so."[27]

Testimony by other school officials, however, revealed less than complete enthusiasm for desegregation. Board of Education president C. Melvin Sharpe, although claiming that "we have made great advances," judged that "present events indicate if we had been a little more moderate we would have succeeded better." Roosevelt High School principal Elva Wells, representing a school with a 45 percent black enrollment, blamed the "belligerency" of her new black students for upsetting integration progress, and Macfarland Junior High School principal Arthur Storey recommended the removal of problem youngsters to special adjustment classes. Research on the District's four-track pupil assignment scheme revealed that 315 whites and only 50 blacks attended college preparatory courses, while 645 whites and 1,453 blacks went to "terminal" courses and 158 whites and 1,319 blacks were assigned to "basics" classes for slow learners. As expected, the Southern-dominated subcommittee's majority report blamed integration for white flight from the school district, increases in juvenile delinquency and sexual offenses, staff and teacher demoralization, spiraling costs, and an overall regression in educational quality. Pointing out that the District "cannot be copied by those who seek an orderly and successful school operation,"[28] it called for the reinstitution of segregation.

26. Ibid., 151, 154.
27. *New York Times*, Jan. 25, 1956 and Jan. 28, 1956; Rogers, "Nation's Showcase," 156–58.
28. Rogers, "Nation's Showcase," 158–60.

Criticism of the subcommittee because of its anti-integration bias quickly surfaced. The subcommittee's minority filed its own report challenging the majority's findings, asserted that integration could not be blamed for the social ills cited, and accused the subcommittee staff of selectivity in presenting evidence. The Washington Committee for the Public Schools, a pro-integration organization formed in the same month as the subcommittee hearings, issued its own refutations of the majority report. The following year, in a study sponsored by the Anti Defamation League of B'nai B'rith, Assistant Superintendent Carl F. Hanson labeled the District's program a "miracle of social adjustment." The Washington *Post* sent out its own "truth squad" to rebut the subcommittee's findings and published a series of articles by Erwin Knoll entitled "The Truth about Desegregation," which were reprinted in pamphlet form.[29]

Successfully weathering the initial storms of controversy, the Board of Education could point to an upgrading of black achievement levels and an overall improvement in student performance by the 1959–60 school year, despite increasing proportions of black pupils. However, school officials still could not honestly claim that the abolition of official segregation had produced a truly integrated school system. White abandonment of the city school system had produced a drop in white pupil enrollment to only 20 percent of the District total in 1960. Because of "white flight" and black in-migration, as late as 1958 seven of every ten city schools were 90 percent or more of one race, and usually the majority race was black. By 1960, nearly 14 percent of District schools remained totally segregated, another 40 percent were still 98 percent of one race, 23 percent were 90 percent of one race, and only 23 percent of the school system could claim better than a 9–1 racial mixture.[30]

The failure of the District of Columbia to become a national model of racial progress in education was matched by an inability to provide sufficient employment opportunities for its black citizens. Upon the direct intervention of Vice President Richard M. Nixon, the District Board of Commissioners issued an order in late September 1953 requiring city contracts with private firms to contain nondiscrimination employment clauses. On November 25, the board followed up its earlier proclamation with an additional decree stating that all District personnel actions would be

29. Ibid., 161–62; Derthick, *City Politics*, 220–21.
30. Schlundt, "Civil Rights Policies," 32; Derthick, *City Politics*, 221.

based entirely "on merit and fitness." Despite the assurances of the commissioners, much of the actual task of promoting equal employment by private city contractors fell upon the President's Committee on Government Contracts, chaired by Nixon, and its subcommittee on District affairs, headed by Representative James Roosevelt of California. Other active members of the District subcommittee included George Meany, president of the American Federation of Labor, and publisher Helen Rogers Reid.[31]

Following a series of liaison meetings with local civil rights organizations and civic groups, the Roosevelt subcommittee targeted a select number of city firms for its lobbying efforts, beginning with the city's major bus and streetcar employer, the Capital Transit Company. With the cooperation of the White House and the District's Public Utilities Commission, Roosevelt garnered a private session with the transit company's president in early November. However, fearing work stoppages by white employees opposed to integration, company officials resisted taking any remedial action, which forced Roosevelt to go directly to chief stockholder Louis Wolfson. Despite Roosevelt's success in getting Wolfson's grudging consent to begin black hiring, the company took an additional fourteen months after the February 1954 meeting before acting. Awaiting a specific union promise not to initiate a work stoppage, Capital Transit eventually responded only after the city Public Utilities Commission threatened to withhold company dividends until "further notice." Stockholder Wolfson soon sold his assets to a successor company, the District of Columbia Transit Company, which by May 1960 had hired forty-four black workers, of whom only twenty-six were currently employed.[32]

The subcommittee's next major case, against the Chesapeake and Potomac Telephone Company, stemmed from a complaint originally filed by the NAACP in late 1951 and renewed the following year. Once again, White House and subcommittee officials sought results through quiet persuasion. Roosevelt, administration aide Maxwell Rabb, and CIO representatives conferred

31. Spencer to Richard M. Nixon, Oct. 26, 1953; James P. Mitchell Papers, Box 125; Jacob Seidenberg, "The President's Committee on Government Contracts: An Appraisal," 57–59, Mitchell Papers, Box 130, DDEL.
32. "Report of the Subcommittee on Liaison with Interested Groups," Nov. 30, 1953, "Minutes of Meeting of the Committee on Government Contracts," Dec. 1, 1953, Mitchell Papers, Box 125; Seidenberg, 60–62, Mitchell Papers, Box 130, DDEL.

with company officials who indicated that resistance centered among telephone operators in the "traffic" department. On February 8, 1954, the company announced its initial plans for desegregating clerical and stenographic employees by transferring two blacks. By December, however, no changes had been reported in either the traffic department or skilled craft jobs. Another year later, Clarence Mitchell of the NAACP protested Chesapeake and Potomac's continuing footdragging to the Vice President. Abandoning its prior strategy of private negotiations, the Government Contracts Committee ordered the General Services Administration to undertake a full investigation. The GSA's report of March 26, 1956 indicated that although general departmental desegregation had begun, many job categories within departments had not been touched. Following exasperating delays at both the Washington and Baltimore offices of Chesapeake and Potomac, officials promised to employ black telephone and teletype operators, and in May the first two black operators were hired.[33]

Roosevelt and his subcommittee colleagues encountered similar frustrations in their dealings with Government Services, Incorporated, the major operator of government cafeterias in the capital. Eighty percent of the cafeteria work force was black, but these workers primarily were confined to menial job categories. Ironically, the initial complaint against GSI had been filed by a white employee. The subcommittee eventually was able to "close" the case in 1957 when a minority representative was added to the company's board of directors, and officials promised to recruit college-educated black dieticians and nutritionists. However, by the end of the administration, GSI had only managed to hire four additional black cashiers, four supervisors, and one assistant manager.[34]

Probably the District subcommittee's greatest frustration, however, lay in its failure to make a major impact upon the segregated hiring practices of capital building trades. The subcommittee's lack of success carried special weight because of the number of major construction projects under way in the city in the 1950s, including the Southwest Redevelopment Project Area B, the alteration of the east front of the U.S. Capitol, and the erection of the new House Office Building No. 6. Electricians' union locals, despite protests from the Urban League, excluded black workmen

33. Seidenberg, 65–68, Mitchell Papers, Box 130, DDEL.
34. Ibid., 68–72.

with the consent of the GSA, which invariably ruled "no discrimination" when contractors turned down black electricians and rodmen as unqualified. By 1959, the city still employed no black stonemasons, tile setters, asbestos workers, glaziers, lathers, painters, paperhangers, or iron workers on its projects, and it hired few black steamfitters, sheet-metal workers, plumbers, and carpenters. The District's bricklayers' union maintained separate black and white locals, and only the roofing and masonry trades contained significant numbers of black workmen.[35] Following the formation of a new Committee on Government Contracts subcommittee on District employment problems in 1959, labor chief George Meany lobbied local contractors and union officials to hire more black construction workers. The subcommittee as a whole also called upon government agencies to direct contractors to meet nondiscrimination requirements, but although the rodmen's union did refer several blacks to union projects, it continued to resist their admission to the local. The hiring of three black rodmen under the auspices of Local No. 20, in April 1960, took place only after intensive lobbying by the Committee on Government Contracts, AFL-CIO officials, and the District Commissioners' Council on Human Relations.[36]

The ability of Meany and his colleagues to encourage black hiring was limited even further by internal quarrels between Eisenhower administration members and labor representatives on the Government Contracts Committee over the relative responsibilities of contractors and unions for discrimination. After disputes between committee staff director Irving Ferman and labor members Meany and Boris Shiskin, in February 1960 Meany accused Labor Secretary James Mitchell, the committee vice-chairman, of ignoring his offer to find black electricians in return for the secretary's agreement to pressure a local contractor. The labor leader added his insistence that "the contractor can't hide behind the restrictive practices of the local union." Although Mitchell maintained that he had never received the offer from Meany, he noted privately that Ferman had "gone out on a limb" in antagonizing the labor chief, and in May Ferman resigned from committee duties for "personal reasons." Further attempts by Meany to provide black electricians were blocked by union locals'

35. Ibid., 73; "Minutes of Committee on Government Contracts," Feb. 5, 1957, Mitchell Papers, Box 125, DDEL; Guichard Parris and Lester Brooks, *Blacks in the City* (Boston, 1971), 356; NAACP, *Annual Report* (1959), 53.
36. *Washington Post*, Apr. 30, 1960.

claims that the workers were unqualified. Only in October 1960 did a federal project hire a black electrician, and it did so only after GSA administrator Franklin Floete bypassed a subcontractor and confronted the chief contractor, Democratic national committee treasurer Matthew H. McCloskey.[37]

The meager progress of the District in advancing black employment at federal projects mirrored deficiencies in black hiring and promotion within federal agencies and city departments. A 1956 survey revealed that blacks comprised only 24 percent of federal employees in sixty-two agencies. Of these, 53 percent were classified as "white collar," but 84 percent of the positions were lodged in the four lowest grades and the rest consisted of blue-collar or post-office clerical positions. The District of Columbia Fire Department, which had five all-black and nineteen all-white stations in 1954, did adopt the Board of Commissioners' ban on segregation in September of that year after prodding from the Government Contracts Committee. But by 1957 twenty-two of thirty-five fire squads remained segregated, and a 1958 survey added that 90 percent of black firemen (compared to 75 percent for whites) were in the bottom rank. Blacks were totally unrepresented in all but the lowest positions of two out of five administrative divisions of the fire department. The D.C. Police Department, owing to an unofficial 10 percent black quota, contained only 13 percent minority officers by the middle of 1959, and most squad cars remained segregated. A 1960 study of the hiring practices of the District government revealed that although blacks comprised nearly half of the employees, they were overrepresented in the lowest service grades.[38]

Accompanying changes in housing patterns perpetuated the capital's heritage of racial segregation and discrimination. Although the Supreme Court in *Shelley* v. *Kraemer* in 1948 had eroded government sanction for restrictive covenants, a report in the same year by the National Committee on Segregation in the Nation's Capital noted the growing problem of residential segregation. Although the 1950 census revealed that blacks had penetrated an additional 459 city blocks, these gains owed more to white withdrawal than to genuine integration.[39] Efforts to provide

37. *New York Times*, Feb. 28, 1960 and May 26, 1960; *Washington Star*, Oct. 20, 1960; Seidenberg, 86–93, Mitchell Papers, Box 130, DDEL.

38. NAACP, *Annual Report* (1954), 44; *New York Times*, July 27, 1959; Schlundt, "Civil Rights Policies," 27; Javits, *Discrimination — USA*, 222.

39. McCoy and Ruetten, *Quest and Response*, 333.

greater amounts of low-income housing for minorities and to reduce segregation in the capital were hampered by the District's
divided sources of housing authority. The National Capital Housing Authority (NCHA), the agency responsible for administering
public housing programs in the city, found its capacity to represent minority interests limited by its small size (six members) and
its composition, both predetermined by presidential order. Only
one NCHA member, Colonel Campbell C. Johnson of the District
Parole Board, was black. Although the NCHA announced the
official end of segregation in its public housing projects in June
1953, its efforts to obtain low-cost public housing were stymied by
the Board of Commissioners. When Commissioner Robert E.
McLaughlin, Samuel Spencer's successor on the board, tried to
obtain approval for an NCHA proposal to purchase private apart-
ments for conversion to public units rather than to construct expensive new units, fellow commissioners David Karrick and
Alvin C. Welling blocked the program. McLaughlin's colleagues
based their opposition on the argument that public housing authorities should not enter the private housing market. With the
Board of Commissioners unwilling to intervene in the private
sector, minority housing supporters found little additional encouragement within the community. The Washington Housing
Association, an advocate of public housing, rent control, and integration, was ejected from the Community Chest in 1953, re-
portedly at the urging of the real estate industry, despite the claim
of its executive director, Anna Miller, that "we only paid lip
service to integrated housing."[40]

If minority housing needs were overlooked in public housing
decisions, District urban renewal and construction projects
directly contributed to discriminatory patterns of dislocation of
black families. Once again, divided District authority over the
renewal projects contributed to the problem. The National Capital Planning Commission approved urban renewal plans and
boundaries, but the Redevelopment Land Agency participated in
project plans and the Board of Commissioners possessed final
approval rights over Planning Commission boundaries. The Redevelopment Land Agency demonstrated a dangerous proclivity
for authorizing the demolition of more housing than could reason-
ably be replaced in a given period, and with redevelopment in the
hands of private firms, low-income housing frequently was re-

40. Derthick, City Politics, 71–72, 107, 201–3.

placed with more expensive units. The awarding of redevelopment rights itself often was secretive and overly generous to outside developers, shunting minority investor interests out of the bidding. Construction on other city projects, particularly freeways, disproportionately affected low-income areas less able politically to resist displacement or to secure new housing.

Attempts to ease the pains of relocating minority residents received little aid from the Board of Commissioners. A 1957 proposal of the WHA for a separate agency to provide relocation services was initially ignored. Instead, the commissioners tried an "interagency referral system," followed by a six-month trial of a sparsely staffed Service to Displaced Families within the Department of Public Welfare. Among the commissioners, Engineer Commissioner Welling became a special target of liberal housing critics. The Washington *Post* charged on July 29, 1960: "The office of the District Engineer Commissioner is the last place in which Washington is likely to find effective leadership for its lagging urban renewal program, whoever happens to be filling the post at the moment. Retiring Commissioner Welling has more than once attempted to sidetrack the renewal program."[41]

Lacking effective political support inside the District government or assistance from white private housing interests, blacks seeking housing placed increasing reliance upon the limited resources of black borrowing institutions, the D.C. Industrial Bank, and the North Carolina Mutual Life Insurance Company. Blacks found housing unavailable west of the Rock Creek Park section of the city, and restrictive covenants barred access to other outlying areas. In transitional areas with mixed housing, black residents reported incidents of cross burnings and vandalism. Displacement caused by renewal projects hit low-income blacks the hardest, and relocation pressures increased the overcrowding of black neighborhoods, heightened class tensions among blacks for scarce housing, and pushed more affluent minority families into competition with white property seekers. The result was an increasing residential segregation by class and race and continuing quarrels between the advocates of public and private housing.[42]

By the end of its term, the Eisenhower administration could point to executive actions that had removed official sanction from a wide range of discriminatory practices in the capital. Formal segregation had ended in theaters, hotels, restaurants, public

41. Ibid., 190–93, 209–11.
42. Ibid., 123–25.

housing, and federally sponsored employment. Recreational facilities and swimming pools had been integrated; blacks had gained initial entry into professional societies. And in April 1958, following NAACP charges of police brutality, the Board of Commissioners had created the District Council on Human Relations. But the actions of administration and District officials had been outpaced by demographic change and the adaptability of racial discrimination. White flight had contributed to an overall city population decline of 38,000 within a decade, despite a black increase of 130,000. Median family income in the city stood at only $5,993, compared to $7,577 for the entire metropolitan statistical area. The black unemployment rate in 1960, 5.7 percent, was more than double the white rate. Forty-five percent of District whites possessed at least a high school education; only 25 percent of blacks had attained a similar level. Most strikingly, from 1956 to 1960 the average monthly number of persons receiving general public assistance had risen from 596 to 1,574, of whom 85 percent were black, and aid to dependent children requests had jumped from 8,957 to 18,878, of which 93 percent came from blacks.[43] Despite the intentions of the administration, by the end of the decade Washington, D.C., far from being a national showplace of racial progress, was a city under siege by the forces of urban decay.

43. "Civil Rights in the Nation's Capital," 7; Derthick, *City Politics*, 20, 28, 123, 146.

4.

A Government of Merit

The employment practices of the federal government provided yet another opportunity for the Eisenhower administration to demonstrate its adherence to the principle of equal opportunity. A national government intent on presenting itself as an exemplar of democratic idealism clearly required a federal service apparently based upon merit rather than color. Although equal opportunity in federal employment purportedly had existed since the passage of the Civil Service Act of 1883, race had not been designated as a specific category of discrimination, and application photographs had not been eliminated until 1940. Motivated by the renewed interest in civil rights after World War II, the Truman administration had created the Fair Employment Board, which had utilized the investigative resources of the Civil Service Commission. Although it had lacked independent enforcement powers, the board had possessed the authority to bypass agency chiefs and to bring complaints directly to the President in cases of agency unwillingness "promptly and fully" to carry out committee recommendations.

Within the upper echelons of the executive branch, presidents also had begun to learn the symbolic value of selective minority appointments to visible (though not challenging or controversial) administrative positions. In the 1952 campaign, Eisenhower had stated his intention of incorporating "qualified" blacks in his lists of cabinet possibilities and he directed assistant Sherman Adams to seek out black candidates for administration posts.[1] Actual preparation of a list of minority candidates for administrative positions was assigned to Val Washington, Republican national committee director of minority affairs, who provided the names to the director of the administration's appointment process, Attorney General Herbert Brownell. Following the screening of the candidates' qualifications and partisan loyalty, the Eisenhower administration sprinkled blacks in symbolic posts throughout the executive departments. In the White House, Lois Lippman joined the secretarial staff, and in 1955 E. Frederic Morrow became the first member of his race to hold the position of administrative assistant to the President. Conscious of the importance of international opinion, the State Department tabbed Frank Snowden of Howard University as cultural attaché in Rome in 1954, and in 1958 it made Clifton Wharton the first black chief of mission to a white country, as minister to Rumania. Robert Lee Brokenburr, Charles H. Mahoney, and Archibald J. Carey joined the American delegation to the United Nations, and John B. Eubanks became the head of the Rural Improvements Staff for the U.S. Operations Mission of the International Cooperation Administration.[2]

Slating blacks for a select number of domestic policy positions as well, the administration appointed Jewell Stratford Rogers as an assistant U.S. attorney, Julia Cooper as an attorney in the Criminal Division of the Justice Department, and Scovel Richardson as chairman of the Board of Parole. Responding to White House pressure to name a black assistant, Secretary of Agriculture Ezra Taft Benson reluctantly tabbed John W. Mitchell in October 1953 as head of black agricultural extension work within his department. And J. Ernest Wilkins, appointed as an assistant secre-

1. New York Times, Sept. 6, 1952; Eisenhower, Waging Peace, 149; Adams, Firsthand Report, 333.

2. New York Times, Apr. 11, 1954 and Aug. 19, 1954; Donovan, Eisenhower, 154. Not all administration appointments showed an equal sensitivity to the American racial image. The appointment of James F. Byrnes as a member of the UN delegation in July 1953 brought sharp criticism from the NAACP, and Josef Malek, Soviet delegate to the UN, called him the "No. 1 Racist." New York Times, July 28, 1953 and Oct. 14, 1953.

tary of Labor in 1954 and the principal department representative to the International Labor Organization, became the first black to participate officially in a cabinet meeting. Wilkins owed his opportunity to a suspiciously arranged "accident" which prevented higher-ranking Labor Department officials from attending the cabinet session.[3]

The nature of the positions given to blacks in the executive branch clearly reflected the belief of high-ranking officials that the value of black government employees lay in their presence as symbols of national racial democracy rather than in their usefulness as policy makers. The President himself was far more ready to acknowledge publicly the virtues of loyalty and bravery in black Americans than he was their intellectual or leadership capacities. Black appointees were carefully positioned to avoid domestic political controversy while still offering a visible counterpoint to Soviet charges of "false" American democracy in race relations. One indication of the administration's fear of appearing too fervent an advocate of minority interests was the fact that its informal adviser on minority problems, Maxwell Rabb, was not a black. Rabb—a Jew, a lawyer, and a former volunteer assistant to Henry Cabot Lodge—became known by colleagues on the White House staff as the resident "liberal" on racial issues, and E. Frederic Morrow praised him as the sole staffer who took racial problems seriously. But Rabb's primary duties were those of a political troubleshooter who assumed responsibility for containing politically embarrassing racial incidents, providing the administration's response to minority complaints, and promoting Republican interests in the black community. After the murder of black youth Emmett Till in Mississippi in late 1955 and the release of Gallup Poll results indicating declining Eisenhower popularity with black voters, Rabb initiated a series of meetings with black administration officials. However, Rabb's primary aims were to provide a forum for black personnel complaints and create an early warning system for administration problems with minorities. The meetings of the group, which was dubbed the "Emancipation Committee," were kept from public knowledge to avoid the label of a "kitchen cabinet."[4]

The administration's concern with the superficial problem of projecting a color-blind image in personnel policies concealed a

3. *New York Times,* July 24, 1953, March 5, 1954, Sept. 29, 1954, and July 10, 1955; Eisenhower, *Waging Peace,* 149.
4. Morrow, *Black Man in the White House* 29–31, 223.

constant pattern of discrimination and segregation in federal agencies and offices throughout the country. Nothing demonstrated the gap between the promise of equal opportunity displayed by visible black appointees and the reality of discrimination in the Civil Service more clearly than the sad history of the President's Committee on Government Employment Policy. The Truman administration's Fair Employment Board, despite its limited powers, was seen by officials of the new administration as a potential source of political embarrassment. The holdover panel immediately justified Republican officials' fears by investigating an NAACP complaint against the Bureau of Engraving and Printing in 1953 and discovering discrimination in the Treasury Department's termination of black apprentices' employment in an "economy move." Noting the outrage of Treasury Secretary George Humphrey at the investigation, Maxwell Rabb stated to Sherman Adams in September 1954 the need to eliminate the Truman committee because of its "over-age" members and its tendency to issue rulings embarrassing to administration officials. Rabb did add, however: "We cannot abolish the Committee altogether or there would be very severe and justified public criticism."[5]

On January 18, 1955, the President solved the political headache created by the Truman board by replacing it with a new President's Committee on Government Employment Policy. Press Secretary James Hagerty claimed that the new body possessed "increased stature," since it was authorized to issue summary reports to the President. Actually, the new committee's effective authority had been reduced, in keeping both with Eisenhower's distaste for "coercive" federal agencies and the complaints of administration members about the Truman Committee's powers. The new advisory body initially included only five members (among whom were representatives of the Defense and Labor departments and the Civil Service Commission), although it was later increased to seven (with another private member and an additional representative of the Defense Department). No longer able to employ the investigative resources of the Civil Service Commission, the committee had only a three-member staff of its own, could not go over agency heads directly to the President, and had to rely upon the accused agencies themselves to investigate charges of discriminatory practices. Commit-

5. NAACP, *Annual Report* (1953), 42; Maxwell Rabb to Sherman Adams, Sept. 20, 1954, Official File, Box 473, DDEL.

Source Uncertain/Dwight D. Eisenhower Library
White House minorities adviser Maxwell N. Rabb (*left*), shown here with
Secretary of Labor James P. Mitchell in March 1954.

tee members, screened by their home-state senators and the Republican national committee, included Maxwell Abbell, honorary president of the United Synagogues of America; black minister and lawyer Archibald J. Carey of Chicago; Charles H. Kendall of the Office of Defense Mobilization; J. Ernest Wilkins of the Labor Department; and Civil Service Commissioner W. Arthur McCoy. Eisenhower hailed the creation of the new committee as a clear indication that "it is the policy of the United States Government that equal opportunity be afforded all qualified persons, consistent with law, for employment in the Federal Government."[6]

Despite the President's claims, the Committee on Government Employment Policy did not have the power to provide equal opportunity to all workers within the federal service. Ironically, because the federal government had phased out the collection of racial data on its employees the committee could not even determine exactly how many blacks worked within the federal service at any given time. Instead, it directed its efforts to issuing guidelines for supervisory personnel, preparing pamphlets for federal workers, and issuing procedural checklists to employment policy officers. The practical impact of the committee's work was less to uproot employment discrimination than to educate agencies in forestalling successful charges of discrimination by following proper formal procedures. The committee's complaint procedure, relying as it did upon the goodwill of accused agencies, could be manipulated in several ways. First, the investigation of complaints was performed by the accused agency itself. In addition, the "findings of fact" in cases were prepared by employment policy officers of the agencies in Washington, D.C., often far from the complaint source, and the reports relied upon information provided by field investigators in the offices charged with discrimination. Local complainants were never provided with the information contained in field reports, and could not defend themselves from false or misleading statements. Finally, although the full burden of proof rested with the complainant, he was never allowed to know the contents of the case file, and he was denied access to the employer's files on employment patterns, application results, or test scores to support his contentions of discrimination.[7]

Heads of agencies suspected of discriminatory practices natu-

6. Peters, *The Southern Temper*, 244.
7. Ibid., 252.

rally saw nothing wrong with the committee's procedures for investigating employment complaints. J. Edgar Hoover, director of the Federal Bureau of Investigation, praised the committee in 1957: "You have proceeded along lines of a broad program of guidance and education calculated to create a progressively favorable atmosphere." Ross Clinchy, executive director of the Committee on Government Employment Policy, admitted that such factors as fear of reprisal, lack of information about complaint procedures, procedural delays, lack of access to legal advice, inaccessibility of evidence, and awareness of the poor odds for complainant success contributed to a misleadingly low number of cases filed. Nevertheless, he expressed the conviction that federal agencies had given "darn good cooperation." The committee's second chairman, Archibald Carey, admitted, "I do not feel that the job is done," but still claimed, "I do feel that our committee has made a change in the social climate in government agencies on this question." Carey added, "We have not had occasion to complain to the President."[8]

The obvious limitations of the committee's investigative resources and techniques did not prevent the administration from making expansive claims of success in eliminating federal job inequality. In the 1958 edition of *The People Take the Lead*, a publication of the American Jewish Committee, Vice President Nixon asserted: "Ten years ago, Government employment did not always mean fair employment. Today it does. Americans are now assured that Government service — from the highest ambassador to the lowliest clerkship — is open to one and all, on the basis of ability. By scrupulously following fair employment practices, the Government not only sets an example for other employers but directly protects the rights of more than two million workers to equal opportunity." The Committee on Government Employment Policy's own December 1958 report accepted at face value the claims of executive departments that segregation had been completely eliminated, and in its final report, the committee stated that of more than 1,000 complaints submitted, only 225 had needed investigation and only 33 corrective action. In a letter of congratulations to chairman Carey, the President underscored the "moral imperative to make our practices of democracy measure up to our professions."[9]

8. Ibid., 253; U.S., President's Committee on Government Employment Policy (PCGEP), *Second Report*, 11.

9. Peters, *The Southern Temper*, 242; Eisenhower to Archibald J. Carey, Jan. 6, 1961, Whitman File, Administrative Series, Box 17, DDEL; PCGEP, *Fourth Report*, 29.

Despite assertions by administration spokesmen to the contrary, the hiring practices of the federal government had not been transformed into a model of equal opportunity in action. Simply by following administrative guidelines, agencies still could discriminate freely against black applicants. Employers could infer the race of applicants through information provided on educational background, through past employers and references, or by conducting personal interviews. Although after a federal hiring all applicants on the same register moved up the list, black job seekers again could be excluded because of rules permitting employers to cease consideration of an individual passed over three times. Other methods available to employers included filling positions with retired former employees seeking reinstatement, changing job vacancy descriptions in order to secure a different register, or simply leaving positions vacant. With these available loopholes only supplementing continuing blatant discrimination, the actual pattern of unequal employment in the federal government probably was changed little by the Committee on Government Employment Policy. A June 1956 committee study of five cities — Washington, D.C., Chicago, St. Louis, Los Angeles, and Mobile — indicated that over 80 percent of black employees were in Civil Service grade four or lower. In Mobile, Alabama, discrimination was even more widespread, with no blacks over grade six and 84 percent in the first three grades. Although a 1960 survey of the same five cities showed an increase from 3.7 percent to 5.9 percent in the share of black employees in grades five to fifteen, almost all of the gains occurred in Washington, D.C. and Chicago and were concentrated in the lower grades.[10]

Independent studies of the Southern cities of Greensboro, North Carolina, Charleston, South Carolina, Birmingham, Alabama, Knoxville, Tennessee and Atlanta, Georgia, showed an even more dramatic picture of black underemployment and concentration in menial categories. In Greensboro, only two of twenty federal agencies employed blacks above the janitorial and laborer levels. In Charleston, no blacks were employed in the U.S. Customs House, and none above janitor level could be found in the offices of the Internal Revenue Service. Birmingham offices of the IRS and the Labor Department's Bureau of Apprenticeship, Office of Solicitor, and Wages and Hours Division had no blacks in nonmenial positions, and the Federal Housing Authority office lacked a black race-relations officer. In Knoxville, offices of the

10. Peters, *The Southern Temper*, 251.

departments of Agriculture, Commerce, and Health, Education and Welfare; the FBI; the FHA; the Geological Survey; the Small Business Administration; and the Veterans Administration had not a single black employee, and fewer than 100 of the city's federal work force of 2,200 were black. In Atlanta, only five of thirty federal agencies hired blacks above the laborer level.[11]

The only "exception" to the pattern of racial exclusion from white-collar federal jobs in Southern cities was the post office, where segregation itself mandated separate services. As a result, larger numbers of black clerks, mail handlers, and carriers slightly brightened an otherwise dismal performance by federal agencies in the South in providing opportunities for blacks. The United States Employment Service's own lack of black employees in field offices further frustrated national directives that called for the rejection of discriminatory job orders filed by federal departments. As late as January 1962, the four-state regional office of the U.S. Bureau of Employment and Security for Texas, Arkansas, Oklahoma, and Louisiana did not have a single black federal employee.[12]

The impact of federal employment discrimination upon whose who depended upon the federal government for services, particularly poorer blacks, was graphically illustrated in the performance of the Department of Agriculture. Of approximately 30,000 department employees in the five lowest grades, blacks numbered only 1,600, and none occupied positions in the department's five highest grades. Within the Farmers Home Administration, the primary authority for the issuance of housing loans lay with county committees, and of all such committees, *none* had black members. The outcome of such exclusion was predictable — minorities received only 4.3 percent of farm housing loans in 1960, and in Florida, Georgia, and Tennessee not a single such loan was made to a black farmer. The Federal Extension Service contained only 12 blacks out of 238 direct employees and only 700 in a force of 15,000 cooperative employees. Blacks hired as county extension agents received pay ranging from one-third to one-half less than their white counterparts. Black farmers received much less federal assistance than their white neighbors, and shared minimally in aggregate increases in farm income. An elderly black in Tuskegee, Alabama, voiced his reaction to administration

11. Ibid., 244–49; PCGEP, *A Five-City Survey of Negro-American Employees of the Federal Government* (1957).
12. Aptheker, *Soul of the Republic*, 92.

claims of increased farm income to three times previous levels: "You don't have to be a college graduate to know that one times something is more than three times nothing."[13]

The most tragic example of the consequences of continuing government exclusion of blacks from policy positions, however, involved the shameful excesses of the federally sponsored Tuskegee, Alabama syphilis experiments. Begun in 1932 by officials of the U.S. Public Health Service, the experiments, which denied medical treatment to a group of infected sharecroppers in order to observe the long-term effects of the disease on blacks, continued unchecked until 1972. Reflecting the Eisenhower administration's preoccupation with symbolism even at the cost of perpetuating its own ignorance of institutionalized racism, in 1958 HEW presented the Oveta Culp Hobby Award for distinguished service to Eunice Rivers Laurie, a black public health nurse who served in the Tuskegee project as a go-between for white researchers and their black subjects. Secretary Marion Folsom saluted her for "notable service covering twenty-five years during which through selfless devotion and skillful human relations she has sustained the interest and cooperation of the subjects of a venereal disease *control* [italics added] program in Macon County, Alabama." In addition, the Public Health Service distributed certificates of appreciation and cash payments of twenty-five dollars to the infected sharecroppers for "twenty-five years of active participation in the Tuskegee medical research study."[14]

Hiring by no means signaled the end of the black federal employee's problems. A government of individuals willing to discriminate against his hiring did not hesitate to subject him to harassment on the job, assignment to menial responsibilities, and social exclusion. Such experiences were shared by the public symbols of racial progress in the upper echelons as well as those further down the federal employment ladder. The career of E. Frederic Morrow in the Eisenhower White House illustrated the prevalence of prejudice and insensitivity at even the highest levels of an administration publicly dedicated to equal opportunity.

E. Frederic Morrow, the third of five children, grew up in a middle-class Republican section of Hackensack, New Jersey. His father, the son of a slave, was a Methodist minister who taught

13. Ibid., 95; Morrow OH (1968), DDEL, 93.
14. *New York Times,* July 26, 1972 and July 28, 1972. For an admirable study of the Tuskegee experiments, see James H. Jones, *Bad Blood: The Tuskegee Syphilis Experiment* (New York, 1981).

seminars on the educational philosophies of Booker T. Washington and W.E.B. Du Bois and identified himself as a member of the "talented tenth." According to Morrow, the black population of Hackensack were "treated like children" by the city's political leadership, and most community leaders "fell for the flattery and chicanery of the white politicians." The Morrows, however, insisted that their children attend integrated schools and pursue self-improvement, even at the cost of social isolation from both blacks and whites. "I have never recovered from the surprise of escaping the devastating futility of life in a community that offered neither opportunity nor hope to a child born black," Morrow later noted; but his "never-ending struggle" to escape was not without ordeal. Nella Williams, his sixth-grade teacher, observed, "Fred had a difficult and painful childhood. I remember so distinctly how the whites hated him because he refused to act 'colored,' and the Negroes hated him because they thought he was trying to be white."[15]

Upon completing high school in Hackensack, the young Morrow entered Bowdoin College in 1926, one of only two black students at the school. At the outset of the Depression, he took successive jobs as a social worker in a WPA project and as a bank messenger. With the aid of black graduate fraternity contacts, in 1935 he joined the staff of *Opportunity,* the organ of the National Urban League. After two years with the Urban League, Morrow shifted to the NAACP as a branch coordinator, traveling throughout the country on chapter visits and funding campaigns. Soon after the outbreak of World War II, he entered the army and successfully contested a discriminatory ruling barring him from Officers' Candidate School. Despite his hopes of an overseas assignment, Morrow spent the war stateside countering attempts to drive him from the service. Mustered out in 1946, Morrow enrolled in the Rutgers University Law School, received his degree in 1948, and joined the public affairs division of the Columbia Broadcasting System in 1950.[16]

Having inherited the Republican loyalties of his native community, Morrow led a successful fight in 1948 to admit blacks into the Young Republicans organization of New Jersey, and in 1952 he sought a position in the Eisenhower campaign. Morrow's wish to work for Eisenhower coincided with the candidate's own de-

15. E. Frederic Morrow, *Way Down South Up North* (Philadelphia, 1973), 5–14, 32–37, 107.
16. See E. Frederic Morrow, *Forty Years a Guinea Pig* (New York, 1980), 13–72.

sire, conveyed through Sherman Adams to Republican national committee official Arthur Summerfield, for a "bright young man" to assist in black voter appeals. Eisenhower uncharacteristically hired Morrow as a campaign consultant without prior clearance from New Jersey Republican officials, who viewed him as a "maverick" within their ranks. Any doubts about Morrow's loyalty to the Eisenhower campaign, however, were dispelled by his willingness to distribute anti-FEPC columns written by conservative black journalist George Schuyler in Northern black communities.[17]

A few days after the election, Morrow discussed a possible administration appointment with Sherman Adams, and he received a letter from the aide advising him to notify CBS of his resignation. But Morrow disagreed with minorities adviser Rabb over an appropriate starting salary, and his telephone calls requesting information on the appointment were not returned. Three months after the inauguration, Morrow learned without further explanation from White House special counsel Bernard Shanley that no position would be available for him at the White House. Efforts by Val Washington to obtain fuller information failed, although some administration officials privately admitted embarrassment over the incident. With the help of Washington and Adams staffer Charles Willis, Jr., Morrow finally received an offer from the Commerce Department as adviser on business affairs in April 1954, a full seventeen months after the election.[18]

After another year's delay, with administration officials gearing up for efforts to court black voters in the 1956 election, Morrow finally received his long-sought White House appointment. But his official responsibilities — arranging for executive office physical security, office space for special projects, and parking space — were hardly more than a higher-level form of domestic service. Even given his inconsequential duties, in late 1957 the administration shifted Morrow out of the White House over his objections to a "make-work" position as an assistant speech writer under Arthur Larson. Although the transfer was part of an effort to show a lower White House profile on civil rights following the Little Rock crisis, Morrow's threats to Sherman Adams to air his discontent led to his reinstallation at the White House in "special projects" work. Following the resignation of Maxwell Rabb in 1958, Rabb's minority affairs responsibilities were parceled out

17. Morrow, *Way Down South Up North*, 26.
18. Morrow, *Black Man in the White House*, 11–13.

among several staffers, and Morrow acquired additional duties of replying to black correspondence. Nevertheless, he still did not receive an official White House commission as administrative officer for special projects until January 1959, almost four years after his initial White House appointment. Adding a final insult, President Eisenhower did not even attend the ceremony.[19]

From the beginning of his service in the administration, Morrow found himself shut out from serious policy discussions by the White House staff. Eisenhower career aides viewed him as "window dressing," and although Sherman Adams occasionally showed a "fatherly interest," his lieutenant, Alabaman Wilton B. Persons, vocally opposed his appointment and threatened to walk out with the female clerks on the first day he arrived at work. According to Morrow, Eisenhower financial adviser George Allen nearly had a "nervous breakdown" upon seeing him in the White House. Morrow found great difficulty obtaining secretarial help because, as he explained, "No one wants the onus of working for a colored boss." Under scrutiny from higher-ups at all times, the new aide requested that his personal staff meet him in pairs to avoid any damaging gossip. Staff resistance to Morrow's presence became manifested in actions that frustrated his efforts to improve the administration's image with blacks. When Morrow asked Harold Stassen and Howard Pyle to speak before the National Federation of Colored Women's Clubs in 1954, Stassen declined on the grounds that one officer of the organization had belonged to a "blacklisted" group, and Pyle refused at the request of Democratic governor LeRoy Collins of Florida. Later in the fall, Pyle further infuriated Morrow and Val Washington by suggesting in Southern speeches that "as a white Southerner, he would take his chances and support Eisenhower rather than Stevenson." In spite of the hostility and the suspicion of White House staffers that he was a possible "traitor" to administration civil rights policy, Morrow offered advice on racial matters when asked, insisting that "I know and understand the innate honesty of the President."[20]

Morrow found himself the butt of cruel talk and insensitive jokes by other staffers. At a White House Christmas party, he was singled out for ridicule by being given an off-key bell to ring during a rendition of a carol. Morrow brushed off the incident gracefully, responding to the President's comment that "I didn't know you were a musician" with "Sir, after that dismal perfor-

19. Ibid., 107–109, 112, 181–85, 195, 208, 275.
20. Ibid., 17, 27, 37, 79–82, 102–3; Morrow OH (1977), DDEL, 3, 17.

mance, your doubt is still sustained." More serious harrassment came after the resignation of Sherman Adams in 1958: "The present atmosphere among staff members indicates that I will be in for heavy sledding in the future," Morrow noted. Adams's successor, General Persons, did not even bother to meet Morrow officially until February 1959. At that session, Persons informed him that subsequent civil rights matters would be brought to White House counsel Gerald Morgan because racial issues had divided Persons's family and caused emotional hardship. In a later incident, administrative assistant Jack Anderson embarrassed Morrow before fellow staffers by repeating Persons's description of another aide as "a nigger rat running into an ambush of white mice."[21]

Living in a racially segregated city where "my every move is open to observation," Morrow endured a hermitlike social life in the capital. Some members of the White House staff, including presidential secretary Ann Whitman, staff secretary General Andrew Goodpaster, press secretary James Hagerty, and executive clerk William Hopkins, tried to make Morrow more comfortable in the administration. After being told by Morrow of his unsuccessful attempts to play golf at local country clubs, Vice President Nixon arranged a game for him at his club. Morrow subsequently looked upon the vice president, himself something of an outsider from White House consultations, as a "very capable, qualified, dedicated young man." White House legal counsel Gerald Morgan invited the Morrows to social gatherings at his home, including dinners with the Persons family. However, such gestures of friendship remained the exception rather than the rule in the Eisenhower White House, particularly after the departure of Adams.[22]

On a number of occasions, Morrow demonstrated his loyalty to the administration by taking actions questionable to the interests of his race. In November 1955, Morrow reversed his previous advice that Vice President Nixon address the National Council of Negro Women because of the group's intention to invite "pro-Soviet" Indian ambassador Krishna Menon as its "International Night" speaker. Attending the 1956 Republican convention at the request of Adams (in order to avoid possible press questions about his absence), Morrow spent virtually the entire convention in the White House's operations center out of sight except during the President's acceptance speech. In September 1958, it was Mor-

21. Ibid., 112, 258–59.
22. Ibid., 23–25, 42–43, 193.

National Park Service/Dwight D. Eisenhower Library
President Eisenhower with staff assistant E. Frederic Morrow, October
4, 1956.

row who was assigned to explain to the NAACP's Daisy Bates why a group of black students from Little Rock Central High School could not see the President. And earlier that year, in May, following Justice Department reports that the proposed Youth March on Washington included radical infiltrators, Morrow privately advised march leader Jackie Robinson not to participate. The subsequent release, without his authorization, of Morrow's warnings to Robinson resulted in sharp criticism by black leaders.[23]

Morrow's main service to the administration, however, was as a spokesman defending the Eisenhower record before black audiences. He gave more than three hundred speeches during his White House service, and in the process opened himself to the abuse and insensitivity of local party officials and private citizens. Morrow's speeches were frequently cut in length or eliminated entirely from scheduled ceremonies. His clashes with party officials included his refusal at a California meeting to accept coaching in the appropriate behavior of a "Negro assistant." A series of complaints were directed at him from Republican National Women's Club representatives for his vocal advocacy of black membership. At a reception following a February 1956 speech at the Kansas Day celebration in Topeka, Morrow was mistaken for a servant and asked to summon a taxicab; and on one of his speaking trips, in Birmingham, Alabama, he was refused service at a downtown office of Eastern Airlines. After registering a complaint with company president Eddie Rickenbacker, Morrow noted that his action was "one of the few times that I have ever used the prestige of my office to try to rectify a situation that could affect a whole racial group."[24]

As an adjunct to his role as administration spokesman, Morrow sought inclusion in foreign trips to Third World countries, but White House aides gave permission only with great reluctance. After persistent lobbying, Morrow attended his first state dinner, in honor of President Achmed Sukarno of Indonesia, in May 1956. Winning official approval to accompany Vice President Nixon to Ghana statehood ceremonies in March 1957, Morrow remarked jokingly to the President upon his return, "For the first time in my life I was a member of the majority; it was a damned nice feeling." Following the African trip, rumors abounded of an ambassadorial appointment for Morrow, but he insisted on an assignment in a

23. Ibid., 20, 88–90, 244–45.
24. Ibid., 39–40, 99–102, 201; Morrow OH (1977) DEEL, 13; Morrow OH (1968) DDEL, 95.

nonblack nation as "an excellent move for combatting Russian propaganda about the falseness of our democracy." Eventually it was not Morrow but his brother John who received a diplomatic nomination in 1959 as ambassador to the Republic of Guinea. A later request by Morrow to accompany Nixon on his South American trip received a reply from one official, "If anything, he ought to have an Indian." Selected, after delays, for a January 1960 trip to Liberia for the inauguration of President William V.S. Tubman, Morrow found that his wife was denied seating for space reasons, and he angrily rejected the trip.[25]

Because of his sacrifices in behalf of the administration, Morrow became the focus of criticism from blacks outside as an ineffectual or unwilling advocate of their concerns. Following the Emmett Till murder, Morrow described his dilemma within the White House to William G. Nunn of the Pittsburgh *Courier*: "I make no effort to advise anyone in this regard, since interfering in another's province in the White House is an unpardonable sin. However, I would not want those who believe in my integrity to think I would sit still during this crisis and do and say nothing." In a June 1957 letter to Morrow, Roy Wilkins of the NAACP questioned his effectiveness in the administration: "It may not be politic to say this to you in your elusive and aloof perch far from the arena of brass-knuckle politics, but the Republicans could have wrapped up at least 65% of the Negro vote for the next three presidential elections (at least) if they had early and emphatically backed the Supreme Court decision."[26]

Completely ignored in the discussions concerning the Little Rock school integration crisis of September 1957, Morrow also was frustrated by his inability for three years to persuade the President to meet with black leaders. Following the expulsion of Autherine Lucy from the University of Alabama in early 1956, Morrow sought permission to confer directly with Alabama black leaders, but was dissuaded by Adams, who cited FBI reports claiming a "tremendous" Communist presence. Only after several years of requests from A. Philip Randolph, Martin Luther King, Jr., Roy Wilkins, and other civil rights leaders did Eisenhower agree to meet Randolph, King, Wilkins, and Lester Granger in the summer of 1958. After the meeting of June 23, Morrow praised Randolph in particular for his moderate presentation, but ob-

25. Morrow, *Black Man in the White House*, 69, 125, 155, 203, 220, 290–91.
26. Morrow to William G. Nunn, Dec. 8, 1955 and Roy Wilkins to Morrow, June 17, 1957, White House Staff Files, Morrow Records, Box 10, DDEL.

served that the prevalent sentiment among other staffers had been, "Let the old man speak and get it over, because this is his shining hour."[27]

Throughout Morrow's service in the White House, staff remarks conveyed a similar attitude of condescension toward blacks generally and an impatience with the "disloyalty" of minority voters. Morrow's attempts to explain black reluctance to support the administration in the absence of official Republican backing for economic proposals, the *Brown* integration decision, or greater influence in party councils fell on deaf ears. White House adviser Howard Pyle, sitting in on a meeting of the "Emancipation Committee," bitterly complained that "Negroes aren't grateful" for the administration's civil rights actions. "We must get out into the field and preach loyalty to those who are not loyal to us." Responding to an earlier Morrow attempt to arrange a meeting of black leaders with the President, Rabb complained that "responsible officials" in the White House were becoming disgusted at the "aggressiveness" of black demands, which displayed an "ugliness and surliness" that had "driven most of the liberals to cover." Although he asserted that he had "stuck out his neck" to help blacks before, Rabb could no longer honestly tell the President that black support was a political asset.[28]

Pressured by his divided loyalties as a "black man in the White House," Morrow flirted with the idea of resignation on several occasions. Early in his White House service he noted, "The time may come when I will find that these two responsibilities are incompatible and that will mean that I will choose." After the Little Rock crisis, Morrow lamented that the vacillating White House stance on civil rights made him "feel ridiculous," but he ruled out resignation on the grounds that "while I am certain that many things are not done despite my presence, it does prevent some anti-Negro acts from being attempted." Probably the deeper motivation, however, was Morrow's open admission that "I could never be disloyal to Dwight Eisenhower."[29]

Early in 1960, Morrow sought release from his White House duties in order to work in the Nixon presidential campaign. Nixon had befriended Morrow at various times, but his support had bordered on condescension and he had praised Morrow for not

27. Morrow OH (1968), DDEL, 46; Morrow, *Black Man in the White House*, 51–52, 233.
28. Morrow, *Black Man in the White House*, 28, 31, 47.
29. Ibid., 48, 184.

using his color as an "excuse" for his misfortunes. With the help of campaign liaison man Bob Merriam, Morrow was granted two minutes of air time for a brief statement at the Republican convention, and he proudly proclaimed, "One hundred years ago today my grandfather was a slave. Tonight, I stand before you a trusted associate of the President of the United States." His remarks, however, were cut from live television coverage in favor of a commercial announcement. Following the Republican convention, Morrow received a two-month leave to work in the Nixon campaign, and he was promised important duties by manager Leonard Hall. But the promised campaign role never materialized, and the pleadings of Morrow and others for a Nixon statement of protest at the arrest of Martin Luther King, Jr., in mid-October were ignored by Nixon's chief advisers. A completely frustrated Morrow left the campaign trail and returned despondently to the capital.[30]

Morrow's disappointments did not end with his departure from the administration. At the White House staff Christmas party, he was informed by a penitent President Eisenhower that he had been unable to secure his former staffer a position in private business. Seeking to boost his income and justify his position in the administration to critics, Morrow contacted a number of publishing firms interested in obtaining the rights to his White House memoirs, including Doubleday. However, apparently fearful of criticism of administration civil rights efforts, representatives of the President threatened to withhold rights to Eisenhower's own White House memoirs to Doubleday if Morrow's were accepted. In addition, friends of the President discouraged other major book publishers from accepting his former aide's manuscript. Suggestions that Eisenhower had "blacklisted" Morrow were supported by an incident between the two men in 1964. Inviting Morrow to Gettysburg for a staff reunion and a discussion of Republican party strategy, an angry Eisenhower then threatened him, saying, "I'm going to throw you to the dogs." Addressing the entire gathering, the former President announced, "There is a man here today who I felt was my friend, but he wrote a book. I don't know whether he's my friend now or not. But I'm going to let him get up here and tell you whatever he has on his mind." A startled Morrow defended his authorship of the White House memoir to the group by claiming that it had been his reply to critics of his support of the administration.[31]

30. Ibid., 240, 293–94; Morrow OH (1977) DDEL, 8.
31. Morrow OH (1977) DDEL, 36, 42–47. Eisenhower similarly tried to block

Despite the lack of assistance from most administration officials, Morrow did attain financial success after leaving public
service. With the help of Robert Anderson, by then an advisory
board member of the Bank of America, Morrow joined the same
organization in 1964, was voted to a vice-presidency three years
later, and became a division head in 1969. He still chafed, however, at the restrictions placed upon him as a black man in a largely
symbolic position. Reflecting upon his career in 1973, he wrote
bitterly: "I do not believe we are any nearer a solution to the
black-white controversy than we were in 1870 . . . Furthermore, I
do not believe it is possible for a black to ever be fully accepted,
without any reservation, into the power structure of this country,
or even accepted generally as a complete man. It matters not what
his social or educational credentials might reveal — a black may
penetrate and be within the structure, but never of it." Despite
sitting "in the seats of the mighty" and receiving "commendations
from presidents of colleges and of our country," Morrow lamented, "we awake each day to the ignoble scourge of color and
caste, and feel its corrosive power eat away our faith in the American credo 'All men were created equal.' If this is the ignoble fate
of those who spent a lifetime training for acceptance, what must it
be like not to be one of the talented tenth!"[32]

Scarred by his White House experiences, a weary Morrow had
taken many blows to his dignity and self-respect in the course of
his public career. At a moment of his deepest doubt, he declared,
"I am grateful that my parents died before they saw their children
grow bitter green around the edges of their souls from years of
facing the problems of America's intransigence in the matter of
color." Critically assessing the man he had served in the White
House, Morrow wrote, "he was a great, gentle, and noble man;"
but, he added, "his background and viewpoint on civil rights was
Southern. He was fair and honest in most things, but he couldn't
take that single bold step of courageous pronouncement that
would have moved the blacks another mile toward freedom . . . In
my many talks with him in this area, I found him neither intellec-
tually nor emotionally disposed to combat segregation in
general."

Morrow's disappointment was doubtless shared by many of the
federal government's black employees at all levels. Despite the
promises and the optimistic assertions of the administration, the

publication of Emmet John Hughes's critical memoir of the administration. William Bragg Ewald, *Eisenhower the President* (Englewood Cliffs, N.J., 1981), 239.
    32. Morrow, *Way Down South Up North*, 120.

federal service remained far from a model of equal opportunity. The first comprehensive federal employment census by race, conducted in 1961, revealed that although Afro-Americans constituted one-fifth of all federal workers at levels GS1 through GS4, they made up only one percent of employees at level GS12 or above. Three out of every ten blacks in federal employment were still confined to service in the postal department. Black government workers could only look to the future for hope and share the determination of Morrow that "despite the bitter memories and heartbreak of the past, I shall not turn back, nor sit in a corner and sulk away my remaining days. I remain a true believer that, with God's help, we shall overcome someday, someday."[33]

33. Ibid., 121–22; Dorothy K. Newman, Nancy J. Amidei, Barbara L. Carter, Dawn Day, William J. Kruvantz, and Jack S. Russell, *Protest, Politics, and Prosperity: Black Americans and White Institutions, 1940–75* (New York, 1978), 113–14, 128–30, Morrow, *Forty Years a Guinea Pig*, 234–35.

5.

The "Good Business" of Equal Employment

The Eisenhower administration's actions in removing official barriers to equal opportunity in the military branches, the District of Columbia, and the federal service gained it a measure of respect from civil rights advocates. Yet the declarations of administration officials in these policy fields did not violate any of the President's strictures against the use of "coercive" federal power in areas of divided federal-state jurisdiction or likely community resistance. The President's spokesmen on national employment policy, strong believers in the capacity of the American "mixed economy" to provide sufficient economic opportunities for all who earnestly sought them, similarly repudiated an employment strategy based upon federal regulation in favor of a policy of moral exhortation, employer "education," and mild jawboning. The administration's subsequent attempts to confront unequal employment in the private sector through these methods provided additional illustration of the limited effectiveness of a civil rights philosophy that denied the federal government the use of strong enforcement tools.

The Eisenhower team in 1953 faced a formidable task in stimulating additional fair employment gains for blacks, despite the progress engendered by postwar defense production. A Senate Labor and Management subcommittee report in November 1952 had noted that the average annual salary of blacks in 1950, $1,300, was only 52 percent of white wage levels (a drop of 5 percent from 1945). War production for the Korean conflict had boosted black earnings, but by 1953 black median family income was still only $2,461, compared to $4,392 for whites. Lesser incomes stemmed partly from restricted avenues for black employment, for according to 1950 figures, only 2,190 blacks in the entire nation were employed as apprentices, and only 42,500 were classified as "self-employed." Black employment opportunities also were limited by discrimination practiced by labor unions receiving federal certification. Although National Labor Relations Board rulings held that unions could not cause the discharge of nonunion workers denied membership by discrimination, and the Taft-Hartley and Railway Labor acts required "fair representation" of worker grievances, unions freely segregated or excluded minority members. As a result, blacks outnumbered whites in the unemployment ranks by a greater than 2-to-1 margin, and the number of unemployed adult blacks not even counted in the labor force exceeded that of whites by nearly 50 percent.[1]

Because black advances in employment had been stimulated by federally assisted and subsidized defense production, the enlarged federal role in the private economy gave the government additional leverage in promoting fair employment practices. By the early 1950s, about $3 billion traveled from Washington, D.C., to the private sector in direct federal grants, and another $16.5 billion was transmitted to private industry through domestic credit programs. By 1953, however, none of this federal largesse required nondiscrimination. During World War II, the War Labor Board had outlawed wage differentials according to race, the U.S. Employment Service had refused for the first time to honor racially restricted job applications, and the NLRB had declared its intention to refuse certification to unions practicing racial exclusion. However, these wartime measures to promote fair employment by private firms holding government contracts had disappeared with the conversion to peace.[2]

1. Keesing's Research Reports, *Race Relations in the USA, 1954–1968* (New York, 1970) 48; Nathan Wright, *Black Power and Urban Unrest* (New York, N.Y., 1967), 1–2.

2. "Grant-in-Aid and Loan Programs of the Federal Government," Oct. 2, 1953, Mitchell Papers, Box 125, DDEL.

The history of the Fair Employment Practices Committee, the federal wartime agency that had offered the greatest initial hope to fair employment advocates, had demonstrated the severe limitations of the federal government's commitment to equal employment opportunity. The creation of the FEPC itself had been a product not of deep official concern, but of political pressure exerted by black representatives connected with the March on Washington movement of June 1941. From the beginning, the FEPC had suffered from shortages of funds, personnel, and effective authority. It could not initiate action without first receiving a formal complaint, and then could only investigate the charges and issue a directive to the offending contracted employer. The actual authority to cancel a contract lay not with the FEPC but the contracting federal agency, and government departments demonstrated little willingness to jeopardize war production by disciplining discriminatory employers. In addition, the FEPC's ability to take independent action was restricted by its subordinate position within larger federal departments with other priorities, including the Office of Production Management, the War Production board, and the War Manpower Commission. In May 1943, President Roosevelt did grant the FEPC a brief reprieve by placing it within the Executive Office of the President, raising its appropriation, and expanding its authority to investigate and insert antibias clauses in contracts. Even then, however, the FEPC did not specifically consider employment segregation as a cause of investigation, and it still relied upon the willingness of other agencies of the administration to enforce its fair employment decrees. Only one-third of the eight thousand complaints registered with the FEPC, and only one-fifth of those received from the South, were resolved successfully. Discriminatory employers and unions disregarded thirty-five of forty-five FEPC compliance orders. Even these meager gains of the committee were halted in 1945, when the Congress slashed its budget in half and provided for its dissolution within a year.[3]

Any subsequent plans of utilizing federal regulatory action to ensure fair employment by private firms under government contract were stymied by the Russell Amendment of 1944, which permitted agencies created by executive order to exist for only one year without legislative appropriation. Additional provisions stated that no existing federal agency could use its funds to carry out the functions of an executive agency eliminated as a result of

3. For a brief account of the wartime FEPC, see Richard Polenberg, *War and Society: The United States, 1941–1945* (New York, N.Y., 1972) 113–23.

the Russell Amendment. These restrictions effectively prohibited the creation of a new FEPC in the absence of specific legislative authorization. Although the Truman administration regularly submitted FEPC legislation as part of its civil rights proposals, and the Truman Committee on Civil Rights recommended a new FEPC and executive mandates for open hiring in its final report, Congress resisted all such overtures. Some states did respond on their own to provide greater fair employment guarantees. Before 1945, thirteen states possessed fair employment laws, and eight others joined by 1950. New York and New Jersey enacted antidiscrimination laws in 1945, followed by Massachusetts in 1946, Connecticut in 1947, and New Mexico, Oregon, Rhode Island, and Washington in 1949. As with the federal FEPC, however, many of these state mandates lacked effective enforcement mechanisms, and in other sections of the country, most notably the South, employers remained free to discriminate in private employment on the basis of race.[4]

Advocates of federal enforcement of fair hiring had found little to encourage them in the 1952 presidential campaign, for Democrat Stevenson's support of FEPC was lukewarm at best and Eisenhower advocated only state responsibility. Despite Eisenhower's refusal to support any "compulsory" federal fair employment agency, Republican campaign adviser Henry Cabot Lodge had insisted that an Eisenhower victory would speed FEPC passage in Congress. Despite Lodge's optimistic rhetoric, FEPC had no realistic chance without strong White House endorsement, and only a slim chance even with it. Eisenhower's second secretary of labor, James P. Mitchell, did endorse FEPC proposals offered by the NAACP and the Urban League, and he sent a message of support to the Senate Labor and Public Welfare Committee for FEPC bills sponsored by Republican senator Irving Ives of New York. But when questioned about Mitchell's advocacy of FEPC, the President separated the secretary's remarks from the official position of his administration and restated his own view that employment problems "are not best handled by punitive or compulsory federal law." When Louis Lautier of the National Negro Press Association asked pointedly whether the President had even broached the subject of state fair employment guarantees to state governors at a recent conference, Eisenhower replied, "I didn't address them this time except most informally."

4. Seidenberg, "Committee on Government Contracts," 23.

Nevertheless, Eisenhower still insisted that the states "will move on this in an enlightened and forward-looking way."[5]

Having rejected a "compulsory" FEPC despite its track record of impotence in compelling fair employment, Eisenhower and his advisers instead endorsed the creation of an interagency advisory committee on government contracts, which would lack the power to report cases directly to the President or to issue compliance orders, but would act as a "clearing house" for complaints. Formation of such a committee was not a new idea — the Truman administration had created a similar ten-member body during the Korean War that included six "public" members and four representatives of government contracting agencies. As long as the committee did not assume regulatory functions, Truman administration officials had judged, it would not violate the restrictions of the Russell Amendment. Created by executive order, the Truman committee was funded out of the general revenues of contracting departments rather than through a separate legislative appropriation. It did not receive full staffing until April 1953, however, and it spent its brief life studying the history of federal fair employment contract clauses since the beginning of World War II.[6]

At Eisenhower's request, in May 1953 White House minorities adviser Maxwell Rabb sought out Truman Committee staff director Jacob Seidenberg to help design a new antidiscrimination program directed at government contractors. Seidenberg responded by preparing a draft proposal for a new government contracts committee, and on August 13, 1953, Eisenhower announced the creation by executive order of his own President's Committee on Government Contracts. The new committee began its work with a staff of nine and a budget of $125,000, which eventually by 1961 grew to a twenty-five member staff and a $375,000 appropriation. The allocation, however, never represented a major federal investment in eliminating job discrimination, for the New York State Committee Against Discrimination (SCAD) alone received over $650,000 for its work, and the starting figure of the later Civil Rights Commission in 1957 was $850,000. Budgetary responsibility for the new body was divided among the Department of Defense (50 percent), the Atomic Energy Commission (17.5 percent), the General Services Administration (17.5

5. *New York Times*, Aug. 5, 1952 and March 4, 1954; Schlundt, "Civil Rights Policies," 64.

6. Schlundt, "Civil Rights Policies," 65–66; Seidenberg, "Committee on Government Contracts," 17.

Source Uncertain/Dwight D. Eisenhower Library
Eisenhower administration representatives on fair employment, April
17, 1956. *Left to right:* Vice-chairman Archibald J. Carey and Chairman
Maxwell Abbell of the President's Committee on Government Employ-
ment Policy, and Chairman Richard M. Nixon and Vice-chairman James
P. Mitchell of the President's Committee on Government Contracts.

percent), and the departments of Commerce and Labor (7.5 percent each).[7]

The President's Committee on Government Contracts included seats for eight "public" members, and the administration spread the appointments among business, labor, and professional representatives. Among the original committee members were labor chieftains Walter Reuther of the United Auto Workers and George Meany of the AFL, Congressman James A. Roosevelt of California, publisher Helen Rogers Reid of the New York *Herald-Tribune*, John L. McCaffrey of International Harvester Company, and Fred Lazarus of the American Retail Federation. The most visible spokesmen for the committee, however, were its government representatives, in particular chairman and Vice President Richard M. Nixon and secretary of labor and vice-chairman James P. Mitchell, who joined the committee in October 1953. Responsibilities were divided between subcommittees on liaison with interested groups, the armed forces, atomic energy, common carriers, contract clause revision and enforcement, District of Columbia affairs (see chapter 4), education and public relations, personnel, policies and program, and research.[8]

Following the President's lead, administration spokesmen on the Government Contracts Committee described the primary functions of the body as providing an educational forum on fair employment and projecting official concern for the democratic principles of equal opportunity. In his letter of congratulation to Vice President Nixon upon his appointment to the committee, Eisenhower noted the duty of the group to counter skeptics of American idealism "both as answer to that doubt and proof of our faith."[9] To publicize their faith to the public in the fulfillment of racial democracy in the marketplace, committee members employed a variety of public relations techniques, including leaflets, brochures, films, appearances by members on radio and television, two television commercials, equal opportunity posters on 1957 Postal Service vehicles, Spanish language publications

7. Schlundt, "Civil Rights Policies," 69; Seidenberg, "Committee on Government Contracts," 44–48; Maxwell Rabb to Seidenberg, Aug. 13, 1953, Whitman File, Subject Series, Box 30, DDEL; Wallace Mendelson, *Discrimination* (Englewood Cliffs, N.J., 1962), 85.

8. U.S., President's Committee on Government Contracts (PCGC), *First Report*, Sept. 1954.

9. Eisenhower to Nixon, Aug. 15, 1953, Whitman File, Diary Series, Box 3, DDEL.

(from 1958 on), and speeches before business, labor, civic, and civil rights groups.[10]

In their official pronouncements, committee spokesmen consistently tried to depict themselves as exponents of aggressive action on behalf of fair employment rather than mere boosters. Vice President Nixon asserted in 1958: "Our committee has prided itself in its relatively brief existence in this field on this fact. We don't get out many fancy reports. We don't do an awful lot of talking. We do try to make up in action for what we do not do in talking. We believe that in this whole field of equality of opportunity, that there has been a little bit too much balance on the talk side and not enough on the action side."[11] However, the group's lack of independent enforcement authority and the political and philosophical reservations of its members to vigorous federal enforcement belied Nixon's claims. Even the rhetoric of committee members lacked the sense of genuine outrage at, or understanding of, the effects of job discrimination on blacks themselves. Whether addressing white audiences or black, spokesmen rarely explained the daily consequences of discrimination for a black job seeker. Instead, they congratulated themselves and their audiences for their avowed moral sensitivity, and they praised the goal of equal opportunity as "good business," a more "efficient" use of national labor resources and purchasing power, and a testament of American democratic principles in the face of foreign criticism. The vice-president actively discouraged wider public discussion of the stark realities of American racial discrimination, lamenting that "we commonly discuss the issue of discriminatory employment practices in completely negative terms."[12]

A major part of the Committee on Government Contracts' program of selling Americans on the benefits of equal employment was its series of conferences and subcommittee meetings with representatives of business, labor, religious, and civil rights organizations. The first two such meetings, in November 1953 and June 1954, brought together the liaison subcommittee with members of "interested groups," including the NAACP, the Urban League, the American Friends Service Committee, and the American Jewish Congress. The full committee followed up these

10. Schlundt, "Civil Rights Policies" 77; Seidenberg to Mitchell, June 19, 1957, Mitchell Papers, Box 126, DDEL.
11. Peters, *The Southern Temper*, 260.
12. "Speech of James P. Mitchell before the Urban League of Cleveland, Ohio," Jan. 21, 1956, in Bryce Harlow Records, Box 21, DDEL; PCGC, *Newsletter*, No. 18 (March–Apr. 1959), Mitchell Papers, Box 127, DDEL; PCGC, *Equal Opportunity Is Good Business* (1954).

initial meetings with sessions with trade association representatives in December 1954, leaders of organized labor in March 1955, and business executives in October 1955. At the October meeting, held behind closed doors, Secretary Mitchell exhorted his audience to discard discriminatory practices as it would "outmoded machinery," and Vice President Nixon praised the businessmen for not waiting for federal compulsion before making progress in minority employment. In return, the business leaders claimed "splendid" advances in providing employment opportunities.[13] Businessmen understandably liked the committee's low-key, "soft-sell" approach, and they showed their appreciation by helping it trumpet its claims of success. Hailing the committee's accomplishments, the trade journal *Factory Management and Maintenance* attributed them to its members' "prestige in business circles." *Business Week* added its voice to the chorus of applause emanating from private executives, and RCA chief executive David Sarnoff saluted what he called the group's "practical approach."[14]

In some instances, committee-sponsored conferences with private groups did produce tangible results. A 1957 Youth Training Incentives Conference in Washington, D.C., stimulated the development of programs in six cities to encourage minority youth training and private employment. In 1959, leaders of religious organizations were called to the capital, and they responded by establishing a Religious Advisory Council which assumed the task of exhorting local communities to expand minority job opportunities. In these conferences, as well as their other public relations efforts, committee members called upon representatives of the private sector to promote equal job opportunity voluntarily, but the effectiveness of their cheerleading was severely limited. Improvements beyond the cosmetic level required a federal agency with the powers both to issue compliance orders and to enforce them, and the Committee on Government Contracts possessed neither. The committee did not even have the authority to take complaints over the heads of contracting agencies directly to the President, for Eisenhower had insisted from the outset that the new committee not be given the power to bring compliance recommendations to his desk. The President reasoned, according to Maxwell Rabb, that such recommendations would only "serve as

13. *Radio Reports, Inc.*, Oct. 22–25, 1955, in Mitchell Papers, Box 41, DDEL.
14. PCGC, *Youth Training Incentives Conference Proceedings* (1955); Steven M. Gelber, *Black Men and Businessmen* (Port Washington, N.Y., 1974), 114.

an embarrassment to the President because he can't carry them out."[15]

Aware of the political resistance to a strong fair employment agency, particularly among Southern representatives, and unconvinced of its pressing necessity, administration spokesmen stressed the fact that the Committee on Government Contracts was not another FEPC and would never become one. Vice-chairman Mitchell notified fellow member Fred Lazarus soon after the committee's creation that he would not support any requests for additional enforcement powers. In September 1953, responding to the concerns of South Carolina governor James F. Byrnes and other Southern politicians about the new body, Eisenhower contacted Nixon and urged him personally to ease Byrnes's fears that it represented a new FEPC.[16] Administration members never sought greater enforcement authority from Congress, and their silence reflected not only an awareness of the political difficulties, but also their philosophical reservations. A speech drafted for Mitchell declared, "Society cannot be, and should not be, made to conform, or be regimented, or be operated on analytically." Instead, the vice-chairman's text continued, "the way to reform is a longer one, and a more patient one, and a more moderate one."[17]

Eschewing "coercion," the Committee on Government Contracts adopted an approach of engaging the accused employer in an informal process of conciliation and sporadic appeals by individual members for voluntary cooperation. Actual enforcement of nondiscrimination by private firms under government contract was left to the contracting agencies and their compliance officers. Vice President Nixon sent letters to the federal government's twenty-seven contracting units requesting compliance reports, and Mitchell, as head of the military services subcommittee, did persuade the Defense Department to revise its contracting regulations. The subcommittee on enforcement, headed by Deputy Attorney General William P. Rogers, drafted a new standard nondiscrimination clause for government contracts, which the President installed by executive order on September 3, 1954. However, the committee went no further in seeking greater fair

15. Schlundt, "Civil Rights Policies," 76; Rabb to Sherman Adams, July 8, 1953, Official File, Box 430, DDEL.

16. James F. Byrnes to Eisenhower, Aug. 27, 1953, Whitman File, Name Series, Box 3; Eisenhower to Nixon, Sept. 4, 1953, Whitman File, Diary Series, Box 3, DDEL.

17. Mitchell to Fred Lazarus, Oct. 31, 1953, Mitchell Papers, Box 125; John W. Leslie to Mitchell, June 5, 1959, Mitchell papers, Box 68, DDEL.

employment enforcement powers, and it maintained that "primary reliance should be upon educational persuasion, mediation, and conciliation rather than enforcement by the imposition of penalties."[18]

The new nondiscrimination clause adopted by the administration made fair employment mandatory in all but two major types of federal contracts—agreements held by American companies overseas and subcontracts for standard commodities. However, eighteen other exemptions were granted for financial institutions holding contracts with federal lending agencies, businesses engaged in the federal crop support program (following pressure on the Agriculture Department by Governor Byrnes and other Southerners), and public utility companies possessing regional monopolies over their services. The net effect of the many exemptions was to shoot gaping holes in the compliance program. For example, Clarence Randall, former board chairman of Inland Steel and special assistant for foreign economic development, condemned in 1958 the "undemocratic and almost uncivilized" attitudes of American employers abroad. At home, Fred Lazarus attempted to use his personal influence to urge compliance from utility executives in the South and Southwest, but with little success.[19]

Even for employers still covered by the nondiscrimination clause, the "conciliation" process adopted by the government proved long and tedious. The long sequence of complaint procedures included referral of the complaint by the Government Contracts Committee to the appropriate contracting agency, notification by the agency of the employer's violation, personal conferences of committee and agency representatives with the employer, public hearings as a last resort, and only then the issuance of a cease-and-desist notice and possibly the initiation of legal action. The process of routing a complaint to the appropriate compliance division of a federal department alone could produce interminable delays. In one extreme instance, a single complaint was referred to four different sections of the air force.[20]

Because the Committee on Government Contracts lacked legal enforcement standing, its enforcement role was limited to routing complaints it received to department compliance officers. The

18. Seidenberg, "Committee on Government Contracts," 155–162; PCGC, "Subcommittee Report on Compliance," Dec. 11, 1953, Mitchell Papers, Box 125; William P. Rogers to Edward Mansure (GSA), May 28, 1954, Rogers Papers, Box 50, DDEL; PCGC, *First Report* (1954).

19. Schlundt, "Civil Rights Policies" 71; Mendelson, *Discrimination*, 86.

20. Schlundt, "Civil Rights Policies," 73; "Subcommittee Report on Compliance," Dec. 11, 1953, Mitchell Papers, Box 125, DDEL.

contracting agencies and departments themselves generally were unwilling to pursue litigation to force compliance when conciliation failed, and they refused to exercise their powers to disqualify employers from future contracts; cancel contracts; seek injunctive relief, arbitration, or damages; or cancel government certification necessary for payment. In the area of union-sanctioned discrimination, despite the fact that 20 percent of complaints by the end of 1956 cited union exclusion, the Committee on Government Contracts judged that investigations lay beyond its jurisdiction. Members' actions in investigating union discrimination were limited to the informal "good offices" provided by labor representatives Meany, Reuther, and alternates Boris Shiskin and George L.P. Weaver. Only in 1958 did the committee in its compliance guide even request agency compliance officers to indicate whether or not charges of discrimination stemmed from union practices.[21]

Members of the Committee on Government Contracts gradually recognized the inadequacies of their ad hoc approach even in collecting information on private employment discrimination. Proposals to upgrade the Government Contracts Committee also coincided with the administration's newfound interest in civil rights after the 1956 election and the personal desire of Vice President Nixon to heighten public exposure of his committee's efforts. Staff increases were recommended and approved, and an additional position was created of executive vice-chairman. Regional offices were established in Chicago, Los Angeles, Atlanta, and Dallas, and the industry-wide compliance survey program began in 1957. Even with these actions, however, the committee still could not enforce fair employment clauses, and political quarrels with state antidiscrimination agencies further weakened federal equal employment efforts. Disagreements between committee members and New York's State Commission Against Discrimination prevented the adoption of joint action to spur black employment in the New York headquarters of the airline industry. The Committee on Government Contracts' limitations were sharply criticized by the Governors' Committee on Civil Rights, and representatives of civil rights organizations complained of a lack of communication with the group. Roy Wilkins noted in 1958 that no progress report had been issued by the committee in several years on the status of NAACP-sponsored discrimination complaints, and only after he personally complained to Nixon did

21. Seidenberg, "Committee on Government Contracts," 163–90; F. Ray Marshall, *The Negro and Organized Labor* (New York, 1965) 219–26.

the NAACP receive the information it sought. In addition, despite the potential gains in compliance through public exposure of recalcitrant employers, the Committee on Government Contracts began releasing the results of its compliance studies without first obtaining the permission of employers only in 1958. The new public scrutiny given to employers' discriminatory practices in turn brought angry responses from businessmen complaining that they "could not find" qualified minority workers.[22]

In the Committee on Government Contracts' final two years, its emphasis shifted from increasing the size of the black work force to upgrading the positions of existing black workers, especially those within technical and scientific fields. The change illustrated newfound popular and political concern over Soviet advances, symbolized by the Sputnik launch, as well as the committee's own failure to expand markedly the overall number of black workers. The focus on white-collar employment and technical training also reflected the employment views of Vice President Nixon, who privately criticized social welfare and public jobs programs as outdated relics of an earlier time in which "mass employment was our major domestic problem." Committee staff director Irving Ferman observed: "Nixon insisted that the disadvantaged minority groups must be educated to provide the work force required by the new technological orientation of our economy." The vice president himself described the task as one of preparing minorities "to apply themselves so that they can qualify for the positions that currently are open" as well as future opportunities.[23] Seeking to elevate the committee's status, the administration followed recommendations of Secretary of Labor Mitchell and asked Congress for authority to establish a permanent Committee on Equal Job Opportunity in 1959 and 1960. However, Eisenhower personally did not give the proposals high priority, and they died in committee in both legislative sessions. In its final report to the President, the Committee on Government Contracts revealed both its consistent preoccupation with white consciences and its failure in confronting discrimination by con-

22. Seidenberg, "Committee on Government Contracts," 236; "Recommendations of Education Subcommittee," Jan. 8, 1957, Mitchell Papers, Box 125; "Executive Order 10733," Oct. 10, 1957, Mitchell Papers, Box 126; Charles Abrams to Mitchell, Oct. 20, 1958, Mitchell Papers, Box 127, DDEL.

23. Richard M. Nixon to Charles H. Percy, March 21, 1959, Rogers Papers, Box 50, DDEL; Earl Mazo and Stephen Hess, *Nixon: A Political Portrait* (New York, 1968), 214; PCGC, *Report of Discussions — Minority Community Resources Conference,* Jan. 15, 1958, 49, 69.

cluding, "Only when all of us accept this responsibility will the blemish on our national conscience be removed."[24]

Examined on an industry-by-industry basis, the shortcomings of the Committee on Government Contracts and the contracting agencies were easily documented. In the Gulf Coast's petroleum refining facilities, limited gains were owed largely to the personal influence of committee member and lawyer John Minor Wisdom of Louisiana, later an appointee to the federal bench. Industry-wide employment declines hindered black hiring, as did employer skepticism of the qualifications of black college graduates. Union bias also hampered progress, despite the stated non-discrimination policy of the Oil Workers' International Union. In April 1955, the NAACP filed a sweeping complaint against Esso Standard Oil of Baton Rouge, Cities Service Refining Company of Lake Charles, Louisiana, the Carbon and Carbide Company of Texas City, Texas, Lear Oil Company of El Dorado, Arkansas, and several unions, charging a conspiracy to deny blacks advancement by confining them within a single department. Executive Director Seidenberg described the case as "open and shut," and a year later the committee reported to the President that "the oil refining industry offers greater opportunities for minority workers as a result of the satisfactory resolution of a complaint against one of the major companies." But by April 1958 the NAACP still had not received a report on the case, and the following month it discovered that the case had actually been referred to a subcommittee, which had given up hope of encouraging compliance a year earlier and had passed it on to the Defense Department. The only eventual changes occurred at the Esso refinery, which made peripheral wage and classification adjustments. All the refineries continued departmental discrimination, if not plant-wide exclusion. By 1959, only 5.6 percent of 58,000 workers in thirty refineries were black, only 28 blacks held white-collar jobs in eight plants, and five plants still contained no black employees.[25]

The employment picture for blacks was little better in the

24. "Memorandum of Jan. 28, 1959," Henry R. McPhee Records, Box 3; "Information from the President's Committee on Government Contracts," Feb. 24, 1960, Mitchell Papers, Box 127; "Draft Statement to Final Report of the PCGC," Mitchell Papers, Box 130, DDEL.

25. NAACP, *Annual Report* (1957), 53; Herbert R. Northrup, dir., *The Negro in the Petroleum Industry* (Philadelphia, 1968), 36–39; "Minutes of Meeting of Subcommittee on Review and Enforcement," Feb. 27, 1959, Mitchell Papers, Box 127, DDEL.

automobile, aerospace, and farm machinery industries. Compliance surveys of twenty-one Ford, General Motors, and Chrysler plants showed that while blacks comprised 12 percent of all workers, only 0.2 percent held professional, technical, or clerical jobs. In the South, only 9 of 2,991 employees in Dallas, 35 of 1,458 in Memphis, and 9 of 1,628 in Norfolk were black. Ford's Atlanta plant contained only 21 blacks, and an assistant plant manager admitted, "We agreed to abide by local custom and not hire Negroes for production work." In the aerospace industry, the NAACP as early as December 1953 had filed complaints against Chance Vought Aircraft of Fort Worth-Dallas, eventually resulting in the hiring of two blacks as clerical workers and one in the personnel department, plus the initiation of an "orientation" program for workers. By 1957, complaints also had been filed against Boeing and Cessna aircraft plants in Kansas, Hayes Aircraft Company in Alabama, and a Lockheed plant in Marietta, Georgia. At the Marietta plant, nearly 1,000 of 1,350 black employees were concentrated in two departments as "structural assembly helpers," denied promotions, and subjected to racial identification codes. Boeing did agree in 1958 to eliminate racial references in application forms and it promoted three blacks, but by the next year Negroes still constituted only 8.7 percent of all Boeing employees and were concentrated in less skilled positions. Surveys of three Allis-Chalmers farm implement plants also revealed "no information of a satisfactory kind" at the Norwood, Ohio and Springfield, Illinois locations and the absence of any blacks at the Pittsburgh facility. At the Caterpillar assembly plant in Joliet, Illinois, no blacks were included among the company's eighty-eight apprentices.[26]

Similar failures permeated government efforts in the chemicals, tobacco, and electrical manufacturing industries. In the chemicals industry, the Committee on Government Contracts concentrated its lobbying efforts on the executives of DuPont, the industry leader. However, hindered in part by employment declines brought on by automation, eleven plants by 1959 registered only 0.2 percent black white-collar employment and 8.9 percent blue collar. One International Latex synthetic rubber plant in Dover, Delaware did agree to hire seven blacks, but the gesture scarcely

26. "Minutes of Meeting of Committee on Government Contracts," Dec. 1, 1953, Mitchell Papers, Box 125, DDEL; NAACP, *Annual Report* (1957), 53; Peters, *The Southern Temper*, 264; Northrup, dir., *The Negro in the Aerospace Industry*, 24–30; *The Negro in the Farm Implement and Construction Machinery Industries*, 38–39; NAACP, *Crisis*, 64 (1957): no. 3, 146–48.

altered the racial composition of the plant's 1,700 workers. Under committee lobbying of the tobacco industry, Liggett and Myers Company and the American Tobacco Company began negotiations with the segregated Tobacco Workers' International Union to open more jobs to blacks. Liggett and Myers hired twenty-five minority workers for its Durham, North Carolina facilities, and American Tobacco took on fifty more blacks at its Richmond, Virginia operation. But industry-wide black employment declined as a result of continued discrimination, changes in product demand, unevenly distributed technological change, and union prohibitions. In electrical manufacturing, lobbying of General Electric produced a 1954 "internal education" program on government nondiscrimination requirements, but later surveys revealed a continuing scarcity of black blue-collar workers and concentration of minority white-collar employees in clerical positions.[27]

As in the tobacco industry, progress in the building trades and in waterfront occupations depended upon the goodwill of member unions, but the committee's uncertain mandate to investigate union discrimination limited its efforts. In the building trades, the temporary nature of construction employment hindered attempts to introduce lasting changes in racial employment patterns. Blacks themselves hurt their chances by filing complaints without a clear understanding of union referral systems or by acting with the intent of openly circumventing the union. In 1958, after complaints were received against the Cleveland local of the International Brotherhood of Electrical Workers, threats from committee member George Meany to withdraw AFL certification produced the initial union acceptance of black electricians in the city. Elsewhere, however, locals of the International Longshoremen's Union in Philadelphia blocked the hiring of black workers as checkers and weighers, and additional charges of union discrimination along the waterfront in New York and New Jersey produced fruitless confrontations between the unions and the Waterfront Commission.[28]

As with matters of employer bias, ultimate enforcement authority in cases of union discrimination lay not with the Committee on Government Contracts but with other recalcitrant federal agen-

27. Northrup, dir., *The Negro in the Tobacco Industry*, 30; *The Negro in the Chemicals Industry*, 29; *The Negro in the Electrical Manufacturing Industry*, 38–46.

28. Marshall, *The Negro and Organized Labor*, 221–23; Langston Hughes, *Fight for Freedom* (New York, 1964), 161.

cies, including the National Labor Relations Board, the National Railroad Adjustment Board, and the National Mediation Board. The unions' duty to provide "fair representation" of workers was stated clearly in the National Labor Relations Act and the Railway Labor Act, but unfair-representation cases brought on racial grounds routinely were dismissed by lower courts for lack of jurisdiction. Federal courts also hesitated to hear fair-representation cases unless the federal labor boards first held hearings before submitting them to the courts. With labor boards and the courts each "passing the buck" to the other for initial responsibility in interpreting "fair representation," effective use of the law to protect minority workers was nullified. Under accepted interpretations of labor law, unions also could enter into agreements with employers to use job qualifications tests skewed against black promotion seekers. As late as 1961, the Civil Rights Commission noted that Congress, the federal courts, and the National Labor Relations Board still refused to consider black exclusion from union membership a violation of fair representation. The Railway Labor and National Labor Relations acts provided that union shop agreements did not apply to employees denied equal union membership opportunities, but attempts to amend the law to specifically prohibit the certification of discriminatory unions failed to gain administration endorsement and were defeated in Congress. Other enforcement tools, including use of injunctions or private suits for damages, entailed long delays, an uncertain reception, and great expense to blacks seeking relief. Black employment interests were in addition ill served by the NRLB's narrow interpretation of the grounds for union decertification. The NLRB consistently ignored racial discrimination as a justification for decertification, for its members viewed prohibition of such practices as incidental to the major purposes of fair labor practices legislation.[29]

Also left unaddressed by the President's Committee on Government Contracts were the large sums of money extended by the federal government for grants-in-aid and construction projects. Highway construction aid agreements, administered by the Bureau of Public Roads, contained nondiscrimination clauses from 1941 on, but they were never enforced. Public housing construction grants administered by the Low Rent Housing Program of the Public Housing Authority required a nondiscrimina-

29. Greenberg, *Race Relations and American Law,* 173–75; Marshall, *The Negro and Organized Labor,* 250–66.

tion clause and a hiring quota for each project, based upon the number of local minority construction workers. Local housing authorities were even called upon to keep pay records containing racial data and were subject to inspections at four-week intervals by PHA minority-group advisers. This enforcement mechanism, however, was watered down in 1958 in favor of a review system conducted by PHA engineers untrained in racial hiring inspection duty. In programs financing slum clearance projects, Urban Renewal Administration nondiscrimination clauses applied only to employment in the initial clearing activities, not in the subsequent redevelopment, and URA inspectors never actually applied sanctions to discriminatory contractors. In numerous other areas of federal assistance, from vocational education grants to apprenticeship programs to employment services, private biases similarly were "absorbed into federal law."[30]

Despite President Eisenhower's wishful thinking that states willingly would shoulder the burden of ensuring fair employment in the absence of federal enforcement, only a handful of states added to their antidiscrimination authority during the administration's tenure. In 1955, Michigan, Minnesota, and Pennsylvania created fair employment agencies, followed by California, Ohio, and Alaska in 1959 and Delaware in 1960. In addition, Wisconsin and Colorado added to their existing fair employment powers in 1957. But even in "FEPC" states, state and federal employment service operators hesitated to report violations for fear of losing employer clients, and when violations were reported, employers merely transferred their business to private employment services. In states without FEPCs (including the entire South), local employment service officials continued to fill discriminatory orders from private firms despite reliance upon federal funds and "supervision" provided by the U.S. Employment Service. Only after his presidential election defeat in 1960 was lame-duck Vice President Nixon willing to recommend to an uninterested Eisenhower the extension of equal opportunity clause provisions to the wide range of activities involving federal grants-in-aid and federal housing construction.[31]

For its relatively meager accomplishments in promoting equal employment opportunity, the Eisenhower administration re-

30. Aptheker, *Soul of the Republic*, 91; Mendelson, *Discrimination*, 95–96.
31. Aptheker, *Soul of the Republic*, 92; "News Focus Service — Richard Nixon and Civil Rights," Dec. 21, 1960, Mitchell Papers, Box 130; Milton Konvitz, *A Century of Civil Rights* (New York, 1967), 194–235.

ceived disproportionately high praise from some civil rights advocates. The Committee on Government Contracts received honors from the National Conference of Christians and Jews, Freedom's Foundation, the National Newspaper Publishers' Association, and the American Jewish Congress. In 1960, Eleanor Roosevelt praised Vice President Nixon and his colleagues for a "very good job on elimination of discrimination on work done under government contracts." Reports from Secretary Mitchell's Labor Department in 1960 painted a picture of marked improvement in minority hiring. The NAACP, in contrast, noted the slowness with which the committee had processed employment discrimination complaints. By using the prewar year of 1940 as its baseline date, the Labor Department claimed a drop in the number of teenagers in the job force, increases in black school enrollment, and rises in black median family income from 41 to 58 percent of white levels. The latter figure, however, actually represented a virtual standstill from the minority income levels recorded during the Korean War, and the average black family income, $3,233, still stood at a point far behind the $5,835 figure of whites. Although the black middle class had grown in the 1950s, the percentage of black families in "poverty" had declined only 3 percent from 1947 to 1962 compared to 27 percent for whites, signaling a dangerous growth of class stratification within the black community. In major industries, blacks remained concentrated in lower classifications, racial employment patterns stayed largely unchallenged, and black youth unemployment stood at double the white level. According to Norval Glenn, if the occupational trends of the 1950s continued unchanged, American nonwhites could not expect employment opportunities proportionate to their overall percentage of the population in clerical fields until 1992, among skilled workers until 2005, in professional classes until 2017, as sales employees until 2114, and among business managers and proprietors until the year 2730.[32]

By 1960, the number of self-employed blacks had dropped by 10,000 from 1950 levels, black-owned businesses had declined by one-third, and only one more black was being trained as an apprentice than had been employed ten years earlier. Despite the Vice President's claim that mass unemployment no longer existed in America, black unemployment in the recession of early 1961

32. Mazo and Hess, *Nixon*, 215; NAACP *Annual Report* (1960), 41; Mitchell to Eisenhower, Nov. 2, 1960; James T. O'Connell to Wilton B. Persons, Oct. 28, 1960, Mitchell Papers, Box 41, DDEL; National Urban League, *The Racial Gap* (New York, 1967), 2–5.

stood at 20 percent in Cleveland, 70 percent in South Bend, Indiana, and 39 percent in Detroit. Detroit blacks, although only 20 percent of the work force, constituted 60 percent of the city's unemployed.[33] Because it lacked the political will, the philosophical conviction, the personal understanding of the realities of unfair employment to blacks, and the enforcement tools necessary to make substantial gains in minority employment, the Eisenhower administration handed over to its successors a perpetuating, and in some respects worsening, economic crisis for blacks. For the members of the Eisenhower team involved with the problems of unfair employment, most black job seekers had never ceased being an invisible part of the "other America."

33. Aptheker, *Soul of the Republic* 38, Mendelson, *Discrimination* 69; Theodore Cross, *Black Capitalism* (New York, 1969), 63–64; Louis L. Knowles and Kenneth Prewitt, eds., *Institutional Racism in America* (Englewood Cliffs, N.J., 1968), 118.

6.

A Peculiarly Local Problem

The Eisenhower administration's failure to promote widespread equal employment opportunity resulted in part from its fidelity to free enterprise and its revulsion at any form of "coercive" federal regulation. In a similar fashion, federal government officials rejected direct intervention as an effective strategy for dealing with the problems of insufficient and segregated housing for minorities. Despite the claims of the NAACP and the National Jewish Congress in 1953 that "housing remains the strongest and most tenaciously defended bulwark of racism in the country," the new administration's faith in the distributive powers of the marketplace, its abhorrence of regulatory intervention, and its general lack of knowledge of the extent of urban neighborhood deterioration ruled out a vigorous federal assault on housing discrimination.[1]

Stimulated by the growth of the black urban population, blacks' demand for more and better housing in the nation's cities had accelerated rapidly after World War II. By 1950, the number of

---

1. National Jewish Congress and the NAACP, *Civil Rights in the US — 1952*, 80.

blacks living in cities had increased to over nine million, exceeding the ranks of foreign born by nearly a million. Because of unequal economic access to new housing being constructed and overt exclusionary practices, solidifying patterns of residential segregation accompanied black urban population growth. Although nine million new private housing units were built from 1935 to 1955, only 100,000 went to black applicants. Segregation by class as well as race further complicated the minority housing picture, as middle-income blacks sought escape from inferior dwellings into price-inflated urban "border" zones. For the black poor, housing opportunities were usually confined to the aging, overcrowded, substandard lots of the inner city. Although interracial committees in various communities officially banned discrimination in publicly assisted housing, enforcement of the equal opportunity strictures lagged badly. Blacks found themselves in competition with each other for a limited quantity of available housing that was often substandard, unsuited for mass accommodation, overpriced, and restricted by credit requirements, zoning policies, and selling procedures.[2]

As in the employment field, growing federal involvement in the housing industry provided a number of possible avenues of government action to counter the minority housing shortage. The federal government played a central role in home mortgage and loan programs, licensing, public housing, slum clearance, and the regulation of lending institutions. However, the record of federal involvement in fair housing did not give equal opportunity advocates cause for optimism. The initial mortgage guarantee programs of the Federal Housing Authority (FHA) in 1934 openly had rejected any applications that threatened to mix "incompatible racial and social groups." The FHA's segregation clause was dropped only in 1947, and although racial designations in applications assessment were abandoned two years later, black home seekers continued to be denied help disproportionately.

During the Truman administration, housing officials did call for an expansion of the low-income housing supply and slum clearance, and the Justice Department entered an amicus brief before the U.S. Supreme Court in the *Shelley* v. *Kraemer* restrictive covenant case of 1948. The high panel responded by barring court

2. Irving Berg, "Racial Discrimination in Housing: A Study in the Quest for Government Access by Minority Interest Groups, 1945–1962" (Ph.D. diss., University of Florida, 1967), 9; Foster Rhea Dulles, *The Civil Rights Commission, 1957–1965* (E. Lansing, Mich., 1968), 75; Blake McKelvey, *The Emergence of Metropolitan America, 1915–1966* (New Brunswick, N.J., 1968), 175.

enforcement of restrictive covenants and five years later prohibited enforcement through private damage suits as well. Nevertheless, by the beginning of the Eisenhower administration public housing programs were still in their infancy, and housing assistance was not specifically targeted at the growing needs of the minority poor. Despite the Supreme Court's position on restrictive covenant enforcement, discriminatory zoning patterns and restrictive covenants themselves had not been definitively prohibited, nor had residential discrimination in the sale or rental of public properties or publicly assisted housing construction been outlawed. The Housing and Home Finance Agency (HHFA), for example, although given overall federal responsibility for the administration of housing policies, consistently ignored the pleas of the NAACP for open-occupancy guarantees in public housing projects.[3]

The approach advocated by the new Republican administration placed ultimate reliance upon the foresight and goodwill of the private housing industry to provide sufficient housing for all Americans. Administration officials consciously followed a policy of cooperation rather than confrontation toward private builders and lenders. In September 1953, President Eisenhower appointed the Advisory Committee on Housing, manned primarily by representatives of the building, loan, and realty industries, to examine housing problems and prepare recommendations. Despite complaints from the NAACP against HHFA-sponsored redevelopment projects in Birmingham, Alabama, and Baltimore, Maryland, the committee's December report merely recommended the continuation of the low-rent public housing program of 1949. The study avoided mention of any new open-occupancy machinery and suggested only a modest loosening of mortgage guarantee requirements and slum rehabilitation grant programs. Despite the President's pledge to "assure equal opportunity for all of our citizens to acquire, within their means, good and well-located homes," subsequent Eisenhower housing proposals in 1954 contained only more liberal "section 221" provisions as a major new initiative. The revised Section 221 allowed the FHA to insure additional home loans at full appraisal value with amortization in up to forty years.[4]

3. Schlundt, "Civil Rights Policies," 103; McKelvey, *The Emergence of Metropolitan America,* 181.

4. Berg, "Racial Discrimination," 129–30; Schlundt, "Civil Rights Policies," 103; Dulles, *The Civil Rights Commission,* 76; NAACP, *Annual Report* (1953), 53; U.S., President's Advisory Committee on Government Housing Policies and Programs, *Recommendations,* Dec. 1953.

After the passage of the Eisenhower housing legislation and a Supreme Court ruling in May 1954 against public housing segregation, congressional support for additional housing measures faded noticeably. Southern Democrats openly dismissed any suggestions of additional federal actions to integrate the housing market as an unnecessary provocation. In 1955, additional housing legislation was passed that projected an increase of 35,000 units, but its implementation provisions limited the actual construction of new units to slightly over 10,000. An amendment by Adam Clayton Powell to strengthen antidiscrimination provisions in the 1955 law was defeated on a 112–158 teller vote in the House of Representatives in July. Even the final bill survived only in spite of the grumblings of the President that it had failed to place further limits on new construction by requiring local communities to provide "workable" slum clearance plans. By limiting new public housing construction while providing additional assistance for middle-income home financing, most of the provisions of both the 1954 and 1955 statutes did nothing to alleviate the low-rent minority housing shortage.[5]

Although the President possessed the authority to appoint the major federal housing chiefs and to propose legislative initiatives to the Congress, his own involvement in minority housing questions was sporadic, motivated by short-term political considerations rather than continuing interest or concern. Minority housing problems reached the President's desk only when they posed an immediate threat to domestic peace or to political objectives. In November 1953, after four black families entered the Trumbull Park public project in Chicago, white violence forced the installation of twenty four-hour police patrols. After similar disturbances in Louisville, Kentucky and NAACP protests against racial exclusion at Levittown projects in Pennsylvania and New Jersey, in early 1955 Attorney General Herbert Brownell proposed to the cabinet the creation of a new advisory housing committee specifically designated to examine federal antidiscrimination policies. Although the plan was endorsed in cabinet discussion by White House chief of staff Sherman Adams, Mutual Security Administrator Harold Stassen attributed the Louisville disturbances to Communist agitation rather than to legitimate grievances. Eisenhower himself squelched additional action to monitor minority housing

5. Donovan, *Eisenhower*, 318; Gary W. Reichard, *The Reaffirmation of Republicanism: Eisenhower and the Eighty-Third Congress* (Knoxville, Tenn., 1975), 126–28.

problems by concluding that although it was improper for any person single-handedly to bar members of another race from a community, it was undesirable for the federal government to assume responsibility for ending discrimination in projects assisted through "indirect activities" such as housing loan guarantee programs.[6]

Not surprisingly, additional racial confrontations followed administration inaction. In 1957, a black family purchasing a home in the Levittown, Pennsylvania development faced verbal and physical threats and the efforts of a local "betterment" committee to evict it. One Levittowner conceded that the black father was "probably a nice guy, but every time I look at him I see two thousand dollars drop off the value of my house."[7] With the White House deliberately choosing a course of inaction, responsibility for federal fair housing enforcement fell to the officials of the Housing and Home Finance Agency and its subordinate housing bodies. The HHFA supervised the activities of the Federal Housing Authority (FHA), the Public Housing Authority (PHA), and the Urban Renewal Administration (URA). In addition, the HHFA's federal housing administrator chaired the National Voluntary Mortgage Credit Extension Program and the board of directors of the Federal National Mortgage Association.

Unfortunately, Eisenhower's initial appointee as HHFA administrator, Albert M. Cole, demonstrated no greater willingness to press for antidiscrimination actions than his superiors in the White House. Cole, a former Kansas congressman known for his opposition to public housing, zealously pursued a program of cooperation with the private housing industry instead. Despite his admission in congressional testimony that minorities constituted two-thirds or more of American slum families, Cole insisted, "Federal intervention is incompatible with our idea of political and economic freedom."[8] Although Cole enlisted the voluntary cooperation of the National Association of Home Builders (NAHB), the Mortgage Bankers' Association, and insurance com-

6. Donovan, *Eisenhower*, 317–18; Charles C. Alexander, *Holding the Line: The Eisenhower Era, 1952–1961* (Bloomington, Ind., 1975), 116; "Cabinet Notes," Jan. 28, 1955, Whitman File, Cabinet Series, Box 4; Maxwell Rabb, "Memorandum for Ann Whitman," July 5, 1955, Whitman File, Administrative Series, Box 32, DDEL.
   7. Alexander, *Holding The Line*, 116.
   8. Berg, "Racial Discrimination," 31, 130–31; U.S., Commission on Civil Rights (CRC), *Report* (1959), 144; U.S. Congress, Senate, Committee on Banking and Currency, *Hearings on the Nomination of Albert M. Cole as Federal Housing Administrator*, March 2, 6, 1953, 7, 30.

panies in efforts to provide additional low-income housing, he opposed all legislative initiatives to tie the number of FHA-issued mortgages to the local "effective housing demand." Cole's only major administrative pronouncement to spur greater use of open-occupancy provisions in federally assisted construction was a request to federal housing agencies to "review" their procedures.[9]

Cole's resistance to federal enforcement activity in the fair housing area especially frustrated the personnel of the HHFA's Racial Relations Service. The service's director, Joseph R. Ray, a former board member of the black National Association of Real Estate Brokers, received protests against federal inactivity at a Minority Housing Conference in December 1954, and he carried the case for action directly to the HHFA Administrator. Ray was careful not to voice his complaints publicly, however, and in speeches he advocated a "middle road policy" and reiterated Cole's pledge to "use every appropriate influence at my command to create new standard housing and to improve access to the existing supply of good housing for racial minorities."[10] In private, Cole charged much of the failure of blacks in acquiring housing to the activities of black lending institutions, which "avoided" FHA and Veterans Administration loans and charged higher interest rates. Rather than recommend the creation of additional public housing for minorities, Cole endorsed the NAHB's proposal for a 10 percent voluntary minority housing quota.[11]

Friction between Cole and Racial Relations Service officials led in early 1955 to a reorganization effort by the administration to bring the service into closer political harmony with the White House. The HHFA reorganization plans included the establishment of a coordinating committee of race relations officials and the creation of race relations positions in the HHFA's regional offices. Continued conflict, however, led to an embarrassing political squabble centered upon the "firing" of Frank Horne, special assistant to the administrator. Horne, a holdover from the Truman administration, had been transferred by Cole in 1953 from his

9. Schlundt, "Civil Rights Policies," 104–105; Cole to Jacob Seidenberg, May 17, 1954, Cole to Senator Homer E. Capehart, Apr. 6, 1954, Harlow Records, Box 8, DDEL.

10. Schlundt, "Civil Rights Policies," 106; "Speech by Albert M. Cole to the National Association of Real Estate Brokers," Oct. 12, 1953, Harlow Records, Box 8; Joseph R. Ray, "Federal Policies and Programs for the Elimination of Housing Discrimination," July 11, 1957, Morrow Records, Box 10, DDEL.

11. NAACP, Annual Report (1955), 40; Cole to Gabriel Hauge, May 27, 1955, Official File, Box 704, DDEL.

Racial Relations Service post to a "special assistant" position in "intergroup relations." The transfer may have been motivated by a desire to keep Horne under closer political scrutiny, for in the 1952 election he had openly expressed his preference for a Stevenson victory. Following his initial transfer, Horne and an assistant, Corienne R. Morrow, resisted new orders assigning them to inferior HHFA posts and petitioned the Civil Service Commission to reinstate them in their former jobs. Cole responded by eliminating their old positions from Civil Service classification as well as eight other posts.[12]

Thoroughly disgusted at the "disloyalty" of the Racial Relations Service, Cole authorized the preparation of a reorganization proposal calling for its elimination and replacement by a "Division of Special Operations and Coordination," which would "relieve the White House of further unpleasant experiences . . . caused by the present Racial Relations Service." Despite Cole's willingness to jettison his agency's fair housing machinery, Joseph Ray managed to block the effort by appealing over his head to Maxwell Rabb. After listening to Ray's arguments, the minorities adviser concluded, "I think we would be justified in attempting to strengthen and broaden this service, and also more fully integrate it into the mainstream of housing activities, rather than attempt to abolish the service."[13]

Until his departure from the administration in 1959, Cole persisted in his opposition to the use of federal intervention to fight racial discrimination in housing. "The problems of racial discrimination are peculiarly local," he asserted. "I believe we should rely heavily on local responsibility and local wisdom to work out solutions." A critical assessment of Cole's performance as HHFA Administrator was provided by the *New York Times* in 1958, which claimed that Cole "believed that the federal government had no responsibility to promote the ending of racial discrimination in residential accommodations."[14] Cole's successor, lumber executive and former FIIA commissioner Norman P. Mason, held a more activist view of the role of the HHFA in promoting fair housing. Upon assuming the top position in the HHFA, Mason commented to an NAACP official that his department's racial

12. Schlundt, "Civil Rights Policies," 105, 108; U.S., Housing and Home Finance Agency (HHFA), *Report of the Housing and Home Finance Agency, 1954,* 32; "Capital Close-Up," Aug. 27, 1955, in Morrow Records, Box 11, DDEL.
13. "Memorandum from the HHFA," Feb. 8, 1956; Joseph R. Ray to Rabb, Feb. 10, 1956, Confidential File, Subject Series, Box 32, DDEL.
14. Schlundt, "Civil Rights Policies," 108; Berg, "Racial Discrimination," 131.

policies "stunk." In response, he restored the special assistant position formerly held by Frank Horne, reinstituted the appointment of race relations officials to regional offices, abolished the restrictive HHFA quota system on minority resettlement, and eliminated prior agency practices of selling repossessed housing units exclusively through private realtors.[15]

Mason's actions did help to restore confidence to the personnel of the Racial Relations Service, but in general the new administrator, like his predecessor, shared the administration's philosophical opposition to either legislation or executive action guaranteeing open occupancy in federally assisted housing. The HHFA persisted in rejecting legislation designed to deny mortgage guarantees to those unwilling to pledge nondiscrimination in the selling or renting of properties. Mason, in opposing any "precipitous" action in the housing field before the U.S. Commission on Civil Rights in 1959, admitted that federal fair housing enforcement was "largely done by persuasion." He added, "We accomplish the most in this field by giving rewards rather than punishments." Mason also rejected proposals for the introduction of immediate open occupancy in all federal housing projects, declaring: "This kind of act at this time—this month—this year—might cause problems more serious than the ones now facing us."[16]

The flaws in the administration's cooperative strategy for encouraging private minority housing were illustrated amply by the performance of federal lending institutions, including the FHA, the VA, the Voluntary Home Mortgage Credit Program, and the Federal National Mortgage Association. For civil rights organizations and their spokesmen, private plans for building and financing minority housing sometimes meant a painful choice between maintaining strict insistence upon the principle of integration at the risk of losing new construction and accepting segregation as the price for additional housing. The FHA, responding to a doubling of minority loan applications from 1952 levels in the last nine months of 1953, encouraged the establishment of an open-occupancy project in New York City and discussed loan guarantees with contractors and minority representatives. In May 1954, FHA Commissioner Mason outlined a "positive program" for the agency before the National Association of Home Builders, including "demonstration open occupancy projects in suitable key

15. Schlundt, "Civil Rights Policies," 117–18; CRC, *Conference with Federal Housing Officials*, June 10, 1959, vol. 2, pp. 14, 33.
16. Schlundt, "Civil Rights Policies," 119; CRC, *Conference*, 34–35.

areas." By 1961, fifty-eight demonstration projects were being operated with the assistance of FHA loan guarantees. However, the NAHB's own 1954 plan called only for a limited number of all-black projects as its way of meeting black housing demand. NAHB housing corporations in Pittsburgh, Cleveland, Dallas, and Houston added construction for blacks only within "suitable" districts. Even after the *Brown* school desegregation decision, the NAHB pushed for FHA endorsement of its "separate but equal" construction plans. The NAACP and the National Urban League found themselves resisting NAHB overtures for additional segregated housing on the grounds that they would "confuse the campaign for integration," and insisted that "we do not want Jim Crow dwellings whether they are new or not."[17]

For its part the FHA continued assistance to discriminatory private projects, despite a 1955 federal court ruling suggesting that the FHA "probably" could prevent discrimination under mortgage insurance programs. The FHA did strengthen its open occupancy enforcement policies by issuing a general order to field offices to assist state agencies in their antidiscrimination notifications to builders and lenders and by pledging to deny federal assistance to violators of New York's antidiscrimination law. However, even when it possessed massive evidence of wrongdoing, the FHA refused to cut off loan assistance before the actual conviction of a builder under state law. When evidence of discrimination existed but state conviction did not follow, FHA loan guarantees continued to be offered to discriminatory projects. After taking over the HHFA, Norman Mason conceded that segregated Levittown projects in New Jersey were still receiving federal assistance despite press accounts in which project managers admitted following discriminatory practices. In other instances, the actual enforcement of other FHA rules worked against the interests of black housing seekers. By 1959, FHA space requirements for minimum frontage still prevented the construction of FHA-backed housing in many black areas of Chicago, for the standard exceeded the size of the typical city lot. The net result of FHA enforcement policies was that, of all the FHA-insured homes constructed from 1946 to 1959, only 2 percent were made available for blacks.[18]

17. Berg, "Racial Discrimination" 31; Schlundt, "Civil Rights Policies," 114–15; McKelvey, *The Emergence of Metropolitan America*, 182.

18. Berg, "Racial Discrimination, 40; Schlundt, "Civil Rights Policies," 116; Mendelson, *Discrimination* 124; CRC, *Report* (1959), 172; NAACP, *Crisis* 66, No. 6 (June–July 1959): 340.

The FHA's reluctance to pursue a vigorous antidiscrimination policy in its lending practices was mirrored by the passivity of the Veterans Administration, the Voluntary Home Mortgage Credit Program, and the Federal National Mortgage Association. The VA did not directly refuse loan guarantees to veterans on property under restrictive covenants, but it did deny lenders the right to convert segregated property to VA control in case of foreclosure, thereby providing some antidiscrimination protection. As with the FHA, however, the VA required conclusive state determination of discrimination before taking any action, lacked its own enforcement machinery, and hesitated to oppose local residential patterns or community sentiment. In 1958, the VA did issue directives stating that builders discriminating on racial grounds against veterans faced loan disqualification, and by 1961 it held cooperative agreements with the states of New York, New Jersey, Washington, Oregon, and Connecticut. Under the agreements, the VA advised state antidiscrimination agencies of the existence of new housing proposals awaiting its approval, and the state then issued an advisory notice of its antidiscrimination statutes to the builders. Upon proof of violation and disclosure of conviction by the state, the VA could suspend its guarantees. However, the VA, like the FHA, might not have even needed to follow such a cautious policy, for the U.S. Commission on Civil Rights concluded in 1959 that a 1944 law already empowered it to suspend assistance to discriminatory builders upon its own initiative.[19]

The Voluntary Home Mortgage Credit Program was created by the 1954 Housing Act to provide necessary assistance for housing seekers unable to obtain FHA or VA financing for home loans. Yet the program, supervised by the HHFA administrator and fourteen representatives of the housing industry, relied totally on the good faith of private lenders to make available additional mortgage funding. Under its provisions, if a VA or FHA applicant had been twice refused assistance by lending institutions, he could apply for VHMCP help. In its six and a half years of existence in the Eisenhower administration, the VHMCP did issue over 47,000 loans worth $479 million, of which 22 percent, worth $12 million, went to minorities. However, middle-class blacks were more likely to receive help under the program than those of lower income. Forty-two percent of minority applicants were turned down because of either unacceptable properties or inadequate personal resources. The availability of housing for poorer blacks was hampered further by the unwillingness of local communities to make

19. Berg, "Racial Discrimination," 127–28; CRC, *Report* (1959), 175.

desirable land available and by the escalation of housing prices in crowded areas to levels beyond the means of many VHMCP applicants. The Federal National Mortgage Association, which had the responsibility of buying and selling FHA and VA mortgages in order to provide a secondary market, demonstrated no greater tendency to make direct loans for open-occupancy projects than the other federal lending agencies. Proposals for targeting FNMA funds specifically for the purpose of providing integrated housing were rejected by administrator Mason in 1959.[20]

Federal agencies responsible for administering federally operated housing and slum clearance—the Public Housing Authority and the Urban Renewal Administration—demonstrated a similar unwillingness to push hard for additional housing for the minority poor. Federal responsibility for promoting equal opportunity in its own housing projects appeared obvious, but the PHA obstinately ignored its mandate. The PHA openly attempted to evade antidiscrimination suits filed against it by claiming that such suits were procedurally impossible. If a case charging possible housing discrimination was filed in the District of Columbia, the PHA insisted that the local housing authority also had to be included in the suit. If a discrimination suit was filed outside Washington, D.C., the PHA then claimed that it automatically was invalidated because it had been brought outside the PHA's home judicial district.

Despite its claim of immunity from suits, in *Cohen v. PHA* the federal agency offered defenses in a Georgia segregation case, and the Fifth Circuit Court concluded as a result that the PHA had submitted to its jurisdiction. Nevertheless, the court also held that the plaintiff had not properly applied for public housing before filing suit and therefore lacked legal standing. After an NAACP appeal of the case, the Eisenhower Justice Department, represented by Solicitor General Rankin, argued against certiorari for the PHA and supported the lower court's ruling, a position that the U.S. Supreme Court upheld. PHA policies of neglect persisted throughout the remainder of the Eisenhower administration, for the federal courts generally refused to enforce integration and additional public housing discrimination cases did not reach the Supreme Court.[21]

The PHA's claims that it was powerless to act against segrega-

20. Berg, "Racial Discrimination," 46; Mendelson, *Discrimination*, 130.
21. Greenberg, *Race Relations and American Law*, 288–89; Stephen L. Wasby, Anthony H. D'Amato, and Rosemary Metraler, *Desegregation from Brown to Alexander* (Carbondale, Ill., 1977), 229.

tion in its projects did not prevent it from acting in a variety of ways that assured continuation of segregation patterns, including issuing an "equity formula" for housing distribution based upon the racial housing "need" of a given area. The PHA left issues of segregation to local officials, and it insisted only upon the principle of equal facilities in the event that housing projects were segregated. Site selection for public housing projects stayed in the hands of local officials, who were usually unwilling to upset existing residential patterns of race and class. In early 1955, the PHA eliminated even its vague requirement of equality of facilities from its manual, and it also dropped a requirement that public housing authorities give families displaced by slum clearance and expressway construction first priority for public housing vacancies. By defining any project with more than one family of the other race as "completely integrated," the PHA claimed credit for an increase in the percentage of integrated public housing projects from 11 percent nationally in 1953 to 55 percent in thirty-two states in 1960. However, when the remaining states, predominantly those of the South, were added to the 1960 figures, the percentage of integrated projects nationwide dropped to 19 percent.[22] By the end of the decade, federal housing projects increasingly were becoming the segregated domain of the minority poor. Forty-six percent of public housing units were occupied by nonwhites by 1961, and the U.S. Commission on Civil Rights warned, "Whether 'open occupancy' will prove to be another name for all-Negro projects remains to be seen."[23]

For blacks displaced by urban renewal, slum clearance, and other forms of public construction, federal hesitancy in assuming responsibility led to further inaction and neglect. The Urban Renewal Administration, created in 1954 as a subordinate unit of the HHFA, did not claim jurisdiction over the discriminatory actions of private redevelopers after the completion of initial slum clearance. URA attempts to anticipate the problems of slum clearance by offering credit extensions to those pledging to improve properties in areas earmarked for destruction failed because few black property owners possessed the financial resources to take advantage of the restoration program. New FHA-guaranteed housing provided under the section 221 provisions of the 1954 Housing Act, designed to supplement urban renewal housing,

22. Schlundt, "Civil Rights Policies," 111; Mendelson, *Discrimination*, 131; CRC, *Report* (1959), 173.
23. Mendelson, *Discrimination*, 131; CRC, *Report* (1959), 476.

gave only one-third of its new units to displaced families. Reasons for the inadequacy of section 221 protections included the fact that the displaced lost priority status after only sixty days and official stipulations placed a mortgage limitation of about $10,000.

Until 1959, attempts to promote desegregation in urban renewal projects were discouraged by the URA's supervisor, HHFA Administrator Cole, who directed the agency's Southern race relations officials to minimize their efforts. By the middle of 1956, 112,420 housing units had been approved for destruction, but only 75,168 new units had been authorized. Sixty percent of those displaced by the urban renewal projects were nonwhites. Urban renewal also added to the problem of black concentration in public housing, for nine out of every ten dislocated families moving to public units were black.[24] After the ascension of Norman Mason to the post of HHFA Administrator, some modifications were made in urban renewal programs. Purchasers of URA properties were notified of the need to comply with state open-occupancy laws. The URA rescinded its earlier policy of reserving fixed racial quotas for the relocation of tenants into section 221 housing, and intergroup relations experts were appointed to URA regional staffs. Despite Mason's changes, however, the Civil Rights Commission in its 1961 report still concluded: "Displacement of Negroes from areas designated for urban renewal, expressway, and other public improvements continues to be a major problem."[25]

Unfortunately, federal neglect in providing both an adequate supply of, and equal access to, safe and affordable housing went beyond even the actions of housing agencies. A fundamental contributor to minority housing scarcity and discriminatory residential patterns was the absence of federal supervision of private mortgage lending practices, which encouraged limiting housing credit to blacks. The Federal Home Loan Bank Board, for example, did not even declare a nondiscrimination policy until June 1961. The Comptroller of the Currency defined his particular role in the regulation of lending institutions narrowly and excluded the supervision of the racial practices of lending bodies from his Treasury Department duties. The Federal Reserve Board, without bothering to test its assumptions of powerlessness, claimed

24. Berg, "Racial Discrimination," 62; NAACP, *Annual Report* (1959), 64; Mendelson, *Discrimination*, 134–35; Greenberg, *Race Relations and American Law*, 293; CRC, *Report* (1959), 174–75.
25. HHFA, *Report* (1960), 38.

that it lacked the authority to block discriminatory mortgage loans issued by member banks, despite its history of periodic interventions in the housing market to protect real estate values. The Federal Deposit Insurance Corporation, in turn, made the amazing claim that it "has no reason to believe that race is being used improperly by banks as a criterion in the making of real estate loans," a statement understandable only when taken in the context of the profound ignorance of racial discrimination demonstrated by federal monetary authorities.[26]

The continuing unmet challenge of providing additional housing for minority Americans in all sections of the nation was revealed publicly in hearings conducted in New York, Atlanta, Chicago, Los Angeles, and San Francisco by the U.S. Commission on Civil Rights in 1959 and 1960. The commission, describing fair housing as the "frontier problem of civil rights," sought the testimony and recommendations of city and state officials, civil rights representatives, and executives of real estate and financial institutions. In New York, despite statutes against public housing discrimination, Earl W. Schwulst, president of the Bowery Savings Bank and chairman of the National Commission on Race and Housing, declared: "Housing is apparently the only commodity in the American market which is not freely available to these minority groups who are nonwhite." Local white resistance to integration fed on fears of declining community status and property values, and segregation was perpetuated by loan company denials of mortgages to blacks, disproportionately high interest rates for black borrowers, and the "block-busting" practices of real estate agents, which produced panic selling, resale to minorities at high prices, and the reshaping of segregation zones.

In the New York hearings, descriptions of minority housing shortages were paired frequently with condemnations of continuing federal indifference to housing problems. Baseball star and business executive Jackie Robinson, noting his difficulties in buying a home, observed that federal officials "have been very polite to me, but . . . nothing has been done." Domestic Relations Court judge Justine W. Polier, recounting the human costs of class and race segregation, also criticized federal apathy: "I think this city can properly pride itself on being a leader in the United States to date to use the democratic process of law to end discriminatory housing authorized or tolerated . . . by Federal, state, and local

26. Mendelson, *Discrimination*, 119–23.

governments." Frank Horne, now executive director of the New York Commission on Intergroup Relations, was even more emphatic: "I think the real sin has been that the great weight and power of the federal government has been thrown on the side of the segregated mind."[27]

Hearings before the Civil Rights Commission in Atlanta tested the claim of private developers that additional minority housing could be provided without altering existing residential patterns. The West Side Mutual Development Committee, with three black members and three white, claimed credit for breaking up bottlenecks to black suburban expansion. Whites agreed to open up a limited number of residential districts to minorities in return for pledges from them not to enter other city zones. Advocates claimed credit for the creation of a "magnificent colored section," and some black observers, though less enthusiastic, did see benefits in the plan. However, I.V. Williamson, the president of the Negro Real Estate Board, destroyed the harmonious tenor of the Atlanta hearings when he openly questioned the claims of progress and charged that blacks overpaid for the housing they received. Although he allowed that the "separate but equal" philosophy might be justified as a temporary expedient, Williamson noted that nothing in the plan actually encouraged integration, and he disputed the claim that Atlanta's segregation was strictly a matter of voluntary custom, charging: "You have your political heads of government saying directly what custom is."[28]

In Chicago, housing discrimination patterns more closely resembled those of New York City, but to a greater extent than in New York, the testimony revealed widespread disagreement among experts over housing goals. Some witnesses, including University of Chicago sociologist Philip M. Hauser, implied that segregation occurred by black choice and that blacks, as the "last immigrants," would escape segregated areas once their economic status inevitably improved. Other testimony, however, described the influence of the all-white Chicago Real Estate Board and real estate interests in Chicago in producing inequalities in the distribution of mortgage loans, higher black housing prices, and block-busting practices that led "inevitably to total Negro occupancy." Rabbi Richard G. Hirsch of the Union of Hebrew Congregations decried the futility of educational desegregation and

27. CRC, *Hearings Before the United States Commission on Civil Rights — Housing* (1959), 32–36, 122, 202–12, 270.
   28. Ibid., 442ff., 557–58.

black voting protections as long as housing remained segregated by race and class, and added: "We in the North learned that the distance between Poplarville, Mississippi, and Trumbull Park in Chicago is not so vast as some of us in our complacency would like to believe." Proposals offered at the hearings included "gentlemen's agreements with teeth," in which real estate dealers would agree not to sell to a nonwhite in a block unless it had first been "cracked" by other means, and community-organized quota systems for the acceptance of blacks into all-white neighborhoods. Although these proposals attempted to address the segregation problem in middle-class zones, they promised nothing for increasing the overall supply of housing or for upgrading the housing of minorities lacking the means to migrate to more affluent areas.[29]

The Civil Rights Commission's hearings in Los Angeles and San Francisco in early 1960 added the somber knowledge that minority housing problems prevailed even in areas of rapid economic growth in the West. Noting the absence of legal safeguards for black housing seekers, state attorney general Stanley Mosk testified that harassment of minorities and federal acquiescence in restrictive covenants "permitted, if not encouraged, the translation of racial prejudices into overt community discrimination." Governor Edmund G. Brown, while heralding the passage of the state's fair housing act, admitted that the worst instances of discrimination still occurred in the housing field and imposed segregation upon all other aspects of black life. Although the mayor of San Francisco chose to emphasize the positive powers of public sentiment, using the example of Willie Mays's eventual success in finding a home in the Bay area, others observed that black entry into the suburbs was limited by white fears of depressed property values and by "improvement association" wealth requirements for residence. Frank Quinn, director of the San Francisco Council for Civic Unity, rejected the claim that blacks preferred inferior segregated accommodations: "I do not think . . . I could go along with the implication that people prefer to live under these conditions without improving them." He added the ominous warning, "We are going backward very fast, and we don't know it, in the whole Bay area."[30]

29. Ibid., 632–33, 815, 886.
30. CRC, *Hearings Before the United States Commission on Civil Rights, Los Angeles, California, Jan. 25–26, 1960 and San Francisco, California, Jan. 17–18,* (1960), 3, 30–34, 473–74, 558, 631–35.

The 1959 report of the Civil Rights Commission offered a series of recommendations for federal action to respond to the segregation of middle-class neighborhoods, but relatively less attention was paid to the housing needs of the black poor. Commissioners suggested the creation of a biracial housing commission to investigate discrimination complaints, and urged the President to issue an executive order directing federal agencies to require open occupancy in their housing projects. Other ideas included giving the HHFA greater antidiscrimination responsibility, requiring FHA and VA builders to comply with all local antidiscrimination laws, urging the PHA to push for site selection on open land rather than in occupied areas, and stimulating URA action to incorporate minority representation in community planning. In 1961, the commission called upon the FHA and VA to prohibit the sale or leasing of guaranteed housing, urged the President or the Congress to take action to bar discrimination in mortgage loans by federally authorized financial bodies, and advocated the creation of new authority to protect housing access for displaced families.[31] Despite their recommendations, however, commissioners expressed personal reservations similar to those of President Eisenhower about the ability of federal action to promote fair housing. In 1960 congressional testimony CRC chairman John Hannah remarked: "The eventual end of segregation in housing and community life . . . can be attained only at a tempo supportable by the American people as a whole and by their communities."[32]

But if the ultimate responsibility for fair housing lay with local communities, most had proven themselves inadequate to the task. Attempts at community organization in depressed areas of such cities as Kansas City, Missouri, and Minneapolis, Minnesota, experienced only minimal success, and the greatest progress in community organization occurred in middle-class districts. By the mid-1950s, about fifty interracial housing projects had begun, many of them under the auspices of the American Friends Service Committee and others sponsored by unions, settlement houses, or black churches. These projects, however, were hampered by the reluctance of banks to extend credit and the unwillingness of real estate associations to offer suburban site locations for community housing projects. Although several housing studies refuted the

31. CRC, *Report* (1959), 534–43; CRC, *Report — Housing* (1961), 150–53.
32. John A. Hannah to Sen. John McClellan, March 9, 1960, Gerald Morgan Records, Box 6, DDEL.

claim that property values inevitably declined after residential desegregation, continuing fears spawned new theories claiming the existence of a "tipping point" tied to the degree of black entrance. Washington, D.C., Pittsburgh, Pennsylvania, and New Haven, Connecticut did develop noteworthy community housing organizations, and in St. Paul, Minnesota, black minister Floyd Massey fathered the Rondo-St. Anthony Improvement Association. But although Massey's organization obtained more generous property assessments for displaced families, it could not block a major freeway plan for the Twin Cities or force passage of a municipal open housing ordinance.[33]

A number of states attempted to fill the vacuum in fair housing policy left by the federal government, and by 1961, nineteen states and the Virgin Islands had enacted antidiscrimination housing laws. But in Idaho, Illinois, Michigan, Montana, Rhode Island, Washington, and Wisconsin the statutes only covered public housing and urban renewal projects. In Indiana and Kansas, public housing laws lacked enforcement machinery. In Alaska, California, Colorado, Connecticut, Massachusetts, Minnesota, New Hampshire, New Jersey, New York, Oregon, and Pennsylvania, statutes also covered government-insured private housing, but in most states officials hesitated to challenge entrenched residential patterns. Federal highway programs did not contain provisions for the relocation of displaced individuals, and state highway and building construction programs suffered from similar deficiencies. Alarming instances of block-busting continued — one New York City block was bought from white owners at $7,000–$11,000 per unit and resold to blacks at $12,000–$18,000, and in Chicago, housing markups by race ranged from 35 percent to 115 percent.[34]

By the time of its departure, the Eisenhower administration could claim only limited progress in providing additional black middle-class housing, while urban residential patterns continued to show racial segregation and the housing conditions of the inner city deteriorated further. The black urban population of fourteen million, 50 percent greater in 1960 than a decade earlier, saw the number of white "overcrowded" housing units drop by over one-third while its own number rose by 16 percent. The nonwhite share of the nation's "substandard" housing pool rose from 19 percent to 27 percent in ten years, and 44 percent of nonwhite

33. McKelvey, The Emergence of Metropolitan America, 78, 182, 184–86.
34. HHFA, Report (1957), 45 and (1959), 201; editors of Ebony, The White Problem in America (Chicago, 1966), 82–83; "Civil Rights and the South: A Symposium," North Carolina Law Review 42, 123–25.

housing was listed as substandard in 1960, compared to only 13 percent for whites.[35] Although aware of the symbolic importance of an image of racial equality in the military services, in the nation's capital, and in federal employment, the Eisenhower administration had proven itself incapable of moving beyond symbolism to an open confrontation with racial inequalities in basic human services, employment, and housing. The plight of minorities in the cities had worsened, but for administration officials the emerging black urban underclass, a stark reminder of the "other America," did not exist. It could not, for it posed a fundamental challenge to the idea of an affluent, color-blind, democratic society so coveted by administration proponents that it had become an article of faith.

35. National Urban League, *The Racial Gap*, 34–35; Louis Lomax, *The Negro Revolt* (New York, 1962), 69.

The
Ascendancy
of
Constitutional
Moralism

7.

Initial Skirmishes with Jim Crow

"Americans are accustomed to inscribe their ideals in laws," wrote the race relations expert Gunnar Myrdal in 1944.[1] Nowhere in the American republic has this link between civic morality and legal standards been more firmly forged than in popular attitudes toward the Constitution and its amendments. The Constitution represents for Americans a sacred secular covenant between government and people—a document that defines the limits of federal power and offers protection to the citizen against government-sanctioned intrusions on basic rights. By the 1950s, leading spokesmen of both parties, spurred by a growing list of black legal challenges to official Jim Crow discrimination in the South, were beginning to recognize the threat posed by Southern racial policies to the American democratic image. The growing concern over the moral image of white America merged with the popular identification of constitutional law with national civic morality to provide new momentum for efforts to strengthen protections of minority citizenship rights.

1. Myrdal, *An American Dilemma*, vol. 1, 14.

For the Eisenhower administration, the growing rediscovery of constitutional moralism as a guiding theme of racial activism dictated significant changes in its official responses. Early administration actions had been limited to the use of executive orders in areas of clear federal authority and symbolic national value, including the armed forces, the District of Columbia, and federal employment. With the growing attention paid to the discriminatory practices of the Southern states, however, the administration was forced to consider the use of legal and legislative remedies in fields of divided federal-state jurisdiction in order to promote popular compliance with a revised standard of constitutional morality. For the members of the Eisenhower administration, especially the officials of the Justice Department, fundamental issues would arise concerning the role of the federal government in promoting public compliance with reinterpreted constitutional principles — principles that now marked Jim Crow segregation as illegitimate. Was constitutional law merely intended as a moral beacon, a secular Ten Commandments to which citizens and local units of government assumed sole responsibility for compliance or violation? Or did the new moral demands placed on the Constitution also mandate its increased use by the federal executive as an enforcement tool, even if such use carried the risk of "compulsion" and social unrest? In the main, the Eisenhower administration chose to follow cautiously a narrow definition of the enforcement role of constitutional law, causing critics to complain that administration officials were denying themselves available and necessary means of enhancing black citizenship rights.

From the 1890s until the 1940s, Jim Crow segregation and discrimination in the American South had hidden behind the convenient morality of a "separate but equal" legal doctrine. Yet such works as John Dollard's *Caste and Class in a Southern Town,* Myrdal's *An American Dilemma,* the Truman Civil Rights Committee's *To Secure These Rights,* and other studies of Southern segregation had chipped away at the rhetorical pretense of "equal facilities" to reveal a wide range of discriminatory practices. Jim Crow segregation in actuality meant unequal access and racial stigmatization for blacks in train, bus, and airplane travel; discrimination in restaurants, saloons, boarding houses, and theaters; separation at public drinking fountains and in public washrooms, parks, barbershops, and auditoriums; and prohibition from white juries and educational facilities. In virtually every form of state-supported services, per capita outlays for blacks measured only a small fraction of white levels, and gaps only widened the more heavily black a county's population.[2]

Segregated public education in particular carried a special symbolic importance to the civil rights struggle, for the nation's public schools held a prominent position in American democratic thought as the great "equalizers" of social opportunity. Schools were commonly seen as the means by which those of differing social, economic, and racial backgrounds would receive an equal chance for advancement through a shared educational training. The distance between the promise of "separate but equal" and the reality of unequal education, however, clearly had been documented in a series of NAACP-sponsored legal challenges to segregated education in the South. In *Gaines* v. *Canada, Sweatt* v. *Painter*, and *McLaurin* v. *Oklahoma State Regents*, the NAACP had demonstrated before the Supreme Court the prevalence of unequal educational facilities at the college level. In the *McLaurin* case, the NAACP had encouraged the high court to find racial segregation an inherent cause of unequal education, regardless of the quality of separate facilities. The NAACP's work in undermining Southern segregation by demonstrating the blatant racial inequalities inherent in its practice was crucial in lessening white apathy toward Jim Crow, for as early as 1940 public opinion polls had indicated that most Americans supported the principle of equal tax expenditures for black and white schoolchildren. Nevertheless, the question of whether the Supreme Court would take the next step, declare public school segregation inherently unequal, and thereby challenge years of Southern practices remained an open one at the time of Eisenhower's inauguration.[3]

At the onset of the Eisenhower administration, seventeen states and the District of Columbia legally mandated segregated public education and four other states made segregation optional. During the 1952 campaign, Eisenhower had demonstrated little knowledge of the implications of segregation. When asked about the effect of dual school systems on educational costs, the candidate had responded, "You brought up a feature of this thing that I have not even thought about. I did not know that there was an additional cost involved." The stage was soon set for the new administration's initial encounter with the school segregation

2. See Kluger, *Simple Justice* ch. 3–4.

3. See James C. Duram, *A Moderate Among Extremists: Dwight E. Eisenhower and the School Desegregation Issue* (Chicago, 1981), ch. 3; Kluger, *Simple Justice*, ch. 11–12; Myrdal, *An American Dilemma*, 893–94n.

issue. In December 1952 the Truman administration's Justice Department filed a brief challenging the constitutionality of "separate but equal" in a group of Supreme Court cases entitled *Brown* v. *Topeka Board of Education*. On June 8, 1953, the Supreme Court "invited" the attorney general to file a brief and submit arguments in the pending cases in response to specific questions from the court on the applicability of the Fourteenth Amendment to the school segregation issue.[4]

With the court issuing instructions to the administration to participate in the *Brown* cases, responsibility for handling the segregation issue fell squarely upon the new attorney general, Herbert Brownell. Brownell appeared well trained for the task of defusing the political explosive contained in *Brown*. A Nebraska native and Yale Law School graduate, Brownell had been a five-term member of the New York Assembly and campaign manager for Thomas E. Dewey in 1942, 1944, and 1948. One of Eisenhower's links to the Republican "Eastern Establishment," Brownell had served as his campaign manager in the successful effort of 1952. Skilled in playing off different political constituencies, including both Northern blacks and Southern whites, Brownell approached the *Brown* brief with the political sagacity and caution that had marked his career. Shortly after the Supreme Court's reargument order, Brownell presided at a meeting of Justice Department officials, including Deputy Attorney General William P. Rogers, Assistant Attorney General J. Lee Rankin, Assistant Attorney General Warren Burger, and two Truman administration holdovers in the solicitor general's office, Robert Stern and Philip Elman. Elman later recalled that the prevailing mood was expressed by Rogers, who lamented, "Jesus, do we really have to file a brief? Aren't we better off staying out of it?" Despite the discomfort of department officials, however, involvement in the *Brown* cases could not be ducked, for the court's request was tantamount to a command and the previous administration's position opposing segregation had forced, at the minimum, a response from the Eisenhower administration in oral argument.[5]

Justice Department officials were not alone in requiring prodding to accept the Supreme Court's request for participation. The President himself entertained serious doubts about the wisdom of administration involvement, and his doubts were reinforced by

4. Kluger, *Simple Justice*, 650, 665.
5. Ibid., 650.

his friendships with Southern political supporters and by his goal of building the Republican party in the South. On July 16, 1953, Governor Allan Shivers of Texas advised the President that "this local problem should be decided on the local and state level." Shivers asserted, "The United States is not a party to this lawsuit except insofar as Truman and former Attorney General McGranery intervened."[6] After receiving additional warnings from Governor Byrnes of South Carolina that court-ordered desegregation would result in the elimination of state aid for public schools and the death of Republican hopes in the South, the President responded by declaring his own philosophical opposition to vigorous federal intervention. "I do not believe," Eisenhower asserted, "that prejudice . . . will succumb to compulsion. Consequently, I believe that Federal law imposed upon our states in such a way as to bring about a conflict of the police power of the states and the nation, would set back the cause of progress in race relations for a long, long time."[7]

Believing that the Supreme Court had trapped his administration into taking a politically risky public stance on Southern segregation, Eisenhower outlined his reservations with the attorney general about filing a brief on several occasions. In a "Memorandum for the Record" of August 19, 1953, attached to a memorandum on "Party Organization in the Southern States," the President complained: "It seems to me that the rendering of opinion by the Attorney General on this kind of question would constitute an invasion of the duties, responsibility, and authority of the Supreme Court." He added, "It seems to me that in this instance the Supreme Court has been guided by some motive that is not strictly functional."[8] As late as November 5, 1953, Eisenhower drew sharp distinctions between the requirement of the Justice Department to participate in District of Columbia school segregation cases and involvement in state-supported segregation cases. The attorney general agreed to follow the President's wishes in presenting merely a "resumé of fact and historical record" about the Fourteenth Amendment in the *Brown* written brief, but he indicated that his department's spokesman at the oral argument would be required if asked to state a position on the

6. Governor Allan Shivers to Eisenhower, July 16, 1953, Official File, Box 731, DDEL.

7. Eisenhower Diary, July 24, 1953, Whitman File, Diary Series, Box 2, DDEL.

8. "Memorandum for the Record," Aug. 19, 1953, Whitman File, Diary Series, Box 2, DDEL.

constitutionality of public school segregation—a position opposing Jim Crow.[9]

To ensure complete political control over the drafting of the
Justice Department's "Supplemental Brief," writing supervision
was removed from career officials in the solicitor general's office
and placed in the hands of Assistant Attorney General J. Lee
Rankin, a fellow Nebraskan and a trusted subordinate of Brownell. Rankin shared his commander-in-chief's dislike of the vigorous exercise of federal enforcement powers, and Philip Elman
lamented to Felix Frankfurter: "They've been out in the wilder-
ness [so long] . . . they've come to believe their own propaganda.
Rankin, for example, thinks there is a distinct characteristic of the
New Deal-Fair Deal type of person. Such a person, he told me,
believes in the philosophy that the end justifies the means. The
Republicans—and this too was said with a straight face—do not
share that philosophy." By the end of July, after delays prompted
in part by Eisenhower's own skepticism about the brief, the department was ready to begin drafting, but Brownell requested and
received a two-month postponement of the oral argument, from
October 12 to December 7, 1953. Pleased at Elman's work in the
Thompson restaurant segregation case in the District of Columbia, Rankin assigned primary drafting responsibility for the
new brief to the Truman administration holdover despite misgivings about his liberal politics.[10]

In drafting the new presentation, Elman and his subordinates
were not concerned about the new administration's instructions
that they omit an open declaration of public school segregation's
unconstitutionality, for the brief already had been labeled "supplemental" to the Truman administration's previous stand. In the
initial *Brown* brief, Elman had offered the Supreme Court the
choice of siding with Brown on the grounds of unequal facilities
without overturning the "separate but equal" doctrine, or of rejecting segregation outright as an unconstitutional interference
with the right of individuals to choose their associates voluntarily
as part of equal educational opportunity, as the *McLaurin* decision had implied. The high court thus could prohibit mandatory
racial segregation as a means to, in Elman's words, "enlarge individual freedom, not to limit it." In language anticipating the

9. Kluger, *Simple Justice*, 651; telephone call, Nov. 5, 1953, Whitman File,
Diary Series, Box 3, DDEL.
10. Kluger, *Simple Justice*, 650–51.

justices' later implementation decision, Elman had also urged a "reasonable period of time" for Southern compliance and had proposed that federal district courts act as the designers of desegregation orders and the supervisors of implementation.[11]

Elman's earlier groundwork in placing the federal government in opposition to mandated segregation, however, worried Eisenhower administration officials less than the thought that an antisegregation brief in *Brown* would cause irreparable political damage in the South. The President in particular was eager to disavow any personal connection with the Justice Department's findings. Hoping to soothe Southern worries, Eisenhower called the attorney general on November 16 to ask what would happen if Southern states disavowed public education. Brownell, noting his scheduled dinner engagement with Governor Byrnes the next evening, indicated that he would tell the governor that if the Supreme Court ruled against the Southern states, "under our doctrine it [integration] would be a period of years and he wouldn't have to 'declare war' so to speak." Reassuring the President that education would not become a federal government function, Brownell offered the assessment that the states would work out segregation problems on their own in ten to twelve years.[12]

The President's wish to separate himself from personal accountability for the Justice Department's stance and, through it, the Supreme Court's eventual ruling was damaged immediately by his own words at a November 18 news conference. Possibly referring to his conversation with Brownell of only two days earlier, the President responded to a question about whether he planned to confer with the attorney general on the *Brown* brief by saying, "Indeed I do. We confer regularly. And this subject comes up along with others, constantly." Southern officials worried about the contents of the government's brief concluded that the President was supervising its drafting, and they hastened to lobby him on the merits of the segregationist position. Governor Byrnes, enclosing in his letter pages from attorney John W. Davis's legal brief, asserted that "the Court has no right to legislate," and reminded Eisenhower of his previous position that "states should have the right to control matters that are purely local." Governor Robert F. Kennon of Louisiana emphasized the progress made in race relations, and expressed the hope that "the position of the

11. Ibid., 558–61, 651.
12. Telephone call, Nov. 15, 1953, Whitman File, Diary Series, Box 3, DDEL.

Department of Justice will be towards sustaining the fundamental American conception of state sovereignty."[13]

Eisenhower's reply to the governors, expressed in a letter to Governor Byrnes on December 1, 1953, both suggested the weakness of the Southern case and pressed his own claims of separation from the attorney general's brief. Expressing sympathy with the South's position, Eisenhower held out the hope that measures could be found that would "progressively work toward the goals established by abstract principle, but which would not, at the same time, cause such disruption and mental anguish among great portions of our population that progress would actually be reversed." The President noted, however, that "equal but separate" school facilities could involve "extraordinary expenditures throughout all the Southern states." He also suggested, in an early draft of the letter, that the attorney general could not ignore the precedents of recent Supreme Court cases that had "beclouded" the original *Plessy* decision on "separate but equal" facilities. Eisenhower reiterated that he and the attorney general had agreed that the government's brief "would reflect the conviction of the Department of Justice as to the *legal aspects* of the case, including . . . the legislative history of the enactment of the 14th Amendment." He warned, however, that "it is clear that the Attorney General has to act according to his own conviction and understanding."[14]

By the time Eisenhower drafted his response to Governor Byrnes, the Justice Department had already filed its brief with the Supreme Court. In the document, Philip Elman did not undertake any reexamination of the questions argued during the previous court term or specifically weaken his earlier unequivocal stand against segregation. What the brief did do was to conclude that it was impossible to draw "a definite conclusion" regarding the intent of the framers of the Fourteenth Amendment in the area of school segregation. The Fourteenth Amendement, according to Elman, did establish "the broad constitutional principle of full and complete equality of all persons under the law, and . . . forbade all legal distinctions based on race or color." In a carryover from the earlier brief, Elman also asserted that on the basis of previous decisions, the high court should not be content to deter-

13. Transcript of Presidential Press Conference, Nov. 18, 1953, Whitman File, Press Conference Series, Box 1; James F. Byrnes to Eisenhower, Nov. 20, 1953; Robert F. Kennon to Eisenhower, Nov. 20, 1953, Official File, Box 731, DDEL.
14. Eisenhower to Byrnes, Dec. 1, 1953, Whitman File, Name Series, Box 3, DDEL.

National Park Service/Dwight D. Eisenhower Library
President Eisenhower and Attorney General Herbert Brownell (2nd row,
far right) posing for pictures with the U.S. Supreme Court on November
9, 1953. Three weeks later the Justice Department's supplemental brief
in the *Brown* school segregation cases was delivered to the justices.

mine "whether there is equality as between schools; the Constitution requires that there be equality as between persons." A day after issuing his response to Byrnes, Eisenhower received word through the attorney general that the new chief justice, Earl Warren, had found the Justice Department's brief "outstanding."[15]

Given the Truman administration's groundwork in stating the case for declaring mandated public school segregation unconstitutional, the greatest contribution of the Eisenhower administration to the Supreme Court's eventual determination proved not its "supplemental brief" but the appointment of Earl Warren as chief justice. The appointment itself, despite official denials, was a political payoff to Warren for helping defeat the Taft forces in the 1952 Republican convention's "fair play amendment" vote. Campaign aide Lucius Clay had pledged the California governor an administration position of his choice in return for his help, and Clay had informed Eisenhower of the promise "days later." Candidate Eisenhower had also accumulated additional obligations to Warren for his help in stamping out a California write-in movement for Douglas MacArthur, and shortly after the election, Clay sounded out Warren for the post of secretary of the interior. After Warren's refusal, Eisenhower raised the possibility of a Supreme Court appointment for him with Attorney General-designate Brownell and, months later, also suggested the solicitor general post. Between these two meetings, Eisenhower discussed an offer of the first Supreme Court vacancy directly with the governor himself, and the Californian subsequently held out for the high court position in spite of Brownell's urgings that he "brush up" on the law as solicitor general first.[16]

Nevertheless, even after the sudden death of Chief Justice Frederick M. Vinson on September 8, 1953, the President apparently did not consider himself bound to nominate Warren for the Supreme Court post. Eisenhower considered a long list of other candidates, including Secreary of State Dulles, judges John J. Parker, Orie Phillips, and Arthur T. Vanderbilt, and Supreme Court Justice Harold H. Burton. The President's wish for a Republican of "national stature," sixty-two years of age or under and with ABA approval, however, reduced his final considerations to a choice between Warren and Burton. Eisenhower's skepticism of Burton's administrative abilities improved Warren's chances, for

15. Kluger, *Simple Justice*, 652; telephone call, Dec. 2, 1953, Whitman File, Diary Series, Box 3, DDEL.
16. Ewald, *Eisenhower*, 77–80.

Warren's "assets" included a high public reputation, "sound" opinions on the illegality of the Truman steel seizures and on the validity of state claims to tidelands oil reserves, the earlier promise of an administration position of his choice, and the desire of Vice President Nixon to remove him from California politics through a Supreme Court appointment. With Warren unwilling to accept new overtures from Brownell to wait for the second open position on the bench, a reluctant Eisenhower informed the Californian on September 30 of his recess appointment to the chief justice position. In defending the Warren appointment to conservative opponents, including Texas oilman H.L. Hunt, Eisenhower declared it his intention "to restore the Court to the position of prestige it formerly held." All evidence indicated, however, that Eisenhower did not see the court's pending action in *Brown* to be the mechanism for any such restoration.[17]

With Warren presiding over the reconvened Supreme Court, Assistant Attorney General Rankin presented the Justice Department's findings in oral argument on December 7, 1953. The justices found Rankin's brief so equivocal on the issue of the constitutionality of public school segregation that one of them, William O. Douglas, asked for clarification of the department's judgment. Rankin, as instructed by Attorney General Brownell, replied: "It is the position of the Department of Justice that segregation in public schools cannot be maintained under the Fourteenth Amendment." Rankin upheld the high court's freedom to act on the question: "The whole concept of constitutional law is that constitutional rights are not to be subject to the political forum, which changes from time to time." The assistant attorney general also emphasized, however, the need for local solutions for implementation, rejected a national timetable, and urged the adoption of a method by which the federal district courts supervised desegregation on a case-by-case basis. Acknowledging the possibility of legal delays, Rankin attempted to draw a distinction between legitimate logistical problems during desegregation and "deliberate attempts to evade the judgment of this court," but Justice Robert H. Jackson injected prophetically, "I foresee a generation of litigation."[18]

After the completion of oral arguments, a period of private concern and behind-the-scenes proparation followed within the

17. Eisenhower, *Mandate for Change,* 226–29; Earl Warren, *The Memoirs of Earl Warren* (Garden City, N.Y., 1977), 268; Eisenhower to H.L. Hunt, Sept. 24, 1953, Official File, Box 100, DDEL.
18. Kluger, *Simple Justice,* 675–76.

White House. For his part, Eisenhower had been spared extensive criticism from Southern politicians for the legal position taken by the Justice Department, for he had been careful to separate himself from the department's judgments on the constitutionality of school segregation. After the oral arguments were completed, the President also attempted on at least one occasion to press the Southern case for segregation with Chief Justice Warren. Early in 1954, Warren was invited to a White House "stag" dinner attended by U.N. Ambassador Lodge, Attorney General Brownell, Professor Edward S. Corwin of Princeton, Dean Erwin Griswold of Harvard Law School, and segregationist attorney John W. Davis. Although other subjects, including the Bricker Amendment, were discussed in addition to school desegregation, Eisenhower openly praised Davis in front of Warren, and, overstepping the bounds of propriety, raised the segregationist argument with the chief justice against placing white girls in classrooms with black boys.[19]

While Eisenhower urged understanding of the South's position, however, others in the White House prepared for the expected Supreme Court ruling against segregated schools. Republican National Committee minorities adviser Val Washington drafted a memorandum for White House aide Maxwell Rabb that urged an attitude of "warmth, sympathy, and solid helpfulness" toward cooperating school districts. Washington also took the opportunity to suggest that federal school construction assistance be extended to desegregating districts as an additional way to undercut the "two or three" rabidly segregationist states.[20]

On May 17, 1954, Chief Justice Warren read the long-awaited verdict of the Supreme Court in the *Brown* school segregation cases. In a unanimous decision, the justices declared that racially separated public schools were a violation of the Fourteenth Amendment and that "separate educational facilities are inherently unequal." The decision, which focused primarily upon the unconstitutionality of government-mandated educational segregation, went beyond the mere citation of legal precedent to assail "segregation with the sanction of law" for retarding personality formation and producing black attitudes of racial inferiority. However, the high court declined to spell out an immediate implementation formula for its desegregation. Instead, the justices

19. Ewald, *Eisenhower*, 81–83.
20. Val Washington to Maxwell Rabb, Feb. 3, 1954, Whitman File, Cabinet Series, Box 4, DDEL.

called upon the parties to submit additional arguments in the fall term.[21]

Western European observers overwhelmingly hailed the *Brown* decision, while the Soviet-bloc press maintained a discreet silence. Within the United States, opinion divided sharply on sectional lines. Northern politicians and press spokesmen generally approved of the verdict, although many echoed the reservations of James Reston of the *New York Times* that the judgment had relied too heavily upon social science evidence about the effects of segregation on black attitudes rather than upon strict legal precedents. In the South, although advocates of gradual desegregation urged calm and moderation, official Southern comment was vituperative. Governor Herman Talmadge of Georgia accused the Supreme Court of reducing the Constitution to a "mere scrap of paper" and pledged his defiance. Governor Byrnes of South Carolina announced his "shock" at the decision, and Senator James O. Eastland of Mississippi predicted that the South "will not abide by or obey this legislative decision by a political court."[22]

The *Brown* decision of May 17, 1954 was a landmark event in both American jurisprudence and the modern political consideration of civil rights. After *Brown*, civil rights became, in the words of presidential press secretary James Hagerty, a "different ball game."[23] The school desegregation ruling invested the entire assault upon Jim Crow with a moral urgency and justification previously lacking. *Brown* meant that the full moral weight of the Constitution as interpreted by the Supreme Court was now on the side of the advocates of integration. For Southern segregationists, subsequent strategy became dependent upon their ability to discredit the moral authority of the current members of the Supreme Court to interpret the Constitution. And the pressures upon the members of the Eisenhower administration multiplied, for as they tried to defuse the segregation issue for both philosophical and political reasons, they received intensifying criticism from both sides for avoiding an unambiguous moral stance.

In the immediate aftermath of *Brown*, as civil rights advocates awaited the Supreme Court's implementation guidelines, Southerners renewed their lobbying of the White House. Many of them

21. Supreme Court of the United States, 347 U.S. 483 (1954).
22. See Duram, *A Moderate Among Extremists*, ch. 5–6; Kluger, *Simple Justice*, 709–14.
23. James C. Hagerty OH, 264, DDEL.

held the Eisenhower administration directly responsible for the Supreme Court ruling because of the President's appointment of Warren and the Justice Department's amicus brief. On June 24, the president of the National Association of Attorneys General, Eugene Cook of Georgia, refused to invite Attorney General Brownell to the organization's convention, and an invitation was subsequently tendered only after the meeting site was changed from Biloxi, Mississippi to Phoenix, Arizona.[24] The administration also received an outpouring of mail from Southern and border states that indicated impending political losses among Southern white voters. Federal officials stationed in the South relayed their own soundings of sectional discontent with the administration. Hardy A. Sullivan, Tampa director of the FHA, recounted for James Hagerty the reactions of one local businessman — "I voted for [Eisenhower] as he said he would leave it up to the states or give us real states rights. I won't make that mistake again." The administration could avoid further political damage, Sullivan believed, only by following the advice of the attorney general of Texas and permitting Southern states to "gradually integrate the races in the schools as they would determine themselves."[25]

Sullivan's basic sentiments were shared by the President himself. Although Eisenhower later would claim that he had believed "that the judgment of the Court was right," at the time he worried that "some of the southern states will take steps to virtually cancel out their public education systems" and might restructure them on a "private" basis. His concern at this possibility was magnified at least as much by its effects on Southern "poor whites" as its impact on black children. Faced with increasing moral polarization over segregation and the accompanying political dangers, the President opted to continue symbolic efforts in areas of unquestioned federal jurisdiction, while refraining from any provocative actions against state-imposed segregation. The day after the issuance of the *Brown* decision, Eisenhower called the District of Columbia commissioners and urged their help in making the national capital a desegregation model. Nevertheless, Eisenhower refused publicly to endorse the Supreme Court decision, later claiming lamely that a declaration of support would "lower the dignity of government" by creating "a suspicion that my vigor of enforcement would . . . be in doubt." At a May 19 press confer-

24. *New York Times*, June 25, 1954, July 23, 1954, and Sept. 18, 23, 24, 1954.
25. Hardy A. Sullivan to Hagerty, Oct. 5, 1954, General File, Box 918, DDEL.

ence, the President refused to offer any advice to the South in responding to the decision, praised the "moderate" statement of opposition from Governor Byrnes, and added only that he would "uphold the Constitutional process in this country."[26]

Eisenhower's own caution in commenting on the fate of Southern segregation was matched by that of his staff in responding to the outpouring of messages from Southerners. After a period of experimentation, Maxwell Rabb assigned the responsibility for acknowledging prosegregation correspondence to fellow White House staffers Bernard Shanley and J. William Barba. Citing his position as the administration's minority adviser, Rabb noted, "My name attached to this type of response in behalf of the president would be like a red flag." White House letters of acknowledgement merely thanked the writers and added the pledge that the President "will bear in mind your comments." Rabb's own direct responses to the far smaller number of prointegration letters received by the White House, on the other hand, declared the President's dedication to ending "second-class citizenship."[27]

Even more important than its public relations strategy, the White House did not authorize any new investigative procedures in handling segregation complaints in the period between the initial *Brown* ruling and the issuance of implementation instructions. For its part, the Justice Department merely instructed the FBI to refer school segregation complaints to U.S. attorneys "without conducting an investigation." In August, the President admitted that he had not even considered asking the Congress for any additional desegregation enforcement legislation. Nevertheless, despite its public silence, the administration still attempted covertly to court favorable black reactions. Referring to an administration-inspired story in *Reader's Digest* featuring praise of the President by Adam Clayton Powell, editor Stanley High responded to Rabb, "This was a grand suggestion — both editorially and politically," and he stated his intention to advertise the article widely in the black press.[28]

26. Hagerty Diary, May 18, 1954, transcript of presidential press conference, May 19, 1954, Hagerty Papers, Box 1, DDEL.

27. Rabb to J. William Barba, June 9, 1954, General File, Box 916; Barba to Mrs. John P. Hird, July 12, 1954, General File, Box 918; Rabb to Rev. L.K. Jackson, July 20, 1954, General File, Box 911, DDEL.

28. John T. Elliff, "Aspects of Federal Civil Rights Enforcement: The Justice Department and the FBI, 1939–1964," *Perspectives in American History*, vol. 5 (1971), 641–42; Stanley High to Rabb, July 16, 1954, Official File, Box 731, DDEL.

In the first half of 1954, the major policy developments influenced by the *Brown* decision came not in school segregation, where action awaited the arrival of the fall term, but instead in the field of interstate transportation segregation. On December 14, 1953, a week after the oral arguments in the school segregation cases, the NAACP had filed complaints against eleven railroads with the Interstate Commerce Commission. An internal White House memorandum of March 4, 1954 revealed that the departments of Justice and Interior supported an endorsement of congressional antisegregation legislation in interstate transportation, while the State Department and the Civil Aeronautics Board expressed no opposition and the ICC took no position. Three weeks later, Ethel Payne of *Defender* Publications asked the President at a news conference if he intended to endorse such a bill. Eisenhower replied, "I will take a look because I am not sure. I would have to consult the Attorney General and see what he says about our authority there."[29]

Following the *Brown* decision, the Justice Department concluded that a legal basis did exist for an interstate transportation desegregation bill, and the Bureau of the Budget gave its approval. The President, however, declined to be linked with desegregation legislation so soon after *Brown*, and he turned aside repeated press questions on the subject. When asked if he would press for the release of desegregation bills from House committees, Eisenhower replied that he believed in "progress accomplished through the intelligence of people, and through the cooperation of people, more than law, when we can get it that way." Seeking to avoid further inquiries on the segregation issue, Eisenhower was accused by black White House reporters of ignoring them at press conferences. He responded to James Hagerty, "I'm going to continue to give them a break at the press conferences despite the questions they ask." On July 7, however, an exasperated Eisenhower snapped back at reporter Payne on the subject of interstate transportation desegregation, "I don't know by what right you say that you have to have administration support. The administration is trying to do what it thinks to be — believes decent and just in this country, and it is not in the effort to support any particular or special groups of any kind."[30]

29. *New York Times*, Dec. 15, 1953; "Memorandum from Commerce and Finance Division to.Mr. R.W. Jones," March 4, 1954, Official File, Box 732; Transcript of Presidential Press Conference, March 24, 1954, President's Personal File, Box 829.

30. Transcript of presidential press conference, Hagerty Diary, June 16, 1954, and July 17, 1954, Hagerty Papers, Box 1, DDEL.

With the President studiously avoiding any personal involvement, the Justice Department and the ICC pursued their own policies through less-publicized channels. On August 4, Deputy Attorney General Rogers transmitted his department's support of antisegregation legislation in interstate travel to Senator John Bricker of Ohio. After an ICC examiner concluded in a segregation case involving the Carolina Coach Company that federal provisions did not ban "reasonable segregation," Adam Clayton Powell vigorously protested the ruling. Attempting to mollify the congressman, the ICC replied that the case would be voted upon by the entire commission "in due time." On October 19, the Justice Department filed its own brief with the ICC opposing segregation in interstate transportation facilities.[31]

With the onset of the new school year, attention immediately shifted back to the problem of Southern public school desegregation. In scattered districts in the border states, developments during the summer had brought encouragement to integration advocates. Five days after the Supreme Court decision, the school board of Little Rock, Arkansas had announced its intention of complying with the ruling, and school boards in Fayetteville, Arkansas; Baltimore, Maryland; Washington, D.C.; Louisville, Kentucky; and Kansas City and St. Louis, Missouri followed. However, danger signs were also present. During the summer, the first White Citizens' Council had formed in Senator Eastland's home county in Mississippi. In Virginia, businessmen and prominent citizens joined other whites in local chapters of the Defenders of State Sovereignty and Individual Liberties and the National Association for the Advancement of White People.[32]

Even though a Supreme Court implementation ruling remained months away, a number of border-state schools attempted to initiate desegregation in the fall of 1954 and encountered segregationist protests and student walkouts. In Delaware, two schools closed in the face of segregationist resistance, and on October 1 a newly chosen school board in Milford, Delaware rescinded the district's earlier desegregation decision. Vice President Nixon, noting his children's enrollment in public schools, called for calm in Delaware and in Washington, D.C., where white students had staged "strikes" at the Anacostia schools. Both Thurgood Marshall

31. *New York Times*, Oct. 1, 2, 19, 1954.
32. Kluger, *Simple Justice*, 720–26; Parmet, *Eisenhower*, 439-40. For a fine study of the organization of Southern resistance to desegregation, see Neil R. McMillen, *The Citizens' Council: Organized Resistance to the Second Reconstruction, 1954–1964* (Urbana, Ill., 1971).

of the NAACP and the spokesmen for the American Jewish Congress urged intervention by the Justice Department to quell the disturbances at Milford and the national capital. In the judgment of Attorney General Brownell, however, federal intervention was neither desirable nor warranted, and he observed that with local resistance to desegregation lessening, local authorities were capable of keeping the peace.[33]

Despite the incidents in the fall of 1954 at border state schools, both the Eisenhower administration and Southern state officials realized that the real showdowns over desegregation, if they developed, would take place in the deep South and would occur only after the issuance of the Supreme Court's implementation order. Writing to his longtime friend Swede Hazlett on October 23, 1954, the President observed, "The segregation issue will, I think, become acute or tend to die out according to the character of the procedure orders that the Court will probably issue this winter. My own guess is this — they will be very moderate and secure a maximum of initiative to local courts." Summarizing his attitude on November 23, one day before the Justice Department was to file its implementation brief, Eisenhower commented, "I am sure America wants to obey the Constitution, but there is a very great practical problem involved, and there are certainly deep-seated emotions." He added his assertion that the Supreme Court's duty was "to write its orders of procedure in such fashion as to take into consideration these great emotional strains and the practical problems, and try to devise a way where under some form of decentralized process we can bring this about."[34]

The Justice Department's implementation brief mirrored the President's desire for federal enforcement restraint and represented a compromise position between the states' desires to control all aspects of the desegregation process and the NAACP's insistence on a fall 1955 starting date and fall 1956 completion date. Adopting essentially the same scheme proposed by Philip Elman in 1952, the brief did not call for a desegregation timetable, but asked the Supreme Court to remand cases to federal district courts. The district courts would call upon local school boards to submit desegregation plans within ninety days and would supervise the implementation procedure. Inserted in the brief, according to reporter Anthony Lewis, was one section in Eisenhower's

33. *New York Times*, Oct. 1, 3, 4, 5, 8, 1954.
34. Eisenhower to Swede Hazlett, Oct. 23, 1954, Whitman File, Name Series, Box 18; transcript of presidential press conference, Nov. 23, 1954, Morrow Records, Box 11, DDEL.

own handwriting which urged "understanding and good will" in implementation because of segregation's position in the South as "an institution . . . which during its existence not only has had the sanction of decisions of this Court but has been fervently supported by great numbers of people as justifiable on legal and moral grounds."[35]

In the interim between the filing of the brief and oral arguments scheduled for April 1955, the uncertainty over the eventual shape of the court's implementation order complicated congressional consideration of administration school construction proposals. Responding to inquiries from reporter Sarah McClendon, HEW Secretary Oveta Culp Hobby admitted that the wait hindered department consideration of education issues, saying, "When the Supreme Court formulates its specific decrees, then we will be in a better position to know exactly how it affects us." On February 1, the President submitted his proposal for limited federal aid to the states for classroom construction, but only three days later Roy Wilkins of the NAACP put the White House on notice that his organization would attempt to "make certain that Federal funds are not appropriated to subsidize school systems in states which refuse to comply with the U.S. Supreme Court opinion." Eisenhower was determined that the school construction bill would not become a hostage of the segregation issue through an antisegregation rider, but Secretary Hobby admitted on February 10 that the President's position meant that federal aid would continue to be given for the construction of segregated schools. "As of today," Hobby confessed, "we would be bound by state laws as to what is a public school."[36]

While anxiously awaiting the implementation order, administration officials resisted all pressures from the NAACP and liberal congressmen to attach an antisegregation rider to the school construction bill. On March 30, 1955, New York Democrat Herbert Zelenko, responding to colleague Adam Clayton Powell's calls for an antisegregation amendment, asked the White House for clarification of its position. After determining to keep the President from personal connection with the reply, congressional liaison Bryce Harlow, with the concurrence of Hobby, Sherman Adams, Wilton Persons, Hagerty, Rabb, Gerald Morgan, and Jack Martin,

35. Kluger, *Simple Justice*, 726.

36. Transcript of press conference of Sec. of HEW Oveta Culp Hobby, Oct. 14, 1954, Oveta Culp Hobby Papers, Box 49, DDEL; Eisenhower, *Mandate for Change*, 596; Roy Wilkins to Sherman Adams, Feb. 4, 1955, General File, Box 127, DDEL.

answered Zelenko with a letter urging separation of the school construction and segregation issues and emphasizing local responsibility for educational policy. Meanwhile, with the administration's school construction bill tangled in committee, on April 22 Secretary Hobby admitted to the cabinet that its chances of passage stood at only "fifty-fifty" at best.[37]

On April 11, the Supreme Court began four days of oral argument in its consideration of the school desegregation implementation ruling. Speaking for the Justice Department, Solicitor General Simon E. Sobeloff reiterated the main points of the administration's brief and urged a "middle-of-the-road concept of moderation with a degree of firmness." Public and official waiting for the *Brown* implementation order finally ended a month later, on May 31, 1955. In a tightly worded seven-paragraph statement, the Supreme Court ordered that the school segregation cases be remanded to the federal district courts for their consideration and approval of desegregation plans drafted by local school boards. After approval, the district courts assumed primary responsibility for overseeing the implementation of the desegregation orders. In one major respect, the high court's ruling was more lenient to the South than even the administration had requested. The justices not only refused to mandate a timetable for the completion of desegregation, but they also set aside the Justice Department's recommendations that local officials develop desegregation plans within ninety days after notification. Instead the Supreme Court exhorted Southern officials to go forward with school desegregation "with all deliberate speed."[38]

Within the administration, the President expressed satisfaction with the Supreme Court's advice, and Justice Department officials also accepted the verdict as a reasonable bow to Southern feelings in view of the region's shock at the first *Brown* decision. For the advocates of civil rights and racial integration, the decision meant an end to the period of waiting. To Southern officials and segregationist leaders, however, the implementation decree offered new hope in the struggle to reverse the legal momentum for desegregation and to preserve the Jim Crow caste system. The battle lines finally had been drawn, and for both sides the moral and legal struggle over the fate of Jim Crow could now begin in earnest.

37. Herbert Zelenko to Eisenhower, March 30, 1955, Official File, Box 731; Bryce Harlow to Zelenko, Apr. 21, 1955, Gerald Morgan Records, Box 6; "Statement on School Construction," Apr. 22, 1955, Hobby Papers, Box 44, DDEL; Kluger, *Simple Justice*, 734–35.
38. Supreme Court of the United States, 349 U.S. 294 (1955).

8.

With All Deliberate Speed

In handing responsibility for carrying out school desegregation to the federal district courts, the Supreme Court had taken a calculated gamble. By avoiding a process that made implementation a Northern imposition, the high court had placed desegregation in the hands of the fifty-eight white Southern judges of the U.S. District Courts and two Court of Appeals circuits. Representatives of the white South would be called upon to assume primary responsibility for the legal liberation of Southern blacks. The first action of a Southern district court in the cases remanded by the Supreme Court, in South Carolina's *Briggs* v. *Elliott,* demonstrated the risks inherent in the implementation design. Federal Judge John J. Parker, offering his own interpretation of the *Brown* decision, declared: "The Constitution . . . does not require integration. It merely forbids discrimination. It does not forbid such discrimination as occurs as the result of voluntary action. It merely forbids the use of government power to enforce segregation."[1]

The "Parker doctrine" suggested a rationale for a number of

1. Kluger, *Simple Justice,* 751–52.

schemes to subvert the intent of the *Brown* decisions. Some local authorities adopted "freedom of choice" forms of desegregation, while many Southern state governments passed "pupil placement" laws. In districts that did not resort to complete defiance, these limiting techniques slowed actual racial integration to a token trickle. In the deep South, however, total repudiation of the Supreme Court's mandate prevailed. In Louisiana, mandatory segregation bills won state legislative approval, and the state invoked its police powers to block federal court enforcement of desegregation. In Georgia, Governor Herman Talmadge pledged his state's undying resistance to integration. In addition, private segregationist resistance accompanied the actions of Southern officials. Local opposition to school district desegregation plans took the form of strident calls to the Southern populace to oppose the Supreme Court (though not the Constitution), the provocation of social unrest and employment of forms of intimidation, and the consequent use of heightened passions as an argument for delay.

The emergence of Southern segregationist resistance presented the President with an unpleasant dilemma. On the one hand, Eisenhower believed that "political or economic power to enforce segregation based on race, color, or creed is morally wrong." Yet, at the same time, he did not want to force a showdown with Southern authorities on the desegregation issue. Like many of his contemporaries, Eisenhower adhered to conventional beliefs of the nobility of the South's principles in the Civil War and the subsequent horrors of "radical" Reconstruction. The President was determined to prevent the intensifying moral debate over Jim Crow from escalating into a second confrontation between national and state sovereignty through the federal imposition of integration upon the South.[2] Eisenhower's fear that the segregation issue could polarize public sentiment on sectional lines and heighten an already alarming level of local racial confrontation was not unfounded. Opinion polls conducted at the time of the implementation decision indicated that while a large majority of Americans outside the South supported the Supreme Court ruling against segregated schools, only 20 percent of Southerners did. However, the President's determination to avoid any actions that might be interpreted by the South as provocative also carried the risk of political losses in the North. An August 1955 Gallup Poll illustrated his dilemma, for the fourth most frequent criticism of the President was the assertion that he "encourages

2. Eisenhower, *Mandate for Change*, 234.

segregation."[3] Nevertheless, given his philosophical objections to the use of federal enforcement machinery and his political sensitivity to Southern white attitudes, Eisenhower chose to continue in a path of extreme restraint even in the face of public criticism.

Acceding to the President's calls for restraint and forbearance, the Justice Department rejected a course of vigorous intervention in the school desegregation process. Although Attorney General Brownell pledged "continued Federal interest in the implementation of the Court's findings," department directives reiterated that "for the time being, investigations should not be conducted" and ordered officials to "refrain from independent action."[4] Viewing suits between local school board officials and private citizens as issues between private parties, the Justice Department refused to intervene in desegregation cases unless specifically ordered to do so by a federal court. In addition, the attorney general's own public statements echoed the President's sentiments on the futility of federal "coercion." Speaking in October 1955 before the Interfaith Movement, Brownell stressed the role of voluntarism and citizenship education in achieving racial progress and added, "Laws have their proper place, but the responsibility of worthy citizenship is a personal one."[5]

Unfortunately for the Eisenhower administration, long-entrenched Southern popular resistance to racial integration did not yield easily to mild exhortation. The fall semester of 1955 witnessed only minimal progress in implementing the desegregation of Southern public schools. Southern Educational Reporting Service figures indicated that by the fall 134,000 black students attended mixed schools, but gains were limited to the border states and included children in token desegregated situations. In Maryland, only 4,000 of 92,000 blacks were in desegregated classrooms, and only 1,230 of 10,500 black students attended mixed schools in Delaware. In the South, no desegregation was reported in Georgia, Mississippi, Louisiana, Alabama, Florida, North Carolina, South Carolina, Tennessee, and Virginia public schools. At the college level, Howard University in Washington, D.C. still claimed more accredited black students than all Southern state colleges and universities combined.[6]

3. Gallup, ed., *The Gallup Poll*, 1332–33; Rabb to Adams, Aug. 8, 1955, Official File, Box 721, DDEL.
4. Elliff, "Aspects of Federal Civil Rights Enforcement" 642.
5. *New York Times*, Oct. 17, 1955.
6. Ibid., Oct. 2, 1955.

In states where the initial resistance to the *Brown* decision had been muted, actual attempts to carry out announced desegregation plans met unexpectedly firm resistance. The worst cases of obstruction occurred at Hoxie, Arkansas, where the school board in late June had announced the scheduled beginning of its desegregation plan for the fall. In early August, opponents prepared a boycott plan, a lawsuit against the school board, and public petitions, and they recruited the political support of the mayor of Hoxie, the county's legislative representatives, and sectional segregationist leaders. Although on August 16 the school board declared its intention to stick to its desegregation plan, mass protests forced it to close Hoxie schools four days later. Following an October 4 suit by attorney Amis Guthridge against the school board for refusing to meet segregationist representatives, the board retaliated with its own suit against the White Citizens Council of Arkansas, White America, Inc., and a local citizens' committee. Nevertheless, the Hoxie public schools eventually reopened only after the issuance of a temporary restraining order and a preliminary injunction against the segregationists, and with student attendance cut by 50 to 60 percent.[7]

The resistance even to the gradual integration plans developed at Hoxie and other communities did push the Justice Department toward a slightly more active posture. Civil Rights Section head Arthur Caldwell unofficially began to provide the Hoxie school board with procedural advice in late 1955, and the Federal Bureau of Investigation initiated a preliminary investigation of the White Citizens' Council branch in Hoxie. But the President, sidelined in late September by a heart attack and following a restricted schedule, did not budge from his "hands off" position. On December 29, Eisenhower relayed to the NAACP through HEW undersecretary Harold Hunt the information that the administration would not "embargo" federal aid to segregated schools unless ordered to do so by the federal courts.[8] With the President and the Justice Department avoiding public activity in desegregation, the major antisegregation action of the federal government in 1955 was the Interstate Commerce Commission's ruling of November 25 banning segregation aboard interstate passenger trains and buses. All but one of the ICC's nine commissioners supported the decision, which gave operators until January 10, 1956 to comply. These rulings, however, did not mandate the elimination of all

7. Ibid., Sept. 2, 1955.
8. Elliff, "Aspects of Federal Civil Rights Enforcement" 642.

segregated facilities in passenger terminals, including lunch-rooms, for the Interstate Commerce Act gave the ICC authority only over facilities deemed an integral part of transportation service. Following the release of the ICC edicts, six Southern states —Alabama, Georgia, Mississippi, North Carolina, South Carolina, and Louisiana—vowed defiance, and Governor Robert Kennon of Louisiana called the order "illegal."[9]

Surveying the overall lack of progress in removing Jim Crow and decrying the absence of presidential leadership, Northern liberals yearned for the emergence of a civil rights leader who could dramatize the moral urgency of desegregation. Columnist I.F. Stone observed in October 1955, "The American Negro needs a Gandhi to lead him, and we need the American Negro to lead us."[10] Subsequent developments in the South soon answered Stone's wishes. Although the ICC rulings on bus and train service had banned segregation in interstate transportation, they had not affected intrastate segregation practices. On December 5 Rosa Parks, a black seamstress and NAACP member, refused to obey a seat segregation requirement on a Montgomery, Alabama bus. Under the leadership of Mrs. Parks's pastor, the Reverend Martin Luther King, Jr., Montgomery blacks started a year-long boycott to strike down the remaining official barriers of public transportation segregation. In King, a dynamic public speaker and an advocate of nonviolent protest, the civil rights movement discovered a leader with the commanding moral presence it required.

Sparked by the Montgomery boycott, violent incidents in Mississippi, and the hope of political gain among Northern black voters, scattered voices within the administration also pressed the case for a stronger official identification with the integration cause. Alarmed at the August Gallup Poll findings on the President's racial image, Maxwell Rabb declared, "We have been more than tender in soft-pedaling our accomplishments." A December 16 memorandum from E. Frederic Morrow to Sherman Adams, citing the crisis in Mississippi, pleaded for greater administration visibility on civil rights, and Adams responded that the memorandum deserved a "grade A." On December 22, Joseph H. Douglass, special assistant to the secretary of HEW, urged the President and Vice President both to "take strong stands on the issues." Val Washington also pressed for upgraded efforts to

9. *New York Times*, Nov. 27, 1955.
10. I.F. Stone, *The Haunted Fifties* (New York, 1963), 109.

attract black voters by raising the party's meager $30,000-a-year minorities budget.[11]

During this period of review of the administration's overall civil rights posture in late 1955, the Justice Department unveiled proposals for a civil rights bill that emphasized black voting rights much more than desegregation. At a December 2 cabinet meeting presided over by Vice President Nixon, the attorney general presented recommendations for enhanced civil remedies for voting deprivations, federal authority to seek preventive relief in civil courts, and the elevation of the Civil Rights Section of the Justice Department's Criminal Division to divisional status. Brownell also advocated that the President indicate support for the Supreme Court desegregation decision, but he cautioned against "waving the red flag" at the South.[12] Additional indications of heightened Justice Department interest in civil rights activity surfaced a month later. On December 29, 1955, a "high Department official," asked about the Gray plan in Virginia for tuition subsidies to "private" segregated schools, asserted that such devices would not stand up in court. Although the official indicated that the department's planned legislative agenda would not include school integration provisions, he revealed that White Citizens' Council activities were under observation. On January 17, Deputy Attorney General William Rogers advised press secretary James Hagerty that although the President should not express an opinion on the Gray plan, he should note that its legality would be reviewed by the courts. Following the January 9 issuance of a permanent injunction by federal judge Albert L. Reeves against segregationists in Hoxie, Arkansas, appeals to the 8th Circuit Court of Appeals produced a Justice Department amicus brief supporting the federal court order on February 23. The decision of the department to file a brief in the Hoxie case marked a policy shift away from the previous practice of avoiding involvement in desegregation suits unless first ordered by a federal court.[13]

In other parts of the administration, however, doubts persisted

11. Rabb to Adams, Aug. 8, 1955, Official File, Box 731; Morrow to Adams, Dec. 16, 1955, Morrow Records, Box 10; Joseph H. Douglass to Rabb, Dec. 22, 1955, Morrow Records, Box 11, DDEL; Morrow, *Black Man in the White House*, 32–33.

12. Parmet, *Eisenhower*, 444–45; Adams, *Firsthand Report*, 336.

13. *New York Times*, Dec. 29, 1955; Hagerty to Rogers, "Press Conference Inquiries on the Gray Plan in Virginia," Jan. 17, 1956, Hagerty Papers, Box 58, DDEL. In addition to the White Citizens' Councils, the Justice Department began wiretap surveillance of radical black groups in 1957, particularly the Black Muslims. David J. Garrow, *The FBI and Martin Luther King, Jr.* (New York, 1981), 154.

about the wisdom of greater public advocacy of civil rights and desegregation, and the skepticism was shared by the President. The earlier cabinet discussion had shown sharp divisions of opinion on the merits of an administration program, and on January 6, the President included mention only of a bipartisan civil rights commission in his State of the Union message. At a Republican legislative leaders' meeting with the President on January 10, Eisenhower noted with irritation that his previous desegregation actions had not garnered the GOP any new support in 1954, and he voiced skepticism that any additional steps would change votes. Nevertheless, he conceded that in view of the Supreme Court decision, any congressman's vote against an antisegregation amendment to school construction legislation would appear to oppose the Constitution, and legislative leaders agreed with Eisenhower to maintain a neutral silence on the subject of "Powell amendments."[14]

Administration splits over integration appeared again on January 25 during consideration of the school construction issue. A day earlier, White House aide Lewis Arthur Minnich had recommended that the administration not oppose openly any antisegregation amendments offered. In staff discussion, however, press secretary Hagerty's call for support of an amendment to demonstrate that the Republicans remained the "party of Lincoln" received a cool reception. Chief of staff Sherman Adams instead stressed the immediate need for additional classrooms, and legal adviser Gerald Morgan warned of political difficulties for the President if he endorsed a Powell amendment. Eisenhower himself, while reiterating his general belief in equal opportunity, echoed Adams's comments on the necessity of passing unencumbered school construction legislation. Although he agreed not to refer to any amendments as "Powell" amendments, or to label them "extraneous" — as he had the previous summer — the President refused to commit himself any further to antisegregation riders. In his press conference the next day, Eisenhower straddled the administration's internal divisions by saying, "I think there should be nothing that is put on this thing that delays the construction of the bill. Now when you come down, though, to ask a man to vote against something that he believes to be in

14. "Supplemental Notes by Lewis A. Minnich of Jan. 10, 1956," Whitman File, Legislative Meetings Series, Box 2, DDEL.

furtherance of the Constitutional provisions, then you have got a tough one."[15]

Attempting to force an open presidential declaration on school segregation, on February 6 Powell publicized his conditional offer to withdraw his amendment to the administration's school bill if the White House pledged in return to enforce the *Brown* decision. On February 10, eight other House Democrats, citing Minority Leader Joseph Martin's support for a school construction amendment, asked the President for assurances that in its absence federal funds would not be used to assist openly defiant school systems. The White House response, transmitted by Bryce Harlow, repudiated any executive responsibility for determining the method by which the *Brown* decision would be implemented. Instead, Harlow repeated the administration's call for the creation of a bipartisan commission as a more appropriate legislative action than passage of a school construction amendment. After a second attempt by the congressmen to provoke a more favorable response, a reply authored by Gerald Morgan only reiterated the basics of Harlow's position.[16]

In drafting the rejections to the congressmen, milder Justice Department language that merely reiterated the administration's separation of the segregation and school construction issues had been rejected by the White House, for disagreements between the attorney general's subordinates and more conservative presidential staffers over the administration's civil rights posture had led to administration suspicion of the "Department of Just Us." The decision at the presidential level to reject any responsibility for school desegregation implementation was bolstered by a letter from Russell I. Thackery, the president of the Association of Land Grant Colleges. Addressed to Commissioner of Education Samuel Brownell and forwarded by Milton Eisenhower to Sherman Adams, the message outlined the difficulties school administrators faced in being caught between federal and state law and cautioned against any federal administrative action to enforce desegregation. Following advice from Attorney General Brow-

15. Parmet, *Eisenhower*, 442–43; Minnich to Rowland R. Hughes, Jan. 24, 1956, Whitman File, Legislative Meetings Series, Box 2; transcript of presidential press confeence, Jan. 25, 1956, Whitman File, Press Conference Series, Box 4, DDEL.

16. *New York Times*, Feb. 6, 1956; Thomas L. Ashley, Charles A. Boyle, Frank M. Clark, Edith Green, Don Hayworth, James M. Quigley, Henry S. Reuss, and George M. Rhodes to Eisenhower, Feb. 10, 1956; Harlow to J. Lee Rankin, Feb. 13, 1956; Rankin to Harlow, Feb. 21, 1956; Harlow to Hayworth, March 1, 1956; Ashley et al. to Eisenhower, March 6, 1956; Harlow to Morgan, March 8, 1956; Morgan to Rhodes, March 15, 1956, Official File, Box 546, DDEL.

nell, the President turned aside subsequent press inquiries on Powell amendments by simply reiterating his desire for a school construction bill.[17]

Intensifying Southern resistance to desegregation only reinforced the President's inherent caution in considering any extensions of executive authority. At the University of Alabama, mob protests accompanied Autherine Lucy's attempts to enroll, and university officials suspended her from classes "for her safety." In response to questions about the matter on February 8, Eisenhower admitted that the Justice Department was looking into the case because of federal law issues, but he reiterated that the district court held primary responsibility. "I would certainly hope that we could avoid any interference with anybody else as long as that state, from its Governor on down, will do its best to straighten it out." Three days later, Alabama Republican leader Claude O. Vardaman informed Eisenhower that his statement "was well received by everyone, including the Governor himself." With the Justice Department unwilling to enter the case without first receiving an invitation from the governor, a federal judge's readmission order on March 1 was rejected by school authorities after a three-week "cooling-off" period. The university then expelled Lucy for bringing "false" contempt charges against school officials for permitting the mob demonstrations. In a second hearing, the federal district court refused to reverse the expulsion on the grounds that Lucy had not proven that the expulsion had occurred because of her race. Throughout the legal battle, the Justice Department neglected even to research the cases, and White House chief of staff Adams dissuaded any administration comments or staff visits to Alabama on the basis of FBI information claiming "Communist influence" in the situation.[18]

The administration expressed no greater interest in direct involvement in Southern disputes when it became known that city authorities had sworn out warrants against the Reverend Martin Luther King, Jr. and his supporters in the Montgomery bus boycott. After receiving a telegram from Adam Clayton Powell on February 24 that the arrests of the demonstrators posed "another

17. Ewald, *Eisenhower*, 204; Brownell to Murray Snyder, March 6, 1956, Hagerty Papers, Box 61; transcript of presidential press conferences, March 14, 21, 1956, Whitman File, Press Conference Series, Box 4, DDEL.

18. Transcript of presidential press conference, Feb. 8, 1956; Claude O. Vardaman to Eisenhower, Feb. 11, 1956, Official File, Box 732, DDEL. Richard Bardolph, *The Civil Rights Record* (New York, 1975), 475; Morrow, *Black Man in the White House*, 49–52.

ghastly victory for communism," communications from the Justice Department's criminal division to the White House concluded that no basis existed for federal intervention. White House aide Harlow conveyed the disappointing news to Powell the next day. When asked later for his own assessment of the propriety of the actions of Montgomery authorities, the President merely observed, "As I understand it, there is a state law about boycotts, and it is under that kind of thing that these people are being brought to trial."[19]

By late February 1956, public opinion polls showed continuing sectional polarization over segregation, with over 70 percent of Northern whites supporting the Supreme Court rulings and 80 percent of Southern whites opposed. Confronted additionally with Southern state resolutions proclaiming outright defiance to school desegregation, Eisenhower still persisted in his "hands off" approach to the problem. In a February 29 press conference, William V. Shannon of the New York *Post* observed that four state resolutions asserted the doctrine of "interposition" of state authority between the federal courts and local school systems. Asked for his opinion on the legality of interposition, the President only noted that it represented a "very vast question that is filled with argument on both sides." Eisenhower added his personal conviction that "we will make progress, and I am not going to attempt to tell them how it is going to be done."[20]

Eisenhower's cautious views received a powerful endorsement at a March 9 cabinet meeting at which the administration's civil rights program was reconsidered. In a twenty-four-page briefing on the Southern racial situation, FBI Director J. Edgar Hoover attributed equal responsibility to the NAACP and the White Citizens' Councils for heightened racial tensions in the region. Quoting a Mississippi NAACP leader as saying that in the event of violence, "some white blood will flow, too," Hoover issued dire warnings of the infiltration of the civil rights movement by the Communist party. In contrast, the FBI director began his description of segregationist activities by stating, "In no instance have we been advised that any of the so-called Citizens' Councils advocate violence." He added the belief that the Citizens' Councils "either could control the rising tensions or become the medium through which tensions might manifest themselves." Although Hoover

19. *New York Times*, Feb. 24, 1956, and Feb. 26, 1956; "Pre-Press Conference Briefing," Feb. 29, 1956, Whitman File, Diary Series, Box 13; Harlow to Powell, Feb. 25, 1956, Official File, Box 732, DDEL.

desribed the barring of Autherine Lucy as a "disgraceful incident," he refused to address the illegality of school integration obstruction itself. Instead, he portrayed the primary issue at stake as one of social order versus violence and subversion, with school integration tensions providing the forum for political extremism.[21]

Hoover's frightening assessment provided administration opponents of desegregation activity with additional ammunition. Agriculture Secretary Ezra Taft Benson, never sympathetic to civil rights advocacy, urged the postponement of any legislative proposals until after the election of a Republican Congress. HEW Secretary Folsom declared support only for a bipartisan commission, and Mutual Security Administrator Harold Stassen instead recommended the creation of a special assistant position in the White House on desegregation problems, to be manned by the president of a desegregating Southern university. Although the attorney general emphasized that the program would be recommended to the Congress by his department and not by a presidential message, thereby shielding the President from political fallout, Maxwell Rabb pointed out "the Cabinet's feeling that the conclusions advanced by Director Hoover are good starting points for any statements on this subject." Eisenhower himself praised the "moderate" tone of Brownell's proposals, but he based his judgment on the understanding that the primary focus of any program would be upon voting rights and not upon racial integration. Cautioning that "another system was upheld by the Supreme Court for sixty years" before the court's ruling against segregation, he added, "Ever since the 'separate but equal' decision, they [the South] have been *obeying* the Constitution of the United States."[22]

Only three days after Hoover's alarming presentation on racial tensions and the cabinet's consideration of the civil rights package, one hundred Southern congressmen and all but two of the region's senators issued the Southern Manifesto, pledging themselves to overturn the Supreme Court integration decisions. Anxious to avoid a political confrontation at any cost, Eisenhower refused at a news conference to comment on "their right to confirm or not confirm" the high court's judgment. Instead, the

20. Gallup, *The Gallup Poll*, ed., 1401–1402; transcript of presidential press conference, Feb. 29, 1956, Whitman File, Press Conference Series, Box 4, DDEL.
21. "Notes on Racial Tensions and Civil Rights," March 1, 1956, Whitman File, Cabinet Series, Box 6, DDEL.
22. "Personal and Confidential Memorandum for the Attorney General," March 9, 1956, Whitman File, Cabinet Series, Box 6, DDEL.

President chose to emphasize that the manifesto's signers had promised to use "every legal means" to stop desegregation and that "no one in any responsible position anywhere has talked nullification." Noting the Supreme Court's own calls for "successive steps," Eisenhower observed, "To expect a complete reversal in these habits and thinking in a matter of months was unrealistic."[23]

Refusing to sanction any act that could be interpreted as "taking sides" on the desegregation issue, Eisenhower repudiated attempts to attribute the Supreme Court *Brown* rulings to the Republican administration. Concerned over the frequency with which Southerners linked the *Brown* decisions with his administration, the President rebuked Vice President Nixon for referring to Earl Warren as the "Republican Chief Justice" and firmly denied in his diary any administration responsibility for the Supreme Court's judgments. Rejecting all calls for official conferences with civil rights representatives or segregationist leaders, Eisenhower set aside a proposal by Rabb for a meeting with black leaders and suggestions for the formation of an advisory committee on desegregation problems. In rejecting an offer of Florida governor LeRoy Collins for a presidential meeting with Southern governors and attorneys general, Eisenhower concluded that such a conference would only inflame passions further, because participants would feel compelled to defend their entrenched positions. Revealing that he and the attorney general previously had considered a conference with Southern officials in late 1955, the President ruled out future meeting plans: "I am not sure that we want, at any time, a conference that would exacerbate this situation."[24]

Denying an executive role in resolving moral disputes over segregation, the President instead turned to the pulpits of the South to promote moderation and reconciliation. At the same time that he called publicly upon Southern churches to use their good offices to restore harmony, Eisenhower discussed the segregation problem privately with evangelist Billy Graham. Expressing his conviction that the Supreme Court decision had set back the achievement of racial integration, Graham pledged his efforts to enlist fellow ministers and politicians in support of moderation.

23. Transcript of presidential press conference, March 14, 1956, Whitman File, Press Conference Series, Box 4, DDEL.

24. *New York Times,* March 1, 1956; telephone calls, March 21, 1956, Whitman File, Diary Series, Box 5; LeRoy Collins to Eisenhower, March 22, 1956, Harlow Records, Box 21, DDEL.

The President, observing that "peacemakers are blessed" and that "success through conciliation will be more lasting and stronger than could be obtained through force and conflict," suggested adoption in the South of symbolic actions designed to lessen the wrath of federal courts charged with desegregation. Eisenhower's prescriptions included the election of a token number of blacks to local offices, the admission of university graduate students solely on the basis of merit, and the development in Montgomery of flexible plans for filling buses with blacks who previously had been forced to stand while vacancies existed in sections reserved for whites. These steps, Eisenhower asserted, could then be brought to the attention of fedeal judges as reasons for authorizing a moderate course in implementing desegregation. Graham in turn encouraged the President to continue his restraint from public involvement in racial issues until after the 1956 election. Assuring Graham that he would "remain a moderate," Eisenhower observed regretfully, "There are foolish extremists on both sides of the question who will never be won over to a sensible course of action."[25]

The President's continuing resolve to do or say nothing controversial in the civil rights area ensured that related administration legislative proposals would languish in the Congress. On April 17, Eisenhower privately emphasized the moderate nature of the Justice Department's civil rights bill and noted that the attorney general was under department pressure to ask for additional measures. Eisenhower took the opportunity to inform Republican congressional leaders of his displeasure both at the Southern press, who wanted "to shout whenever they hear the words 'civil rights,' " and at civil rights extremists, "who called for troops in spite of soldiers' inability to educate black children in the event states closed their public schools." All four parts of the attorney general's program were reported favorably by the House Judiciary Committee on May 21, but Republican leaders warned that without major modifications the bill would not pass both houses. With Eisenhower maintaining his public silence, the House of Representatives approved the administration bill on July 23 virtually intact, but the Senate version of the legislation remained buried in the Judiciary Committee.[26]

25. *New York Times*, March 22, 1956; Whitman Diary, March 21, 1956, Whitman File, Diary Series, Box 8; Eisenhower to Billy Graham, March 22, 1956, Graham to Eisenhower March 27, 1956, and Eisenhower to Graham, March 30, 1956, Whitman File, Name Series, Box 16, DDEL.

26. Eisenhower, *Waging Peace*, 152; Adams, *Firsthand Report*, 339.

Administration school construction legislation, also entangled in the controversy over Southern school desegregation, suffered a similar fate. Faced with renewed Democratic attempts to capitalize on the administration's passivity, Rabb called privately for GOP spokesmen in the Congress to point to the Eisenhower record in the District of Columbia, the armed forces, and the federal establishment, but his recommendations did not include administration reconsideration of its silence on an antisegregation "Powell Amendment." In response to a proposal of Representative Stewart Udall of Arizona for federal aid to desegregating districts for their implementation expenses, Harold Hunt, acting HEW secretary, detailed his department's practical reservations and called instead for the adoption of the administration's general school-aid bill. In an attempt to "get the message out" once and for all on the administration's desire to separate school construction from integration controversies, presidential aides Gerald Morgan and Bryce Harlow authorized a statement for HEW Secretary Marion Folsom on April 30, 1956 that declared, "The comingling [sic] of these two issues profits neither school construction nor integration. They are separate issues and they should not be confused." After three weeks of administration consideration of an HEW-proposed appeal to the House Democratic leadership for support of an unamended school construction bill, White House aides, led by Harlow, rejected sending the offer, and on June 6 the President simply reiterated his general appeal for classroom legislation free of undue federal control. Setting aside the administration bill, the House of Representatives debated a more ambitious school aid bill with an antisegregation rider and defeated it by a 224–194 vote.[27]

Confronted with rising Southern tensions, political controversy, and stalled legislation, the President himself wanted nothing more than a lengthy breathing spell on civil rights and integration issues. Given his sentiments, Eisenhower was angered by new desegregation actions taken by the Civil Aeronautics Administration and the U.S. Supreme Court. On April 6, the CAA cut off federal funds for the construction of segregated airport terminals. One month later, the Civil Aeronautics Board banned segregated interstate and intrastate air travel. On April 25,

27. Rabb to Harlow, March 27, 1956, Harlow Records, Box 8; Harold Hunt to Graham A. Barden, March 27, 1956, Official File, Box 544; Folsom speech draft, Apr. 27, 1956, Harlow Records, Box 21; Harlow to Adams, May 20, 1956, Official File, Box 732; "Draft Statement for the President," June 5, 1956, Hagerty Papers, Box 59, DDEL.

1956, following the issuance of a Supreme Court ruling that struck down a segregated intrastate bus system in South Carolina, an angry Eisenhower privately questioned the high court's authority in intrastate matters, and staffers were forced to advise him not to express his feelings publicly.[28]

Eisenhower's advocacy of a hands-off approach to implementation appeared to have general public support, for surveys conducted in May indicated that a majority of Americans favored gradual desegregation but also overwhelmingly rejected "immediatism." Nevertheless, some White House advisers remained concerned that the administration was losing a golden opportunity to make inroads among Northern black voters. Rabb noted that administration policies had "been done so quietly and with so little publicity that, in circles where it has come to general attention, [it] has come to be known as 'the Eisenhower approach,' i.e., action, without fanfare, and effective." In early May, Bryce Harlow pointed out that a *Congressional Quarterly* article had identified sixty-one non-Southern districts where shifts in black votes could help GOP congressional candidates. At a "Citizens for Eisenhower" rally, Republican workers tried out the theme that "a vote for any Democrat is a vote for Eastland," and Richard Tobin, public relations counsel for the Republican national committee, proclaimed, "In the context of Supreme Court decisions under a Chief Justice appointed by President Eisenhower, decisions as historic as the Emancipation Proclamation of Lincoln, we have a wonderful story to tell." He concluded, "It is my opinion that it has not been told sufficiently well to the average Negro voter." Tobin's point was borne out by the Gallup Poll of August 5. Northern blacks surveyed still judged by a 67 to 16 percent margin that the Democratic party had done more for them, and the respondents directly favored Stevenson over Eisenhower by a slightly smaller margin of 62 percent to 32 percent.[29]

Nevertheless, the President resisted all efforts to strengthen the party's desegregation plank at the 1956 national convention in San Francisco. Privately he revealed to Ann Whitman, his secretary, his belief that the Supreme Court should have set forth a more gradual program of desegregation, beginning with graduate

28. NAACP, *Annual Report* (1956), 38; Morrow, *Black Man in the White House,* 62–63.
29. Parmet, *Eisenhower,* 446; Shoemaker, *With All Deliberate Speed,* 118; Gallup, ed., *The Gallup Poll,* 1438–39; Harlow to Rabb, May 3, 1956, Harlow Records, Box 8, DDEL.

schools and working on down. Although publicly Eisenhower stated, "I don't know . . . how the Republican plank on this particular point is going to be settled," behind the scenes the President declared to platform committee chairman Prescott Bush that "leaders must be encouraged to appeal to the moral obligation of our people rather than refer only to the law." On August 18, Eisenhower telephoned his version of the platform plank to Deputy Attorney General Rogers, and, in a reference to a stronger earlier draft by Rogers, chided, "What are you going to do, get an injunction against the governor of Georgia, for instance?"[30] Upset over suggestions that the platform committee would link his administration with the *Brown* decision, Eisenhower insisted that he had never taken a stand on the constitutionality of segregation, and he reminded Attorney General Brownell in a private conversation that he had appeared before the Supreme Court in the *Brown* case "as a lawyer, not as a member of the Eisenhower Administration." Had the subject of an *administration* position on *Brown* surfaced at the time at cabinet level, Eisenhower asked, "could the Attorney General imagine what a storm Mrs. Hobby would raise?" After relaying his threat not to come to San Francisco if platform committee members "did not come around," Eisenhower received a platform plank that met with his approval; it indicated only that the Republican party "accepted" the decision of the high court.[31]

With Eisenhower dictating a bland position on desegregation, the Justice Department refused to venture from a passive role in investigating acts of obstruction. No new FBI investigations of racial segregation were conducted. Instead, following Director Hoover's lead, the FBI treated the furor over school desegregation primarily as an issue of public disorder. FBI reports were prepared only on disturbances stemming from desegregation confrontations, were treated as "domestic intelligence" reports for internal security purposes, and were sent initially not to the Civil Rights Section of the Justice Department but to the Internal Security Division. Five to ten days later, Civil Rights Section attorneys received copies of the reports. Because of their emphasis on internal-security questions, the FBI investigations also dramatized the social dangers of desegregation implementation

30. Whitman Diary, Aug. 14, 18, 1956, Whitman File, Diary Series, Box 8; "Memorandum for the Record," Aug. 18, 1956, Whitman File, Diary Series, Box 17, DDEL.
31. Telephone calls, Whitman Diary, Aug. 19, 1956, Whitman File, Diary Series, Box 8, DDEL; John W. Anderson, *Eisenhower, Brownell, and the Congress* (Birmingham, Ala., 1964), 121–22.

and gave most prominent attention to the actions of "subversive groups." The FBI, rejecting greater participation in investigating obstruction of court integration orders on the grounds that it forced the bureau to "take sides" in an unresolved question of social policy, refused all Justice Department overtures for greater intelligence gathering. Civil Rights Section chief Arthur Cald-well, citing the FBI's unwillingness to survey pending desegrega-tion litigation, unofficially solicited Assistant Attorney General Warren Olney III's permission to obtain lists of filed or pendings suits from Thurgood Marshall of the NAACP. Citing the depart-ment's need to avoid an "advocacy" position, Olney refused, replying, "I do not approve of any inquiry on this being made to anyone in the NAACP."[32]

At the beginning of the 1956 fall school term, incidents at Texarkana and Mansfield, Texas and Clinton, Tennessee demon-strated the unpreparedness of the Justice Department to respond to officially supported segregationist obstruction. At Clinton, twelve blacks entered the public high school in August, only to be met by mob resistance incited by segregationist leader John Kas-par. Despite a restraining order against Kaspar, the opposition succeeded in forcing the temporary removal of the students and causing the state governor to send in the National Guard to main-tain order. Even with the presence of state authorities, resistance to the admission of black students continued throughout the fall. Responding to similar obstruction at Texarkana Junior College and Mansfield High School, Texas governor Allan Shivers ordered Texas Rangers to remove black students from the schools on the pretext of preserving public order. Refusing to criticize Shivers's action against the black students and turning aside a Dallas NAACP request for federal assistance, the President only condemned "extremists on both sides" and added that "the youngsters that are indulging in violence are not being counseled properly at home." Instead of decrying the resegregation of the schools that the actions of the Texas authorities produced, Eisenhower gave his apparent sanction to Shivers's order, stating, "Under the law the federal government cannot . . . move into a state until the state is not able to handle the matter." He asserted, "Before anyone could move, the Texas authorities had moved in and order was restored, so the question became unimportant."[33]

32. Elliff, "Aspects of Federal Civil Rights Enforcement" 648–50.

33. Parmet, *Eisenhower*, 464; transcript of presidential press conference, Aug. 31, 1956, Whitman File, Press Conference Series, Box 5, DDEL.

Condemning the President's acquiescence in the Texas desegegation resistance, Thurgood Marshall charged that Eisenhower had given "support to many in this country who have sought to confuse the issue by trying to divide responsibility for such situations between lawless mobs and other Americans who seek only their lawful rights in a lawful manner." Despite Marshall's attack, Eisenhower's only answer was a request to the attorney general to ask for the Texas and Tennessee case records in the event federal courts issued contempt citations. Rather than advocate a more vigorous role for the federal government in enforcing school desegregation, the President seized upon and publicized the example of the peaceful limited integration of Louisville, Kentucky schools. Under the "option plan" administered by Superintendent Omer Carmichael (brought to Eisenhower's attention by aides E. Frederic Morrow and James Hagerty), parents were permitted to transfer their children out of a desegregated school if they wished. Carmichael, invited to the White House by the President to describe the Louisville plan, was praised as a "very wise man." Hagerty added his own opinion that Carmichael's approach exemplified "the truly American way in which to carry out the basic principles" of equality.[34]

Aware that the incidents in Texas and Tennessee had raised public concern over civil rights issues, Eisenhower occasionally claimed credit during the 1956 campaign for administration actions outside the realm of state-mandated segregation, including desegregation of the armed forces and the District of Columbia and stipulations for fair hiring under federal government contracts. But he continued to reject all suggestions for a White House conference on desegregation, either before or after the election. Nevertheless, largely for reasons of mutual political expediency, on October 11 Adam Clayton Powell endorsed the President's reelection bid, following a half-hour meeting with Eisenhower. Powell had been implicated in tax-evasion charges in an IRS investigation, and rumors spread among the Washington, D.C. press corps that his support for Eisenhower had been predicated on White House help in forestalling the tax inquiry. Powell maintained that his endorsement was motivated solely by dismay at his own party's vacillation, and he claimed that the President privately indicated to him his support of the arrest of those who disobeyed desegregation orders. However, White House officials

34. Thurgood Marshall to Eisenhower, Sept. 6, 1956, General File, Box 916; Morrow to Hagerty, Sept. 11, 1956, Hagerty Papers, Box 62, DDEL; Shoemaker, *With All Deliberate Speed*, 185.

hastily moved to get a retraction from Powell of his description of the President's attitudes on desegregation enforcement.[35]

The principal campaign duty of issuing stronger statements on desegregation fell not to the President but to the Vice President. At the Alfred E. Smith Memorial Dinner in New York City, Nixon predicted, "Most of us here will live to see the day when American boys and girls shall sit, side by side, at any school — public or private — with no regard paid to the color of their skin. Segregation, discrimination, and prejudice have no place in America." To avoid possible conflict with his superior, however, Nixon added the qualification that the "will must come from within us." Adam Clayton Powell, calling for a Republican presidential vote as a repudiation of "Eastlandism," also spoke in Eisenhower's behalf in Harlem. For his part, though, the President continued to place greater personal emphasis on Southern white voters, particularly those in the border South. In a late campaign swing through the region, Eisenhower assured his audiences that they could handle racial matters at the local level, and he praised anti-integrationist Senator Harry Byrd of Virginia for upholding the "great heritage of efficiency in government, elimination of extravagance, and strong local government."[36]

The President's political caution was rewarded in November with an overwhelming reelection victory over Adlai E. Stevenson, a victory that, however pleasing, provided only a momentary respite from the administration's desegregation headaches. The President did succeed in increasing his overall margin over the Democrat, and he managed to garner additional black voters without alienating significant numbers of whites. In Arkansas, Kentucky, Alabama, and North Carolina the Republican ticket actually gained between two and six percentage points over its 1952 levels. Owing mostly to the Supreme Court's actions and to good economic times, Eisenhower also made modest inroads among middle-class blacks in border South and Northern urban districts,

35. Transcript of presidential press conference, Oct. 5, 1956, Whitman File, Press Conference Series, Box 5; "Appointment of Congressman Adam Clayton Powell with the President," Oct. 11, 1956, Whitman File, Diary Series, Box 19, DDEL. Rumors that Powell exchanged politial support for White House help in halting an IRS investigation are still unproven. Eisenhower privately denied the rumors and claimed he had actually rejected Powell's requests for meetings. "Legislative Leadership Meeting," May 13, 1958, Whitman File, Legislative Meetings Series, Box 19, DDEL.

36. Anderson, *Eisenhower*, 134–35; Sundquist, *Politics and Policy*, 229–30; Parmet, *Eisenhower*, 464; Moses Rischin, *"Our Own Kind": Voting By Race, Creed, or National Origin* (Santa Barbara, Calif., 1960), 13–22.

including (with the aid of Powell) Harlem. In Harlem, the Eisenhower vote rose by 16.5 percent, and the President's totals in Chicago's largest black district climbed by 11 percent. Republican gains among Southern blacks, led by a 25 percent increase in the Eisenhower black vote in Memphis, contributed to victories in Tennessee and Kentucky. Although between 60 and 65 percent of Negro voters nationwide still preferred Stevenson, Eisenhower's percentages among blacks increased by at least 5 percent nationwide.[37]

In mid-November, however, the administration's short "breathing spell" ended abruptly. The Supreme Court's decision in *Browder* v. *Gayle,* which upheld the desegregation of Montgomery's bus system, troubled the president because it was a ruling against an intrastate transportation system. Drawing comparisons between the *Browder* decision and the troublesome desegregation of Southern schools, he asked, "How could the Federal Government enforce a ruling applying to schools supported by state funds?" Eisenhower feared the possibility of a "general strike in the South," and lamented, "Eventually a district court is going to cite someone for contempt, and then we are going to be up against it." Following the Supreme Court's decision, Attorney General Brownell met the executive committee of the National Association of Attorneys General and called a conference of U.S. attorneys from the Southern states to review enforcement measures. Little actual department action in transportation desegregation followed the meetings, but on December 3, the Justice Department received a request from school officials to enter the Clinton, Tennessee school desegregation case. Soon afterward, the department joined in contempt proceedings against segregationist leader Kaspar and his associates in Clinton.[38]

Nevertheless, the President still persisted in his refusal to intervene directly in desegregation matters. Invited to speak before the Conference on Christian Faith and Human Relations in Nashville in April 1957, Eisenhower merely transmitted a bland written greeting to the group. After receiving a letter and accompanying copies of a state nullification resolution from Florida governor LeRoy Collins, the President turned aside the opportun-

37. Numan V. Bartley, *The Rise of Massive Resistance: Race and Politics in the South during the 1950's* (Baton Rouge, 1969), 166–68; Sundquist, *Politics and Policy,* 230; Parmet, *Eisenhower,* 465–92; Rischin, "*Our Own Kind,*" 23–24; Schlundt, "Civil Rights Policies," 139.
38. "Pre-Press Conference Briefing," Nov. 14, 1956, Whitman File, Press Conference Series, Box 5; John V. Lindsay to Jack Toner, Nov. 28, 1956, Dec. 3, 1956, White House Office, Staff Research Group, Records, Box 12, DDEL.

ity to publicize his staff's legal judgment on the unconstitutionality of nullification and merely acknowledged receipt of the letter
through chief of staff Sherman Adams. Feeling increasingly
trapped by the furor over desegregation, Eisenhower privately
grumbled about the political "stupidity" of the Supreme Court's
decisions in the civil rights field and in other areas. Public revelation of his sentiments forced an embarrassed Eisenhower to
issue a letter of apology to the chief justice, but his private sentiments remained unchanged.[39]

The President's sympathies with Southern white concerns over
desegregation continued to influence his stance on school construction and civil rights legislation in the 1957 congressional
session. Calling for a school construction bill "uncomplicated by
provisions dealing with the complex problems of integration,"
Eisenhower saw his administration's bill rejected, and a substitute with a Powell Amendment attached also defeated in the
House of Representatives in late July. Earlier in the month of July,
Eisenhower received warnings from Republican Senate leaders
that Democrat Richard Russell of Georgia, who viewed the administration's civil rights bill as a "forcing act" against the South,
was marshaling opposition to any increased court suit authority
for the Justice Department. Russell contended that the new legislation would authorize the use of federal troops to enforce federal court desegregation orders. Despite the attorney general's
advice that the President already possessed enforcement authority even in the absence of new legislation, Eisenhower heeded
the advice of legislative leaders and backtracked on key portions
of the civil rights bill. After conferring with Russell, the President,
who had admitted that there were parts of the bill "I didn't completely understand," added on July 17 his belief that the attorney
general should only be permitted to bring desegregation suits
upon the request of school authorities. "If you go too far too fast,"
Eisenhower cautioned, "you are making a mistake." Lacking
administration backing, Part III of the civil rights bill, which had
empowered the attorney general to initiate civil suit action, was
eliminated from all areas except voting rights by the Senate on a
52-to-38 vote.[40]

39. LeRoy Collins to Eisenhower, May 6, 1957, Adams to Collins, May 10, 1957,
General File, Box 123, DDEL; Jack Harrison Pollack, *Earl Warren* (Englewood
Cliffs, NJ, 1979), 178.
40. Eisenhower, *Waging Peace*, 138–40, 157; Whitman Diary, July 10, 1957,
Whitman File, Diary Series, Box 9, DDEL; Emmet John Hughes, *The Ordeal of
Power: A Political Memoir of the Eisenhower Years* (New York, 1963), 242; Adams,
Firsthand Report, 341–42.

Eisenhower privately revealed the thinking behind his reversal in a letter to his personal friend Swede Hazlett on July 21. The administration bill "was conceived in the thought that only moderation in legal compulsions, accompanied by a stepped-up program of education" could succeed, he observed. The President sided with Southern critics of the bill by saying that "some of the language used in the attempt to translate my basic purposes into legislative provisions has probably been too broad." Only after having reassured himself that the focus of other provisions for increased federal activity was black voting rights rather than desegregation, Eisenhower resisted additional efforts by Russell and others to attach a jury-trial requirement to all federal criminal contempt cases. Despite his opposition, however, the Senate attached the jury-trial amendment to the bill, a setback Eisenhower described to the cabinet as "one of the most serious political defeats" of his administration. With the President suddenly demonstrating unusual resolve, the Justice Department warned that the new jury-trial amendment, besides placing black voting rights in the hands of white Southern juries, could jeopardize enforcement of antitrust law, labor law, and other federal statutes. The final version of the civil rights bill, which emerged from private negotiations between Majority Leader Lyndon Johnson and the White House, modified the Senate provision by removing the jury-trial requirement from contempt cases outside the civil rights area and leaving its imposition in civil rights suits to the discretion of judges.[41]

The success of the Southern opponents of desegregation in diluting the civil rights package only added to a growing sense of racial crisis. As of the end of the 1956–57 school year, no integration had occurred in Alabama, Florida, Georgia, Louisiana, Mississippi, North Carolina, South Carolina, or Virginia. Southern states had passed 130 separate pieces of prosegregation legislation, and eight states had adopted pupil placement laws. A Gallup Poll of August 6 revealed that a plurality of respondents felt that the coming year would see worsening racial confrontations, and in the South a 2-to-1 majority expressed similar fears. With the President unwilling to impose federal enforcement authority upon the South, the likelihood of additional official defiance of federal court desegregation orders, already tried out at Mansfield, appeared to be growing. Nevertheless, Eisenhower himself con-

41. Eisenhower to Swede Hazlett, July 22, 1957, Whitman File, Name Series, Box 18, DDEL; Hughes, *The Ordeal of Power*, 243.

tinued to hope that the confrontations over segregation could be resolved somehow without the injection of federal force. Despite the heightened sense of public alarm, the President still insisted: "I can't imagine any set of circumstances that would ever induce me to send Federal troops . . . into any area to enforce the order of a federal court."[42]

42. Transcript of presidential press conference, July 17, 1957, in Branyan and Larsen, eds., *The Eisenhower Administration, 1953–1961: A Documentary History*, 2 vols. (New York, 1971) 1119.

9.

Little Rock and Its Aftermath

The Eisenhower administration's hopes of avoiding direct involvement in the South's school desegregation agonies dramatically ended on September 24, 1957. Throughout the morning Woodrow Wilson Mann, mayor of Little Rock, Arkansas, frantically called White House aide Maxwell Rabb and pleaded for the intervention of federal troops to quell growing mob violence at Central High School. After administration officials independently verified Mann's reports with Arkansas representative Brooks Hays, U.S. Attorney Osro Cobb, former governor Sidney S. McMath, and Little Rock school superintendent Virgil Blossom, Attorney General Brownell notified the President. At 9:35 A.M. Eisenhower, on vacation in Newport, Rhode Island, informed Brownell that a statement was being prepared for issuance in the event of continuing resistance. The statement, Executive Order 10730, authorized the federalization of National Guard troops and the sending of guardsmen and U.S. Army forces to Little Rock to prevent obstruction of the court integration order. The President rejected General Maxwell Taylor's suggestion that only guardsmen be used, and he ruled out the placement of

Arkansas forces at the high school, fearing a "brother against brother" confrontation. With U.S. marshals in insufficient numbers to provide help, the President's order meant a six- to nine-hour wait before federal forces could be positioned in the city. Sensitive to public criticism that he had been caught "playing golf" in the midst of a crisis, Eisenhower told General Alfred Gruenther, "The White House office is wherever the President happens to be."[1]

Determined to use force in a calculated manner in order to avoid creating any "martyrs" to segregation, Eisenhower awaited additional information before issuing the executive order. At 10:06 A.M. Mayor Mann again called the White House and repeated his pleas for federal troops. Calling the situation "out of control," Mann stated in a telegraphed message, "I am pleading with you as President of the United States in the interest of humanity, law and order, and because of democracy worldwide to provide the necessary federal troops within several hours." Upon receiving Mann's plea, the President finally issued the troop authorization order. Five hundred troops of the 101st Airborne Division, stationed at Fort Campbell, Kentucky, flew into the city and deployed around Central High School by early evening, and another five hundred arrived from other locations later in the night. Despite his earlier hope of maintaining a normal routine in Newport, the crisis impelled the President to fly back to the capital after preparing a national television message with press secretary Hagerty. In his address to the nation, delivered on the evening of the twenty-fourth, Eisenhower recounted the sequence of events leading to the crisis. Blaming the violence on the work of extremists, Eisenhower noted its adverse propaganda impact abroad, emphasized his duty to uphold the order of a federal court, and expressed his ultimate confidence in the goodwill of the people of Little Rock.[2]

Eisenhower clearly had acted contrary to his long-expressed determination to avoid the use of federal force in the South. Why, then, did the Little Rock intervention occur? Examination of the sequence of events leading up to the actions of September 24 reveals a pattern of vacillation by administration officials, mixed public and private signals, and inadequate preparation that en-

1. Eisenhower, *Waging Peace*, 170; telephone call, Sept. 24, 1957, Whitman File, Diary Series, Box 16; Eisenhower to Alfred M. Gruenther, Whitman Diary, Sept. 24, 1957, Whitman File, Diary Series, Box 9, DDEL.
2. Woodrow Wilson Mann to Eisenhower, Sept. 24, 1957, Hagerty Papers, Box 6; Executive Order No. 10730, Sept. 24, 1957, presidential television and radio address, Sept. 24, 1957, Morgan Records, Box 6, DDEL.

couraged Arkansas authorities to persist in a course of obstruction. Once pushed to the brink of intervention, the absence of previous political restraints upon Eisenhower, and his own sense of having been betrayed by Governor Orval Faubus, encouraged an action otherwise out of character with the president's political instincts.

That Arkansas should have become the setting for a showdown between federal and state authorities over desegregation was ironic, for in 1948 it had been the first state in the South to admit black students to a state university without the prompting of a court order. Immediately after the *Brown* implementation decision, the school board of Little Rock had announced a plan for the gradual desegregation of its public schools, beginning with senior high schools in 1957, junior high schools in 1960, and elementary schools in 1963. After challenges of the plan by the Arkansas NAACP as "too slow" were rejected in court, the board had announced its intention to initiate desegregation at Central High School in September 1957. In August, local segregationists, led by the Mothers' League of Little Rock, began steps to block the program, and Superintendent Virgil Blossom approved a temporary delay in the entry of eight black students to Central High awaiting a briefing. On August 28, the Mothers' League filed suit in Pulaski County Chancery Court to block the desegregation, and petitioned Governor Orval E. Faubus for his assistance.[3]

On the same day that the anti-integration petition was filed, a fateful meeting occurred between Governor Faubus and Justice Department representative Arthur Caldwell. Caldwell had been chosen by the department to discuss the impending enrollment of the black students with state officials partly because of his ties to Little Rock, for his father had served as librarian of the Arkansas supreme court. He informed Faubus that the federal government wanted to avoid involvement in the matter and would assume no prior responsibility for the maintenance of law and order. Claiming, according to Faubus, that "we can't do a thing until we find a body," Caldwell reassured the governor that the government's previous legal involvement in the Clinton, Tennessee desegregation suit had only followed the local school board's request for an injunction and the call of a federal court. Caldwell's unfortunate frankness in stating the Justice Department's lack of enthusiasm for intervention encouraged Faubus and others to pursue a policy of calculated obstruction. Press leaks about the meeting also en-

3. Orval Faubus, *Down From the Hills* (Little Rock, Arkansas, 1980), 174–76; Adams, *Firsthand Report* 344. An overview of the Little Rock crisis is provided by Numan V. Bartley, "Looking Back at Little Rock," *Arkansas Historical Quarterly* 25 (1966), 101–106.

couraged a public posture of resistance by Arkansas authorities in order to pacify the state's segregationists. In a model of understatement, the Justice Department's Warren Olney III noted later of the meeting: "The Governor's subsequent action has given it a significance which was not appreciated by us at the time."[4]

On August 29, with Faubus citing increased weapons sales in Little Rock as evidence of imminent violence, the Pulaski County court issued a temporary injunction against the desegregation of Central High School. School officials, backed by the Arkansas NAACP's Daisy Bates, responded with their own request in federal court for an injunction against all those seeking to interfere with the desegregation plan. Federal judge Ronald Davies, a North Dakotan on temporary assignment to the Eastern District of Arkansas, then reversed the county court and ordered integration to proceed. Meeting the school board after the federal district court hearing concluded, Faubus warned members of his determination to "maintain law and order," but the board still announced that Central High would be opened to all students on September 3. Aware of the precedent set by Governor Shivers' action at Mansfield, Texas, in 1956, Faubus requested his attorney, W.J. Smith, to prepare a proclamation mobilizing portions of the Arkansas National Guard for the purpose of blocking black entry into the school. On September 2, Faubus ordered the guardsmen to Central High School. Faced with the active opposition of the state's police power, the school board directed black students not to attempt entry until all legal obstacles had been removed.[5]

In view of Faubus' open resistance, the Little Rock school board hastily backtracked from its support for desegregation and sought "further instructions" from Judge Davies. On September 3, Davies repeated his desegregation order and asked the board to show why it also should not be cited for contempt. Informed of the Little Rock impasse, Eisenhower personally questioned the authority of the Justice Department to intervene in the face-off between the federal court and the governor of Arkansas, but Attorney General Brownell assured him that the court could rule on the legality of Faubus' action and could also request Justice Department assistance. Eisenhower viewed the crisis as the result of "these people who believe you are going to reform the human heart by law," and he avoided press inquiries on whether he

4. Faubus, *Down From the Hills,*197–98; Richard P. Longaker, *The Presidency and Individual Liberties* (Ithaca, N.Y., 1961), 168; J.W. Peltason, *Fifty-Eight Lonely Men* (Urbana, Ill., 1961), 165.
5. Faubus, *Down From the Hills,* 199–208; Adams, *Firsthand Report,* 345.

would personally contact Faubus. On the morning of September 4, Arkansas guardsmen turned away the black students from Central High. An angry Judge Davies responded by requesting the Justice Department to order an FBI investigation of Faubus's claim that the threat of violence justified a halt to desegregation. Davies also directed federal authorities to collect information on all persons, including the governor, suspected of interference with the court's directives. Anticipating additional involvement, the attorney general requested his office of legal counsel to prepare a memorandum on prospective department legal actions.[6]

Protesting Davies's "extreme stand," Governor Faubus sought assurances from Eisenhower himself that the federal executive would not oppose his actions. In a telegram to the President, Faubus asserted that the issue involved in Little Rock was not school segregation, but rather the authority of a state governor to exercise his police powers to maintain public order. Eisenhower, responding from Newport on September 5, rejected an accompanying Faubus charge that his phone had been wiretapped and denied that his arrest was imminent. The President did inform the governor, however, that the Justice Department was investigating him for obstruction of the federal court order, and he replied to Faubus's call for "cooperation" with a firm pledge to uphold the Constitution and the duties of his office. The next day, a dissatisfied Faubus attempted to prove his argument for delay by informing the President that he had made attorney Smith and Arkansas state police director Herman Linsay available to the U.S. attorney in Little Rock to offer evidence "upon which I acted to preserve the public peace."[7]

On September 7, Judge Davies rejected yet another request for delay, this time filed by the school board. Attorney General Brownell advised the President that the FBI report on the Little Rock situation would be delivered to the court on September 9, and he added that the report's findings and Davies' expected injunction against Faubus and the Arkansas National Guard made federal action imminent. At the federal district court hearing of September 9, Davies requested the Justice Department to "file immediately" both a petition for an injunction and a supporting brief

6. Faubus, *Down From the Hills*, 209; "Pre-Press Conference Notes," Sept. 3, 1957, Whitman File, Press Conference Series, Box 6, DDEL; "Presidential News Conference," Sept. 3, 1957, in Branyan and Larsen, *The Eisenhower Administration*, 1120.

7. Faubus, *Down From the Hills*, 209–13; Faubus to Eisenhower, Sept. 4, 1957, Official File, Box 732; Eisenhower to Faubus, Sept. 5, 1957, Morgan Records, Box 6; Faubus to Eisenhower, Sept. 6, 1957, Official File, Box 732, DDEL.

against the governor and two National Guard officers. Faubus received a summons the next day ordering him to appear before the court on September 20 to show cause why he should not be charged with contempt.[8]

Faubus notified Sherman Adams through Brooks Hays that he desired a way out of the predicament, and urged the President to invite him to a meeting to discuss the matter. The attorney general, who believed that the governor had "soiled" himself badly and should pay the legal price for his resistance, opposed this proposal strenuously. Moreover, he pointed out, at least four previous attempts at mediation, conducted by Senator John McClellan, Winthrop Rockefeller, publisher Harry Ashmore, and former governor James McCann, all had ended in failure. But Adams, placing his confidence in Congressman Hays, argued that Faubus recognized his error and did not necessarily oppose desegregation, for his son attended an integrated college. Upon Adams' advice, Eisenhower overruled the attorney general's call for immediate legal action against Faubus, judging that Brownell did not fully appreciate the sensitivity of Southern feelings. Eisenhower again insisted that the Justice Department's only role was as a "friend of the court" to ensure that Arkansas guardsmen would not be used to block the desegregation order. In a telephone conversation with Brownell, the President stressed that the federal government should avoid any hint of interfering with state police powers, questioning the governor's authority to call the National Guard, or promoting the idea that the President could automatically tell a mob to disperse or a school to integrate. He agreed to Faubus' request for a meeting, but only upon the governor's public request and with the understanding that he would have to comply with the orders of the federal district court.[9]

Private negotiations over arrangements for the Eisenhower-Faubus meeting ensued between emissaries Adams and Hays. Adams approved a Faubus draft of a formal request that stated: "It is certainly my intention to comply with the order that has been issued by the District court." Later on September 10, however, Hays called back Adams to notify him of "minor" word changes in the message, after already having vetoed more extensive changes requested by Faubus and his lawyers. The final version transmitted to the President in Newport changed the words "my inten-

8. Telephone call, Sept. 11, 1957, Whitman File, Diary Series, Box 16, DDEL; Faubus, *Down From the Hills*, 229; Adams, *Firsthand Report*, 346.
9. Faubus, *Down From the Hills*, 238-40; Adams, *Firsthand Report*, 346–47.

U.S. Naval Photographic Center/Dwight D. Eisenhower Library
Eisenhower greets Arkansas Governor Orval Faubus at Newport, R.I.,
September 14, 1957.

tion" to "my desire" and added the limitation that the governor's actions must be "consistent with my responsibilities under the Constitution of the United States and that of Arkansas." Upon receiving the message, Eisenhower and press secretary Hagerty drafted an acceptance letter that stated: "All good citizens must, of course, obey all proper orders of our courts." Under the arrangement agreed upon by the two parties, Faubus and Hays would arrive in Providence on Friday, September 13, and be transported by helicopter to Newport for the meeting on the morning of the 14th. Shortly before Faubus' arrival in Newport, Attorney General Brownell, Sherman Adams, and Gerald Morgan would fly in from Washington, D.C.[10]

In the private portion of the meeting of September 14, Eisenhower lectured Faubus in a "rehearsed" manner, only to encounter claims by Faubus of Arkansas desegregation "successes." Expressing his desire for a peaceful resolution of the impasse, the President indicated, according to Faubus, possession of a letter from an officer warning of possible sectional disloyalty in the ranks in the event troops were ordered to enforce desegregation, a claim Eisenhower dismissed as "nuts." Nevertheless, Eisenhower declared his wish to avoid publicly embarrassing the governor in a showdown, and by the meeting's end he felt that he had obtained Faubus's assurance not to obstruct the court order. After being joined by other administration officials, Faubus renewed an earlier request for a "cooling-off" period, only to be turned down by the attorney general. Seeking once again to reassure the governor of the administration's sympathy, Eisenhower noted that Faubus did not have to pull out the National Guard, but could merely change its instructions to allow the black students in. If Faubus changed his order, the President pledged, he would not be brought to court on contempt charges.[11]

After the Newport meeting, as Faubus and Hays returned to Providence, Brownell, Adams, and Hagerty began drafting a joint statement that pledged Faubus's intention to respect the court's orders and to cooperate with them. Only two hours later, however, Hays warned Adams that Faubus was trying to back out of the

10. Faubus, *Down From the Hills*, 240-41; Eisenhower, *Waging Peace*, 166; Adams, *Firsthand Report*, 348-49; Press Release, Sept. 11, 1957, Morgan Records, Box 6, DDEL.

11. Faubus, Down From the Hills, 255-57; "Notes Dictated by the President Concerning Visit of Governor Orval Faubus of Arkansas on Sept. 14, 1957," Oct. 8, 1957, Whitman Diary, Whitman File, Diary Series, Box 9, DDEL.

agreement, claiming that the attorney general had erred in saying desegregation could not be delayed even at Justice Department request. Adams relayed the White House draft statement to Hays, and after continued negotiations, a final draft prepared for Faubus' delivery stated: "I must harmonize my actions under the laws of Arkansas with the requirements of the Constitution of the United States." Faubus did not directly say that he would change his instructions to the Arkansas National Guard. When asked by reporters, he merely replied, "That problem I will have to take care of when I return to Little Rock."

Although Eisenhower believed that he had gotten Faubus' pledge to comply with the federal court order, others in the White House contingent were less certain. Presidential secretary Ann Whitman noted, "I got the impression that the meeting had not gone as well as had been hoped, that the Federal government would have to be as tough as possible in the situation." As she saw it, "Governor Faubus seized this opportunity and stirred the whole thing up for his own political advantage." Whitman added, "The test comes tomorrow morning when we will know whether Governor Faubus will, or will not, withdraw the troops."[12]

In separate interviews with Mike Wallace and with reporters on CBS's *Face the Nation* broadcast the next day, Faubus refused to commit himself either to removing the guardsmen or to changing their orders. In informal negotiations with the Justice Department, with Hays again acting as an intermediary, Faubus stated that he would remove the guardsmen only on condition that the Justice Department recommend a delay in desegregation pending a Supreme Court test of the state's interposition law. The attorney general not only refused Faubus' demand, but added that he could not promise that the contempt charge against the governor would be dropped even if the Arkansas troops were withdrawn. With no progress reported by Hays in the next several days, administration officials increasingly realized that the governor intended to persist in his obstructionism. Faubus had gained additional time, however, and the Justice Department remained woefully unprepared to intervene. Hoover refused to assign FBI agents to Little Rock for policing purposes, and U.S. Attorney Osro Cobb lamely informed Virgil Blossom that he

12. Faubus, *Down From the Hills*, 257–58; Eisenhower, *Waging Peace*, 166; Adams, *Firsthand Report*, 352–53; "Statements by the President and the Governor of Arkansas," Sept. 14, 1957, Morgan Records, Box 6; Whitman Diary, Sept. 14, 1957, Whitman File, Diary Series, Box 9, DDEL.

lacked the specific authorization from higher officials to seek a court order federalizing additional marshals to defend the school. In spite of Faubus' clear defiance, the President also remained unprepared to take remedial action. In a draft letter, Eisenhower reiterated: "Because it is not in man's nature to accept unhesitatingly the dictation of law of his moral conduct, it is necessary that he be shown the course that is just and right. Then he will accept it if understanding and moderation are used by officials of government at every level of enforcement."[13]

On September 19, a day before his scheduled court appearance before Judge Davies, Faubus an affidavit of disqualification charging the judge with "prejudice." Reports of the governor's action quickly reached the White House command center, headed by staff secretary Andrew Goodpaster. General Goodpaster's memorandum to the President noted: "Governor Faubus is not going to carry out the orders of the Court, but is going to engage in some legal maneuvering to try and block and frustrate the order of the court." Goodpaster and Adams both concluded that in the event the governor persisted in his refusal to obey the court, "an obligation falls upon the Federal government to require Faubus to do so by whatever means may be necessary. At this time the President should speak to the country." An angry Eisenhower wanted an immediate statement prepared against Faubus, but he was persuaded by Adams and Brownell to wait upon further action by the governor.[14]

Faubus did not appear in person at the court hearing of September 20. His lawyers questioned Judge Davies' authority and claimed that the governor's absence did not signal his inflexible refusal to comply with the court. Davies threw out the disqualification petition, Faubus' lawyers then withdrew, and the judge issued an injunction later in the day barring the National Guard and the governor from any further interference with the desegregation of Central High School. With Faubus' intentions toward removal of the National Guard still uncertain, Mayor Mann requested that the attorney general call upon Judge Davies to assign U.S. marshals to the high school. Brownell refused, however, claiming that the sole responsibility for the assignment of marshals rested with the federal court. Davies, in turn, declined to

13. Faubus, *Down From the Hills*, 246, 260; Brooks Hays, *A Southern Moderate Speaks* (Chapel Hill, N.C., 1959), 159, 170–71; draft letter of Eisenhower, Sept. 18, 1957, Harlow Records, Box 11, DDEL.

14. Andrew Goodpaster to Hagerty, Sept. 19, 1957, Whitman File, Diary Series, Box 16, DDEL.

take the action without the official recommendation of the Justice Department. Still seeking to keep law enforcement responsibility in local hands, the Justice Department directed the FBI to sound out the Little Rock department on the possibility of deputizing citizens.

Attorney General Brownell now realized, though, that in the absence of sufficient local police forces or additional federal marshals, the federal government was faced with the likely prospect of sending in military personnel. After informing the President of Faubus's legal maneuverings, Brownell indicated that an appointment with Wilbur Brucker, secretary of the army, had been arranged to discuss the possible use of army troops. A gloomy Eisenhower, frustrated at his inability to avoid the confrontation with Faubus, wished aloud that someone would tell Brooks Hays how low the governor had fallen in his estimation. The President still fretted more openly, however, about the harmful impact of a federal troop intervention than about the consequences of the absence of one. He worried that the sending of troops could produce widespread violence. Afraid that Faubus then might choose to abolish his state's public schools, he directed Brownell to check upon the governor's authority to do so.[15]

Eisenhower's fears of intervention were eased temporarily on the evening of September 20, when Faubus announced on statewide television that the National Guard troops around Central High School would be removed. The governor indicated his continuing opposition to desegregation through legal action, however, and he gave no assurances that state police authority would be used to quell disturbances stemming from attempts to resist black student entry into the high school. Nevertheless, the President's public reply the next day expressed relief at Faubus' action, and again urged moderation to the citizens of Little Rock. Disclaiming any further responsibility for the maintenance of law and order in the city, Faubus flew to the Southern Governors' Conference. But the need for federal intervention had not disappeared, and in Little Rock a small, 175-man police force had been assigned the sole responsibility for keeping the peace. City police officers themselves refused to escort the black children into the school, and left the school grounds unpatrolled. The Little Rock fire department declined to provide hoses for crowd

15. Faubus, *Down From the Hills*, 262–63; Hays, *A Southern Moderate Speaks*, 193; telephone call, Sept. 20, 1957, Whitman File, Diary Series, Box 16, DDEL.

control, and civic leaders kept an uncooperative silence on the need to maintain public calm and order.[16]

On the morning of September 23, 1957, eight black students entered Central High School through a side entrance. Upon hearing of their admission, an angry mob estimated at between five hundred and several thousand surrounded the building, and the school board ordered the removal of the blacks for "safety purposes." Mayor Mann, noting the presence at the disturbances of Faubus intimate Jimmy Karam, concluded that the governor was "cognizant of what was going to take place," even though he was absent. At the White House communications center, General Goodpaster began to receive a series of anxious calls from observers in Little Rock and the capital. The comments of the callers included, "People here not in close touch—not getting up to the minute reports"; "No board of strategy—has gotten diffused"; "Right local people should be speaking out"; "U.S. Attorney in Little Rock a weakling and incompetent"; and "Think that psychologically the Boss should come back." Unable to get through to the White House from 11:00 A.M. until late in the afternoon, Brooks Hays finally reached Maxwell Rabb, who notified the congressman that while troops "are not on their way," the black students had been removed from the school. Upon notification of the disturbances, the President, again vacationing in Newport, issued a proclamation of obstruction of justice—a cease and desist order citing U.S. Code provisions for the use of state militia or federal military forces to prevent obstruction. By the evening of the twenty-third White House officials knew that if mob resistance continued the next day, federal troops would have to be ordered into the city. Sherman Adams remarked to Hays, "You and I can sign off now—it's in other hands, I guess." Twenty-four hours later, army paratroopers were positioned outside Central High School.[17]

To a considerable degree, the rush of events had forced the President to take extreme measures to enforce the orders of the federal court. Yet at Mansfield, Texas a year before, Eisenhower had permitted state authorities to obstruct the entry of black students without complaint. In the Little Rock situation, however,

16. Faubus, *Down From the Hills*, 263; "Statement by the President," Sept. 21, 1957, Morgan Records, Box 6, DDEL; Bartley, 266.

17. Faubus, *Down From the Hills*, 268–169; Hays, *A Southern Moderate Speaks*, 172; "Memorandum for the Record," Sept. 23, 1957, White House Office, Staff Secretariat, Box 13, DDEL.

additional circumstances were present to encourage a different presidential response. Of importance was the fact that the political environment within which the administration acted in 1957 was different from that of 1956. Nineteen fifty-six had been a presidential election year, Texas had been a key campaign target for the President's reelection bid, and Governor Shivers was a personal friend and political ally of Eisenhower. By September 1957 the election was nearly a year past, Arkansas offered far less hope of Republican gain than Texas at the national level, and Faubus was not a political intimate of the President. Eisenhower clearly preferred not to intervene with federal force in the Little Rock situation, and his delays, along with the Justice Department's lack of preparation for the emergency, helped precipitate the ultimate confrontation. But in the President's view, his attempts to show patience and understanding had been met by persistent obstruction and outright deception. The governor's refusal to let the federal government off the hook by carrying out his duty for peaceful desegregation at Central High frustrated Eisenhower's objectives, and Faubus' failure after repeated opportunities to keep his solemn promise to comply infuriated the President on a personal level. Having carried the legal fencing and negotiation as far as possible, Eisenhower, motivated by his perception of his duty, the absence of immediate electoral cost, and his antipathy for Faubus' conduct, performed an act that two months earlier he had been unable to envisage.

Having made the decision to intervene, the Eisenhower administration immediately took steps to insure maximum international propaganda benefit from the action. U.S. Information Service reports already had warned officials that news photographs of the mob actions at Little Rock "were particularly damaging to U.S. prestige." President Eisenhower's television address of September 24 was translated into forty-three languages, and the Voice of America broadcast details of the troop intervention. On September 25, nine black students traveled to Central High School in a U.S. Army station wagon, and soldiers escorted them into the building as a crowd of one hundred watched. Within the White House, a brief controversy surfaced because of staffer Bryce Harlow's concern that the wording of the President's executive order, using the nontechnical term "order" instead of "call" to the National Guard, might provide a pretext for Arkansas guardsmen to disobey. Attorney General Brownell and his assistant, W. Wilson White, quickly reassured Harlow that the order was sufficient

Larry Obsitnik, *The Arkansas Gazette*
Federal troops escort black schoolchildren into Little Rock Central High
School, September 25, 1957.

as worded. During a scuffle, troops nicked one protestor with a bayonet. Capitalizing upon the incident, Governor Faubus claimed on statewide television that evening that the "warm red blood of patriotic American citizens" stained the "cold, naked, unsheathed knives" of the "military occupation."[18]

The following day, Senator Richard B. Russell of Georgia seized upon Faubus' remarks and issued a message to the President assailing the "Hitler-like" and "high-handed and illegal" methods of the Army troops. Eisenhower rejoined: "In one case, military power was used to further the ambitions and purposes of a ruthless dictator; in the other, to preserve the institutions of free government." Army Secretary Brucker also repudiated Russell's charges point by point. Anxious to squelch any doubts about the legitimacy of the government's action, Justice Department attorneys, led by W. Wilson White, prepared a refutation of a David Lawrence column in the September 27 U.S. News & World Report that claimed that the Fourteenth Amendment did not apply to Southern states that had not "fairly" participated in its initial ratification. In addition to defending the legitimacy of the action, administration policy in the aftermath of the President's order was designed to avoid further antagonizing actions and pave the way for the withdrawal of federal troops as quickly as possible. Staffers vetoed a proposal of speech writer Arthur Larson for an open letter to Little Rock students, and the attorney general jotted in his notes on September 26, "Quickly as heat goes out — get troops out — police take over — *Then Faubus responsible.*"[19]

The administration was not alone in wanting a quick pulling out of federal troops and a dignified withdrawal from public furor. At the Southern Governors' Conference, a committee of state leaders sounded out Sherman Adams on the possibility of scheduling a meeting with the President to discuss withdrawing troops. The President agreed to a meeting, but he requested that the agenda be broadened to cover general Southern compliance with the Supreme Court rulings on school integration. One governor — Marvin Griffin of Georgia — refused to attend. Four other gov-

18. Benjamin Muse, *Ten Years of Prelude: The Story of Integration since the Supreme Courts 1954 Decision* (New York, 1964), 142; Harlow to Brownell, Sept. 25, 1957, Harlow Records, Box 11, DDEL; Adams, *Firsthand Report*, 355.

19. Richard Russell to Eisenhower, Sept. 26, 1957; Eisenhower to Russell, Sept. 28, 1957; undated draft, Wilbur Brucker to Russell, Harlow Records, Box 11; "Memorandum for the Attorney General," Oct. 5, 1957, William P. Rogers Papers, Box 51; Brownell to Goodpaster, White House Office, Staff Secretariat, Box 13, DDEL.

ernors, however — Frank G. Clement of Tennessee, LeRoy Collins of Florida, Luther Hodges of North Carolina, and Theodore McKeldin of Maryland — met with the President at the White House on October 1. White House staffers Adams, Hagerty, and Howard Pyle also attended the session, but Attorney General Brownell, seen by Southern officials as the "villain" of Little Rock, did not appear. At the meeting, Eisenhower repeated his assertion that Faubus had pledged compliance at Newport, and he insisted upon a Faubus declaration upholding peaceful desegregation before he would agree to remove federal troops.[20]

In response to the President's statement, the committee of governors drafted a new letter for Faubus. Eisenhower and Attorney General Brownell quickly approved it, and Faubus, through Hays, apparently also gave his initial consent. As originally worded by the governors, the Faubus message stated, "I now declare that I will assume full responsibility for the maintenance of law and order and ohat the orders of the Federal Court will not be obstructed." Faubus added the words "by me" to the end of the sentence, however, thereby absolving himself from responsibility for preventing the obstructionist actions of others. Informed of the governor's revision at a farewell dinner for Secretary of Defense Wilson, Eisenhower joined staffers in drafting a reply that declared that Faubus's statement "does not constitute in my opinion the assurance that he intends to use his full powers to prevent obstruction of the court order."[21]

With Faubus continuing to frustrate his attempts to extricate himself from the crisis, Eisenhower expressed renewed misgivings about the ability of troops to secure public compliance with school desegregation. At an October 3 press conference, he noted that "the very core of my political thinking is that it has got to be the sentiment, the good will, the good sense of a whole citizenry that enforces law." In keeping with his beliefs, the President privately called upon civic, political, and religious leaders in the South to encourage public moderation. Both Eisenhower's firm action at Little Rock and his slowness in arriving at it did enjoy

20. Adams, *Firsthand Report*, 356–57; Whitman Diary, Sept. 14–30, 1957, Whitman File, Diary Series, Box 9; press release, Oct. 1, 1957, Hagerty Papers, Box 6, DDEL.

21. Faubus, *Down From the Hills*, 309; Adams, *Firsthand Report*, 357–58; "Press Conference Notes," Oct. 3, 1957, Whitman File, Diary Series, Box 16; "Statement by the President," Oct. 1, 1957, Hagerty Papers, Box 6, DDEL.

popular support outside the South. An October 4 Gallup Poll indicated that 74 percent of Northerners approved of his action, and 64 percent agreed that he should not have acted any sooner. But the President was frustrated by the lack of public expressions of support from prominent Southerners, and he lamented to former HEW secretary Oveta Culp Hobby that only Ralph McGill, publisher of the *Atlanta Constitution*, had openly defended his action.[22]

Eisenhower ultimately reacted to Southern silence and outright opposition to the Little Rock intervention by increasing private urgings for an acceleration of the troop withdrawal timetable. With segregationist resistance at Central High lessening, on October 14 the President approved Army Secretary Brucker's order to withdraw half of the army forces and to defederalize four-fifths of the guardsmen, reducing the troops in Little Rock to 1,800. Eisenhower himself pressed for a greater reduction, to 1,000 men, and even suggested a total withdrawal. After the dismissal of a complaint of brutality filed by the Mothers' League against commanding general Edwin Walker and his troops, black students attended Central High without escort for the first time on October 23. The NAACP's Thurgood Marshall conveyed the thanks of his organization and of other blacks to the President through Maxwell Rabb. Rabb recommended that a warm reply would have Marshall "purring like a kitten" and also might dissuade him from actions to "rock the boat." Eisenhower forwarded a friendly acknowledgment.[23]

In addition to the troop reductions, the announcement on October 24 of the resignation of Herbert Brownell as attorney general further relieved Southern political pressure upon the administration. Brownell's resignation had been planned well before the disturbances at Little Rock, and he had stayed at his post at the President's request in order to help design the administration's response to the crisis. But Brownell had been dissatisfied with the temporizing attitude of Sherman Adams and other White House staffers, and with the authorization of federal troops to Little Rock, he could no longer communicate with Southern representatives

22. *Public Papers of the Presidents*, Dwight D. Eisenhower, Oct. 3, 1957, 707; Gallup, ed., *The Gallup Poll*, 1517; telephone call, Oct. 19, 1957, Whitman File, Diary Series, Box 16, DDEL.
23. Eisenhower, *Waging Peace*, 175; Goodpaster, "Memorandum for the Record," Oct. 15, 1957, Whitman File, Diary Series, Box 16; Rabb to Whitman; Eisenhower to Thurgood Marshall, Oct. 23, 1957, Official File, Box 732, DDEL.

who saw him as the chief architect of intervention. The Richmond *Times* expressed the feelings of many white Southerners when it asserted, "From Harpers Ferry to the Rio Grande, and in all the land in between, no tears are being shed for the retirement of Herbert Brownell, Jr., as Attorney General. The frightful mess the South, and the country, are in is probably as much his responsibility as that of any living man." In a final official action on November 11, Brownell submitted a "memorandum for the record" that detailed the steps leading to the Little Rock intervention and offered legal justification for his advice to the President. Brownell's successor, William P. Rogers, insisted that he and his predecessor "thought alike" on major issues, but in his previous role as the department's chief liaison man with Capitol Hill the new attorney general had maintained better working relations with Southern politicians.[24]

Following the repudiation of a Faubus charge on October 25 that the continued use of Arkansas guardsmen constituted a "violation of their rights," Brucker cautioned against prematurely pulling out the remaining forces in Little Rock. "The hard core must be broken, irrespective of who does it," the army secretary asserted. Nevertheless, National Guard troops took over responsibility for maintaining order the next day, and twelve days later all remaining army paratroopers were removed from the city. Hoping to encourage continued tranquility, Attorney General Rogers announced that despite FBI identification of mob leaders, the Justice Department would not pursue prosecutions for obstruction of justice through either an injunction or the 1870 Civil Rights Act. The decision was sharply criticized by school officials. "What more encouragement could the White Citizens' Council want?" one school board member demanded. Nevertheless, the administration continued to wind down its involvement in Little Rock. On December 13, the National Guard contingent for the city was reduced again from 950 men to 430.[25]

Assessing the Little Rock intervention in hindsight, the President was convinced above all that the Supreme Court desegrega-

---

24. Parmet, *Eisenhower*, 512; Brownell, "President's Power to Use Federal Troops to Suppress Resistance to Enforcement of Federal Court Orders—Little Rock, Arkansas," *Official Opinions of the Attorney General*, vol. 41, 313–32; Schlundt, 162–63; "Memorandum for the Record," Nov. 4, 1957, White House Office, Staff Secretariat, Box 13, DDEL.

25. Faubus to Eisenhower, Oct. 25, 1957, Bricker to Faubus, Oct. 26, 1957, Official File, Box 732, DDEL; Schlundt, "Civil Rights Policies," 163; Faubus, *Down From the Hills*, 347; Peters, *The Southern Temper*, 85.

tion orders had placed his administration in an untenable legal and political position. During the 1956 campaign the President had lamented to Emmet John Hughes, "I am convinced that the Supreme Court decision set back progress in the South at least 15 years. . . . It is all very well to talk about school integration — if you remember you may also be talking about social disintegration. Feelings are deep on this, especially where children are involved." On a personal note he added, "You take the attitude of a fellow like Jimmy Byrnes. We used to be pretty good friends, and now I've not heard from him even once in the last eighteen months — all because of bitterness on this thing." In the aftermath of Little Rock, on October 3, 1957, Eisenhower seconded Sherman Adams' reservations about the authority of the Supreme Court to issue implementation schemes for its constitutional interpretations. Such an assumption of authority by the judiciary "gets into areas of individual liberties and states' rights," he stated. Eisenhower stated his own fear that "we might have ground torn out from under us by an amendment to the Constitution or 'some law.'" To Arthur Larson he declared directly, "I personally think that the [Brown] decision was wrong."[26]

Eisenhower steadfastly refused to endorse publicly the Supreme Court decisions on school desegregation after Little Rock, and on occasion he even appeared to backtrack from a position of public neutrality. In August 1958, Eisenhower refused to comment on the closing of Virginia public schools and the Supreme Court integration decisions, claiming it "just isn't good business to do so." Any official comment would "weaken public opinion" for judicial actions "where I might agree or disagree." When asked if he was considering an expanded role for the FBI in investigating Southern resistance, Eisenhower responded, "I don't believe that you can start a Gestapo around here." Privately the President revealed to Attorney General Rogers his belief that even desegregation plans in places such as Tennessee "may be thirty or forty years in reaching the ideal." When his private preference for slower implementation of school desegregation leaked to the press, he admitted, "It might have been that I said something about 'slower.'"[27]

26. Hughes, *The Ordeal of Power:* 201; "Press Conference Notes," Oct. 3, 1957, Whitman File, Diary Series, Box 16, DDEL; Larson, *Eisenhower*, 124.

27. *Public Papers of the Presidents*, 1958, 403; "Pre-Press Conference Notes," Aug. 6, 1958, Whitman File, Press Conference Series, Box 7, DDEL; Hughes, *The Ordeal of Power*, 261; "Memorandum for the Record," Aug. 22, 1958, Whitman File, Administrative Series, Box 35, DDEL; *New York Times*, Aug. 28, 1958.

Rejecting a primary role for the federal government in overcoming massive resistance, Eisenhower placed a large burden for progress on the students themselves. Writing to Ralph McGill of the *Atlanta Constitution*, the President concurred that "it is quite possible . . . that the schools must be closed for a period before there is hope of acceptance of the decision." Declaring his belief that "the students themselves will eventually resolve the issue," he went on: "Incidentally it is curious how the extra-curricular activities of school life — the football team, the band, etc. — seem to become more important levers in urging the reopening of the schools than does education." Although he agreed with McGill's criticism that some Southern politicians appeared motivated solely by political expediency, he exempted Virginia's congressmen from that category and limited his personal condemnation to senators Johnston and Thurmond of South Carolina and Eastland of Mississippi as "not only extreme but rigid." Wishing to insure that "progress has the support of law, but should not be so punitive as to get anyone upset," Eisenhower publicly waffled on the basic issue of the morality of segregation — "Well, I suppose there are certain phases of a segregation — you are talking about, I suppose, segregation by local laws — in other words, that interfere with the citizen's equality of opportunity in both the economic and political fields." He concluded lamely, "I think to that extent, that is morally wrong, yes."[28]

With the President carefully avoiding further involvement in school desegregation, the Justice Department was left to pursue its legal intervention in Arkansas to a satisfactory conclusion alone. Ruling out any legislative recommendations for the short term, the department cooperated in winding down the federal presence in Little Rock. Upon the completion of the school term in May, the remaining federalized guardsmen were returned to the control of state authority. School officials, however, had filed yet another request for delay of desegregation, and on June 21, 1958, federal judge Harry J. Lemley agreed to nullify the plan and defer desegregation for two and a half years. Faced with the prospect of having to fight the Little Rock legal battle all over again, Attorney General Rogers assigned his assistant, Lawrence Walsh, to work exclusively on the matter. The Justice Department arranged daily meetings on the Little Rock situation and set up a special telephone line between U.S. attorney's office in the city

28. Eisenhower to Ralph McGill, Oct. 3, 1958, Official File, Box 732, DDEL; *Public Papers of the Presidents, 1959*, 509.

and the department's own switchboard. Further use of troops was rejected, but officials deputized additional U.S. marshals and sent them to the capital for training, prepared briefs in anticipation of new court actions, and delegated representatives to monitor and provide reports on other litigation in Arkansas and Virginia. However, no such arrangements were made in Alabama and Mississippi. With the Justice Department refusing to initiate suits and only reluctantly following the NAACP's lead in determining the location and timing of litigation, the NAACP's own organizational weakness in the two states effectively precluded any possibility of government involvement. Even if the NAACP had been stronger in the Deep South, federal legal activity in all probability would have been limited, for the Justice Department hesitated to jeopardize its legislative proposals in other areas by pursuing suit action in Mississippi, the home state of Senate Judiciary Committee chairman James O. Eastland.[29]

Attempting to defend his department's legal position in view of the President's apparent backsliding, Attorney General Rogers declared that the continuing Southern belief in the constitutionality of segregated schools was misguided. Nevertheless, as columnist Walter Lippmann observed, "Mr. Rogers made a brave attempt to make clear much of what the President has fogged up, but on the crucial question, Mr. Rogers, who had no administration policy to rely upon, resorted to exhortation and pious platitudes." Rogers could do little else, for the White House had vetoed department involvement in the consideration of the Lemley decision by the Eighth Circuit Court of Appeals, and W. Wilson White's nomination as head of the new Civil Rights Division remained stalled in the Senate. On August 18, the same day that White was confirmed by the Senate, the Court of Appeals overturned Lemley's ruling but allowed it to remain in effect pending a final Supreme Court determination. In late August, the Justice Department's J. Lee Rankin gained Eisenhower's assent to file a brief calling upon the Supreme Court to rule directly on the initial Davies order of 1957. In oral argument before the high court, Rankin defended the initial desegregation ruling by declaring, "Opposition to the *Brown* decision expressed in violence cannot justify the abandonment or modification of the plan."[30]

29. Faubus, *Down From the Hills;* 378; Peltason, *Fifty-eight Lonely Men,* 185; *Face the Nation,* Vol. 2, 273.

30. Peltason, *Fifty-eight Lonely Men,* 48–49, 188; Faubus, *Down From the Hills,* 409.

Even before the Supreme Court issued its new ruling on the desegregation of Little Rock's schools, the attorney general contacted city officials to offer them technical assistance through the office of Assistant Attorney General Malcolm Wilkey. Rogers also informed them of the department's retention of 110 additional deputies, at a cost of $390,000. On September 12, the Supreme Court in *Cooper* v. *Aaron* sided with the Court of Appeals and placed the ultimate blame for the Little Rock disorders on the governor and the state legislature. The high court declared, "Law and order are not here to be preserved by depriving the Negro children of their constitutional rights." Governor Faubus responded defiantly by signing a bill empowering him to close the public schools. Arkansas established a state private school corporation, and in Little Rock a local corporation received a charter from the Pulaski County Court. On September 25, Attorney General Rogers transmitted to the President a copy of the department's brief opposing the private school plan, scheduled to be filed with a special three-judge federal court. On September 29, the Supreme Court issued a supporting opinion to its ruling of the twelfth that made clear its disapproval of any forms of public assistance to private school systems. Immediately upon release of the opinion, Justice Department attorneys arranged for its quick transmission to a special federal panel in Omaha, Nebraska. In a ruling made retroactive to September 25 in order to prevent additional appeals, the three-judge appeals court declared that the Little Rock private corporation's plan to lease public school buildings was illegal.[31]

In spite of the Supreme Court's decisive September rulings in *Cooper* v. *Aaron*, Arkansas remained the focal point of Justice Department desegregation activity for yet another year. Although the department observed massive resistance developments in other Southern states, it viewed any immediate attempts at legal action in the Deep South as pointless. The attorney general was not eager to provoke Southern reaction through court tests of "private" school systems. In October he declared, "Private preferences or prejudices, noble or ignoble, present no constitutional question." By the end of the 1958–59 school year, the Arkansas private school system would become bankrupt. In January 1959, the Justice Department answered yet another delay petition from

31. Schlundt, "Civil Rights Policies," 164–67; Faubus, *Down From the Hills,* 414–35, 440; Rogers to Eisenhower, Sept. 25, 1958, Rogers Papers, Box 51, DDEL.

Little Rock officials with a brief charging the school board with violating its duty, and in June the federal district court again ordered the opening of Little Rock public schools to all. Segregated Raney High School in the city closed for lack of funds in August, and the local school board reluctantly reopened Central and Hall high schools. School officials, however, employed the state's new pupil placement law to limit black enrollment to a handful. Rejecting the NAACP's argument that the pupil placement law was invalid in Little Rock, Civil Rights Division head W. Wilson White declared that any department amicus brief should uphold pupil placement, if properly administered, as a way to "continue the moderation in assignments at this time."[32]

The Justice Department's frustrations in overcoming legal obstacles to desegregation might have been expected to stimulate it toward new efforts at drafting remedial legislation. However, the department's legislative recommendations in the field of school integration after Little Rock perpetuated the official emphasis on the control of violent resistance to desegregation rather than on the development of new measures to extend desegregation into the Deep South or the removal of Southern legal obstacles. As had been the case before Little Rock, the Justice Department viewed its primary goal as the preservation of social order rather than the attainment of rapid desegregation. Some changes in outlook did occur within the Eisenhower administration, but they took place not in the Justice Department but in the Department of Health, Education and Welfare. HEW's new willingness to devise strategies to promote desegregation came as the direct result of the appointment of Arthur Flemming as secretary in the late summer of 1958. Unlike his predecessors Oveta Culp Hobby and Marion Folsom, Flemming acknowledged a role for his department in promoting compliance with the Supreme Court decisions, and he named a special assistant, Charles Saunders, specifically to supervise school integration matters. More important, beginning in August 1958, HEW began submitting daily reports to the White House on the status of Southern integration. Excerpts selected from the reports were included in the President's daily briefing book, providing him for the first time with regular information on desegregation developments.[33]

32. "Address of the Attorney General before the California State Bar Convention," Oct. 8, 1958, Morrow Records, Box 10; W. Wilson White to Rogers, Aug. 4, 1959, Rogers Papers, Box 51, DDEL.

33. Arthur Fleming to Eisenhower, Aug. 14, 22, 1958, Whitman File, Administrative Series, Box 16, DDEL.

Responding to the President's invitation in November 1958 to provide recommendations for a new civil rights package in the 1959 congressional session, both the departments of Justice and HEW submitted proposals dealing with desegregation issues. The Justice Department's suggestions — raising criminal penalties for mob obstruction of court orders and making interstate transportation of explosives used against schools or churches a federal offense — remained in keeping with its emphasis on orderly process rather than rapid progress. HEW's proposals, however, drafted by Undersecretary Elliot Richardson, marked a departure from the department's previous insistence upon separating federal aid to education from school desegregation. In a carrot-and-stick approach, HEW proposed grants to desegregating school districts for assistance in the financing of new construction, authority for the commissioner of education to provide information and technical advice upon request, and new powers to assume control over future school buildings constructed with federal funds that refused open admission to all students.[34]

Expressing the hope that through legislation a way could be found to place segregation cases securely in the hands of moderate judges rather than "inflamatory" NAACP lawyers, on January 28, 1959 the President reviewed an eight-point memorandum of civil rights proposals that included the HEW and Justice Department suggestions. Although the President himself endorsed the package on the whole as "moderate" and unlikely to "give rise to argument and dissension," he described HEW's proposals for education grants to cooperating school districts as "not essential." At a February 3 meeting with Republican leaders two days before the presentation of the State of the Union message, Minority Leader Charles Halleck sharply criticized the entire package and questioned the political wisdom of any civil rights proposals. Vice President Nixon defended the HEW recommendations and an additional proposal to make his Committee on Government Contracts a permanent body, and Attorney General Rogers spoke in behalf of his department's program. Rogers later rejected, however, additional suggestions from civil rights supporters during House committee testimony that he seek "Part III" civil suit powers in desegregation cases similar to those previously rejected in the administration's 1956 civil rights package. Rogers observed that the additional authority "might do more harm than good at

34. Whitman Diary, Nov. 19, 1958, Whitman File, Diary Series, Box 10, DDEL.

this time," and the entire set of administration proposals subsequently stalled in the House Rules committee.[35]

In early 1960, the President resubmitted the sections of the administration civil rights package dealing with transportation of explosives, criminal penalties for court order obstruction, and financial and technical aid for desegregating schools. Despite this action, however, the desegregation portions of the package received much less enthusiastic an endorsement from Eisenhower than other administration proposals dealing with voting rights. With the President unwilling to push for "spectacular stuff," particularly in an election year, HEW's carrot of financial assistance to desegregating school districts and its stick of withholding federally financed construction were stricken from consideration by the Congress at committee level and did not appear in the final version of the 1960 Civil Rights Act.[36]

The administration's final skirmishes with Southern opponents of school desegregation occurred in late 1960 and were prompted by the order of Federal Judge J. Skelly Wright for the integration of New Orleans's public schools. In August a three-judge appeals panel upheld Wright's ruling and barred Louisiana Governor Jimmie Davis from interfering with the implementation of the federal order. Concerned that the case could become "another Little Rock" and jeopardize Republican chances in the 1960 election, Attorney General Rogers requested postponement of the appeals hearing arguments in order to "see that nothing happened before the election that would bring out violence." One week after the election, Rogers finally, with Eisenhower's approval, issued a warning to Governor Davis that "any resistance or obstruction or interference with federal court orders will be in violation of federal law." Rogers deployed additional federal marshals to New Orleans and pledged that they were "ready to cooperate fully" with local police in maintaining order. The Louisiana legislature, reacting to court-ordered injunctions against the superintendent of schools and New Orleans school board officials, dismissed the superintendent and the board, reconstituted both under new state segregation laws, and reinstated the previous members with instructions to obey only the state's authority.

35. "Memorandum for the President," Jan. 28, 1959, Henry R. McPhee Records, Box 3; "Notes on Legislative Leadership Meeting," Feb. 3, 1959, Whitman File, Legislative Meetings Series, Box 3; presidential address to the Congress, Feb. 5, 1959, Philip Areeda Papers, Box 7, DDEL.

36. "Notes on Legislative Leadership Meeting," March 8, 1960, Whitman File, Legislative Meetings Series, Box 3, DDEL.

Justice Department attorneys in turn filed suit against the state's nullification resolution and gained an injunction preventing implementation of the state law creating the new school board. With local boycott efforts and public harassment of black students continuing even after the rejection of state interposition claims, the Eisenhower administration gladly handed over the New Orleans headache to the incoming Kennedy administration.[37]

With President Eisenhower unenthusiastic about school desegregation legislation and the Justice Department primarily concerned with keeping a lid on violent passions, probably the greatest contribution of the administration to the long-term struggle against Jim Crow was the appointment of integration supporters to Southern federal courts. Although Eisenhower appointees were not invariably civil rights advocates, several justices did make major contributions to the movement for racial integration. On the 5th Circuit Court of Appeals, judges John Minor Wisdom of Louisiana, Elbert P. Tuttle of Georgia, and John Robert Brown of Texas constituted three-quarters of a voting bloc known as "The Four" — a group of judges later credited with breaking the back of Southern legal resistance to civil rights. At the district court level, Frank Johnson of Alabama joined two other judges on a panel that repudiated Montgomery's segregated bus system, and Axel J. Beck, a Swedish-born South Dakotan on temporary assignment in Arkansas in 1958, overturned the expulsion of three black students in Dollarway, Arkansas under the state pupil placement law.[38]

Eisenhower's appointments to the federal bench in the South, as with his appointment of Earl Warren as chief justice, owed more to partisan loyalty than to any guiding judicial philosophy. Judge Wisdom, a former member of the New Orleans Urban League, the Council of Social Agencies, and the President's Committee on Government Contracts, received his nod for the 5th Circuit position in 1957 because of his chairmanship of the "Southern Conference for Eisenhower" in 1952 and Attorney General Brownell's assessment that he possessed a "better record as a lawyer" than Governor Robert Kennon. Elbert Tuttle of Atlanta, appointed in 1953, had grown up in multiracial Hawaii and had served as vice-chairman of the Southern Conference for

37. Peltason, *Fifty-eight Lonely Men*, 222–33; Jacob Javits to Eisenhower, Eisenhower to Javits, Dec. 1, 1960, Official File, Box 732, DDEL.

38. See Jack Bass, *Unlikely Heroes* (New York, 1981).

Eisenhower before being named general counsel to the Treasury Department. John Robert Brown, a native Nebraskan, had served as an admiralty lawyer and a Republican party leader in Houston before his court appointment in 1955. And Frank Johnson of Alabama, appointed to the federal bench in 1955, had been president of Veterans for Eisenhower in the state in 1953 and U.S. attorney for the middle district of Alabama.[39]

Even though Eisenhower's appointees to Southern federal courts were not chosen specifically because of their previous positions on racial issues, they were in other important ways mavericks from Southern political orthodoxy. Their loyalty to the Republican party itself suggested the possibility of greater detachment from the white supremacist traditions of Southern Democratic politics, and several of them also claimed experience outside the region that promoted more tolerant views of other races. Other Eisenhower selections, however, including 5th Circuit judges Benjamin F. Cameron of Mississippi and Warren Jones of Florida, Clement Haynsworth and Herbert S. Boreman of the 4th Circuit, and district court judges Ben C. Dawkins of Louisiana, Joe Estes of Texas, Claude Clayton of Mississippi, and Harlan Hobart Grooms of Alabama, compiled far less impressive civil rights records. Cameron, a states' rights devotee and Eastland protégé, consistently upheld Mississippi's segregation laws. Jones, a Nebraska native, was a "strict constructionist" who defined his duty as the enforcement of law rather than "doing justice." Dawkins, a Democrat appointed to the bench to succeed his father in 1953, later enjoined the Civil Rights Commission from holding hearings in Shreveport and defended his action by claiming, "It is all part of the game." Clayton, appointed to the court in 1957, joined in abstaining from ruling on Mississippi's segregated transportation system, and Grooms, a Kentucky-born lawyer, upheld the segregated bus system of Birmingham and ruled against black university student Autherine Lucy.[40]

Although some of Eisenhower's judicial appointees would later contribute to the legal eradication of Jim Crow, at the time the administration left office it could claim only meager gains in desegregating the South. Many Southern institutions remained

39. Peltason, *Fifty-eight Lonely Men*, 26–28, 86–87; Morton Inger, *Politics and Reality in an American City: The New Orleans School Crisis of 1960* (New York, 1969), 47; Frank T. Read and Lucy S. McGough, *Let Them Be Judged* (New York, 1978), 388.

40. Peltason, *Fifty-eight Lonely Men*, 24–26, 84, 133.

beyond the reach of federal authority, and by 1961 only twenty-four states had enacted public accommodations laws prohibiting segregation and racial discrimination. In the area of school desegregation, despite being handed a mandate for action "with all deliberate speed," the Eisenhower administration largely had abdicated the field in favor of the federal courts. Without assistance from the executive branch, the U.S. Supreme Court had responded by striking down Virginia's pupil placement law (1957), Tennessee's "voluntary" desegregation plan (1957), and Arkansas' school closing law (1959), and a federal district court had ruled Virginia's private school system unconstitutional (1959). Yet, by the 1959–60 school year, only 6.4 percent of Southern black students in grade and high school attended desegregated classes, and only 0.2 percent did so in the Deep South. From the issuance of the first *Brown* decision in 1954 until the fall of 1957, 750 school districts, mostly in border states, had begun at least token desegregation, but from 1957 to 1960, only forty-nine additional districts followed suit. The U.S. Civil Rights Commission reported that no additional districts reported starting desegregation from 1959 to 1961, and in Washington, D.C. and a number of border-state cities — including Wilmington, Delaware; Kansas City and St. Louis, Missouri; and Oklahoma City, Oklahoma — shifting residential patterns produced an accelerated resegregation of school districts.[41]

Not only had the Eisenhower administration failed to speed up Southern compliance with desegregation, in various ways it had continued to subsidize segregation. Under the Library Services Act of 1956, which provided funds for reading services in rural areas, $7.5 million went to segregated Southern libraries. Of Southern libraries contacted by the Civil Rights Commission, only 109 even bothered to respond, and of those that did, only 61 provided desegregated services. Alabama, Georgia, Mississippi, and South Carolina received $5.3 million dollars in National Defense Education Act funds in 1959, and by 1960, the federal government had provided an additional $7.1 billion to eleven recalcitrant Southern states for public school aid and vocational education programs. Nor could Southern states justify acceptance of federal dollars on the basis that they provided "separate but equal" services: in Alabama, the 1958 state school expenditure

41. Milton R. Konvitz, *A Century of Civil Rights* (New York, 1961), 157; John H. McCord, ed., *With All Deliberate Speed* (Urbana, Ill., 1969), 70; Edwin S. Newman, *Civil Liberties and Civil Rights* (Dobbs Ferry, NY, 1967), 89.

per white pupil stood at $144.10; for black students, only $13.11. Similar ratios prevailed in Florida, Georgia, Louisiana, Mississippi, and South Carolina.[42]

Although the Southern states received the brunt of popular and official attention for their officially sanctioned segregation, Northern and Western de facto segregation, supplemented by zoning laws, pupil assignment policies, and district gerrymandering, loomed as an additional, unaddressed problem. In 1960, one-fifth of New York City elementary and junior high schools reported 85 percent or more black and Puerto Rican concentration, and over 44 percent of the city's schools were equally white. Twenty-eight elementary schools in central Detroit, Michigan reported over 90 percent black enrollment levels. In the West, the cities of Los Angeles, Compton, Monrovia, Enterprise, and Willowbrook, California registered over 85 percent student concentration of blacks, Chicanos, or whites; and in two Berkeley schools, blacks comprised over 90 percent of the student body.[43]

The Eisenhower administration could not be blamed for failing to bring about the end of racial segregation, even in the Southern schools alone, for it had never actually advocated the rapid implementation of racial integration. Administration officials from the President on down, however, had defended a policy that rejected "punitive" enforcement measures on the grounds that a hands-off policy would encourage popular acceptance of desegregation. As measured by public opinion surveys, the administration had failed to make progress even according to this criterion. By July 1959, 59 percent of Americans indicated their support for the Supreme Court decision on school integration, but the figure represented only a 3 percent gain nationally from the level of support registered in May 1955. Eisenhower's personal sensitivity to Southern feelings had not produced any great reversal of Southern white opposition, either, as over 70 percent of the South indicated continuing disapproval. The administration's willingness to accept a mere token desegregation of public schools also carried ominous implications for the improvement of Northern white attitudes toward integration. By the end of the decade, although an overwhelming majority in the North asserted that they did not object to sending their children to a school with a "few" blacks, only slightly more than a third assented to sending

42. Aptheker, *Soul of the Republic,*89–90; Mendelson, *Discrimination,* 63.
43. Mendelson, *Discrimination,* 48.

them to a school over one-half black.[44] The product of the Eisenhower administration's passivity in upholding the new constitutional mandate for desegregation was a nation still polarized along sectional lines on even the abstract morality of integration, and a Northern white population itself unprepared to venture beyond tokenism in its implementation.

44. Gallup, ed., *The Gallup Poll,* 1598, 1616.

10.

Search for a Shield: Voting Rights and the 1957 Civil Rights Act

In the series of racial confrontations that followed the *Brown* integration decisions, violent white defense of Jim Crow forced the Eisenhower administration to consider new means of preserving social order and protecting blacks from economic intimidation and physical harm. The continuing desire of officials to avoid direct federal intervention in civil rights disputes encouraged the administration to turn to voting-rights protections as a solution. Administration officials from the President down generally accepted the assumption that enfranchised Southern blacks would possess sufficient power to ensure their own protection. Armed with the ballot, blacks would not need the administration to undertake intervention actions it deemed politically risky and philosophically objectionable. The administration's assumptions of the effectiveness of the vote echoed the words of the English philosopher John Stuart Mill a century earlier: "Rulers and ruling classes are under a necessity of considering the interests of those who have the suffrage, but of those

204

who are excluded, it is in their option whether they will do so or not."[1]

Equal exercise of the franchise had been a central issue of the nation's first Reconstruction, and the Fourteenth Amendment (indirectly) and the Fifteenth Amendment upheld black entitlement to the vote. However, through a variety of legal and extra-legal devices ranging from the "white primary," poll taxes, and literacy tests to economic intimidation and violence, Southern governments and individuals had effectively limited black electoral participation. The very fervor of the white supremacist defense of the "purity" of the ballot contributed to a belief among both blacks and white civil rights supporters that the vote held the key to minority advance. As young Charles Evers remarked in 1946, the way white Southerners guarded the ballot box "let us know there was something mighty good in voting." For many years before the Eisenhower administration, legislative challenges to the poll tax had been offered in the Congress, and on occasion, popular majorities in both the North and the upper South had favored its elimination. But popular sentiment had not been translated into government action, and with the exception of the abolition of the white primary — invalidated by the Supreme Court in 1944 — the Southern system of voter discrimination had remained unaltered. Although according to the 1950 census some 5.7 million nonwhites of voting age resided in the South, only 750,000 of them had been registered to vote in 1948. The figure rose to over a million in 1952, but exclusively in the border South and in urban areas. The "Black Belt" regions of Deep Southern states unabashedly continued their practices of racial exclusion.[2]

In the 1952 presidential campaign, Eisenhower had proclaimed his devotion to the principle of equal political opportunity. At Wheeling, West Virginia on September 9, and at a second campaign stop a month later, Eisenhower decried the existence of the poll tax as "a blemish upon our American ideal of political equality." But in the first two years of the administration leading up to the *Brown* decisions, the new President and his advisors demonstrated little interest in seeking federal protections for black voting rights. In January 1953, Republican senator Everett Dirksen of Illinois introduced legislation calling for a government commis-

1. John Stuart Mill, *Considerations on Representative Government* (New York, 1958), 131.
2. Stephen F. Lawson, *Black Ballots: Voting Rights in the South, 1944–1969* (New York, 1976), 147; Gallup, ed., *The Gallup Poll*, 48, 75, 271; National Jewish Congress and NAACP, *Civil Rights in the U.S., 1952*, 19.

sion to study civil rights problems, including voting discrimination, but the Senate Judiciary Committee quickly shelved it. The Legislative Conference on Civil Rights, after having removed the "red-tainted" Southern Conference Education Fund from its ranks (despite SCEF's leadership on the poll tax issue), then lobbied the new administration for a legislative program. As part of its effort, LCCR steering committee director Will Maslow advocated the creation of a Civil Rights Division within the Justice Department. But although an LCCR delegation met William Rogers, Arthur Caldwell, and Maxwell Rabb in May 1953, the administration did not indicate any new interest in legislative proposals at that time. On the basis of its own research, the Civil Rights Section of the Justice Department's Criminal Division had concluded that Southern grand juries would not cooperate with federal voter registration investigations. As a result, department attorneys instead pursued a voluntary policy of compliance with Southern county clerks through the mediation of local civic leaders.[3]

After *Brown*, however, the pressures on the administration to protect blacks seeking their constitutional rights in the face of white resistance intensified. In addition to using economic intimidation and both the threat and practice of violence, segregationists in the Deep South further tightened their grip on the franchise. In Mississippi, the White Citizens' Council urged blacks to "voluntarily" remove their names from voter registration lists, and the state legislature added a literacy test to its existing requirements. By the end of 1955, fourteen Mississippi counties contained no black voters. In Louisiana, a joint legislative committee led a purge of registration rolls, distributing a "how-to-discriminate" pamphlet to local officials and urging a reexamination of existing black registration for "errors." Continuing advances in black registration in North Carolina and Tennessee still made the overall number of Southern black registrants rise, but Black Belt totals dropped below even their previous meager levels.

The Deep South's crackdown on voter registration carried implications far more ominous for black citizens than merely the deprivation of the right to participate in elections. For example, although Section 243 of the United States Code, Title 18, barred racial discrimination in jury selection, Southern states could avoid the federal law by drawing lists of jurors from voter registration rolls. Aware of the connection between the vote and the protection of other black rights, after *Brown* the Civil Rights Section

3. Sundquist, *Politics and Policy*, 223; Lawson, *Black Ballots*, 144–47.

predicted a rise in both voting rights complaints and civil rights cases generally. In 1953, the Civil Rights Section had received 92 voting-rights complaints, of which 54 were investigated and only 7 resulted in a prosecution. In 1954, the figures rose to 118 complaints, 68 investigations, and 56 grand jury indictments. Criminal Division chief Warren Olney concluded that in view of the *Brown* decision, "it seems likely an increase must be expected in the area of civil rights matters to be investigated and handled."[4]

With the dangers of violent racial confrontation over Southern segregation growing dramatically, both civil rights leaders and the administration looked with new interest at voting-rights protections. In early 1955, the LCCR concluded that the ballot constituted the one indispensable weapon in defending Southern blacks from attack. Nevertheless, the Justice Department still declined to send a representative to the hearings of the House Judiciary Committee to discuss possible remedies. Scolding the attorney general for his absence, Judiciary Committee Chairman Emanual Celler of New York pointed out, "The Attorney General has stated that he cannot take action in many cases because the existing laws are too weak." The publicizing of incidents of racial violence in Mississippi, however, helped shake the Justice Department from its lethargy. In August 1955 the Reverend George Lee, a Baptist minister and black voter-registration leader, was found murdered on the Lincoln County courthouse lawn. Two weeks later, visiting Chicago teenager Emmett Till was also murdered, for the "crime" of whistling at a white woman. To appeals by the NAACP to the Justice Department to halt the "state of jungle fury" in Mississippi, and additional pleas from the Americans for Democratic Action for an FBI investigation, department spokesman Olney replied only that it was the duty of states to protect their own citizens. A local white storekeeper and his half-brother were brought to trial for the Till murder, but were eventually released because "the body was too decomposed to be positively identified."[5]

Though unprepared to intervene in the Mississippi cases, the Justice Department finally did begin a reevaluation of its legislative program. Attorney General Brownell summoned Maceo Hubbard, a black career lawyer in the Civil Rights Section who had

4. David J. Garrow, *Protest at Selma* (New Haven, 1978) 9–10; U.S. Department of Justice, *Annual Report.* (1955), 131–32.
5. Schlundt, "Civil Rights Policies," 188; Parmet, *Eisenhower,* 440; Lawson, *Black Ballots,* 136, 147; *New York Times,* Sept. 8, Oct. 9, 1955; Adams, *Firsthand Report* 335.

helped draft Truman administration proposals, to prepare a report on the Mississippi situation. Hubbard's analysis, which stressed the increase in White Citizens' Council intimidation efforts, was delivered by Olney to Brownell, who then directed the Civil Rights Section to prepare new legislative recommendations. At the same time that the Justice Department was reexamining its own position, Clarence Mitchell of the NAACP organized a civil rights strategy conference that included sympathetic legislative leaders of both major parties. With a consensus of the conferees favoring a legislative emphasis on voting rights protections, Congressman Hugh Scott of Pennsylvania relayed the group's conclusions to the attorney general.

Alarm at Southern violence and calls for solutions intensified with the shotgun attack upon Mississippi black leader Gus Courts in November. Although the Civil Rights Section asked the FBI to conduct a preliminary investigation in the case, bureau agents conducted only one interview with Courts, performed no tests on the shotgun pellets, and quickly turned over their information to local authorities. The White House's resident black official, E. Frederic Morrow, delivered a stern warning to Maxwell Rabb on November 29, advising the minority adviser of the "dangerous" Mississippi situation. Morrow underlined the risk of widespread racial confrontation, citing both the continuing intimidation practiced by the White Citizens' Councils and the development of a Southern black "underground" for armed self-protection.[6]

On December 2, 1955, with the President inactive because of his recuperation from a heart attack, Attorney General Brownell presented his department's suggested policy responses to the cabinet. Eisenhower's own political plans for 1956 still remained in some doubt, and his absence from the meeting, combined with the uncertainty over the party's fate in 1956, encouraged some of the participants to discuss openly the potential political benefits among Northern blacks of administration civil rights advocacy. The attorney general's legislative recommendations included the creation of a bipartisan civil rights commission to investigate Southern violence, the establishment of a civil rights division within the Justice Department, and amendments to the federal code fortifying voting-rights provisions and providing authority for "preventive" injunction suits for civil rights protection. Brownell noted that the Civil Rights Section had identified "moves

6. Lawson, *Black Ballots,* 149–50; Sundquist, *Politics and Policy* 225; Jack Mendelsohn, *The Martyrs* (New York, 1966), 6–19; Morrow to Rabb, Nov. 29, 1955, Roy Wilkins to Morrow, Dec. 2, 1955, Morrow Records, Box 10, DDEL.

organized to prevent Negro voting and to bring economic pressures," and he added that the department was under considerable pressure to investigate the Mississippi violence, particularly the Till murder. The attorney general advocated the creation of the civil rights commission partly to answer the clamor for Justice Department investigations, for he claimed that any threats issued by his department to the White Citizens' Councils in the absence of incontrovertible evidence would only inflame passions.[7]

Following Brownell's presentation, the cabinet weighed the political risks and benefits of the Justice Department proposals. Secretary of State John Foster Dulles, a skeptic toward administration civil rights advocacy, agreed with the attorney general that the Till murder was a tragedy but questioned the wisdom of additional federal involvement in the South. Representing the other side in the administration's internal debate, Nixon declared his support for the Brownell program. The vice president agreed with the attorney general that the creation of a commission to study racial problems could provide the administration a breathing spell from controversial legal interventions. In addition, although Nixon projected the likely defeat of other legislative proposals by the Congress, he still relished the prospect of Democratic congressional squabbling over civil rights during the election year. Referring specifically to the commission proposal, Nixon suggested that a "seed" be planted with "two or three aggressive fellows" in the Congress to urge an investigation of the Mississippi violence. He added that if the Congress chose not to form its own investigative committee but instead considered proposals for a bipartisan commission, the administration could then recommend that the occupant of the vice presidency be designated by statute as its chairman. Congressional adoption of Nixon's scheme could prove to be a political coup for the administration, for it would make it difficult for the Democrats to balance their 1956 ticket by selecting a Southerner as a vice-presidential nominee and therefore a prospective chairman of a civil rights commission.[8]

Ten days later, Brownell repeated his proposals before Republican legislative leaders. The party leadership, expressing great skepticism that civil rights proposals would clear both houses, requested at the minimum that the administration delay submission of any bills until late in the coming session. Despite the

7. Parmet, *Eisenhower*, 444–45.
8. Ibid., 445; Adams, *Firsthand Report*, 336.

discouraging assessments from the Congress, discussion of the Civil Rights Section's ideas continued within the Justice Department. On January 5, 1956, the attorney general met with Deputy Attorney General Rogers, executive assistant John V. Lindsay, Solicitor General J. Lee Rankin, Assistant Attorney General Olney, Civil Rights Section chief Arthur Caldwell, and FBI Director Hoover to discuss the draft proposals. The early drafts of legislation considered in department session included creation of a five-member civil rights commission, elevation of the Civil Rights Section to divisional status, amendments to Sections 241 and 242 of Title 18 of the federal code permitting civil suit initiation, and additions to Section 594 (the Corrupt Practices Act) and Section 1971 of Title 42 broadening department authority in voting rights cases.[9]

The amendments to the federal code proposed by the Civil Rights Section constituted the most ambitious and controversial parts of the civil rights package. The Section 241 and 242 amendments, the basis of the later Part III of the civil rights bill, extended the coverage of the federal conspiracy statute against civil rights deprivations to the actions of individuals, increased the penalties for violations resulting in loss of life, listed specific civil rights encompassed within the law, and authorized the attorney general to bring civil injunction suits against obstructions of any civil rights covered in the conspiracy statute. The remaining additions, later the bill's Part IV, were targeted directly at voting rights. Section 594 amendments extended legal protections to cover primary and special elections, and Section 1971 additions broadened a Reconstruction era statute to permit individuals to sue for redress of voting violations, granted the attorney general power to seek injunctive relief, and gave the federal courts direct jurisdiction. Although the attorney general also had asked originally for antilynching provisions, the Civil Rights Section, noting the infrequency of lynching incidents, only proposed increased criminal sanctions against a lynch mob (defined as a conspiracy to use violence to prevent an orderly trial). In the Justice Department's subsequent series of discussions, consideration of any antilynching amendments quickly was abandoned.[10]

While the Justice Department continued its own deliberations on the statutory amendments, the White House proceeded with

9. Lawson, *Black Ballots*, 152; "Legislative Leaders Meeting," Dec. 12, 1955, Whitman File, Legislative Meetings Series, Box 1, DDEL.
10. Anderson, *Eisenhower*, 5, 15–17.

its own plans to submit a limited bill, featuring the civil rights commission proposal, to Congress. On January 12, Congressman Hugh Scott informed reporters that the administration was drafting a civil rights message with "specific proposals for legislation." On the nineteenth, reporter Robert G. Spivack of the New York *Post* asked the President at a news conference about reports that the administration would recommend the creation of a commission to study the problem of anti-Negro violence. Eisenhower replied cautiously, "Now, I don't remember that I said "Negroes,' " but he did not deny the reports. On January 30, Scott notified Sherman Adams of his willingness to sponsor the administration's bill, pointing out that his congressional district included 22,000 black and 60,000 Jewish voters. Having been informed of the reservations of Republican congressional leaders toward the other administration civil rights suggestions, the President transmitted from Key West, Florida his initial endorsement only of the commission proposal. Citing "allegations" of voting-rights deprivals and economic intimidation, Eisenhower gave the civil rights commission idea specific mention in his February 5 State of the Union message.[11]

On the same day as the President's message to Congress, the attorney general convened another departmental meeting on the remaining legislative proposals drafted by the Civil Rights Section. In the meeting, section chief Arthur Caldwell stressed the need for legislation to enhance department civil suit authority in behalf of black registration and voting. Caldwell pointed out that the pursuit of criminal prosecutions "after the fact" would not help blacks in time to enable them to vote in local elections, and he urged legislative concentration on preventive suit authority. Caldwell asserted, "The heart of the whole problem of racial discrimination lies in determined efforts to prevent the Southern Negroes from participation in local government through the use of the vote." Prior to the February 5 meeting, the Civil Rights Section had added two amendments of sections 1983 and 1985 of Title 42 to Part III, as well as an amendment to Section 1343 of Title 28 of the federal code. The Title 42 changes permitted the government to bring suit for the injunctive relief of private persons, and the Title 28 amendment allowed the filing of such suits directly in federal courts. However, following Caldwell's advice to empha-

11. Ibid., 25; *New York Times*, Jan. 20, 1956; Lawson, *Black Ballots*, 157; Eisenhower, *Waging Peace*, 153; Harlow to Rogers, Feb. 6, 1956, Gerald Morgan Records, Box 6, DDEL.

size civil suit voting relief and the urgings of other department officials to simplify the legislation, Civil Rights Section attorneys dropped their plans for a list of specific civil rights, greater conspiracy law penalties, and the repetitive amendments to Section 1983 of Title 42. In early March, other "inflammatory" material, including a list of specific Southern civil rights violations that had been compiled in January by the Civil Rights Section, also was trimmed from the bill.[12]

The existence of the Justice Department's sessions on civil rights legislation could not be concealed indefinitely from the press, and late in February details of the deliberations leaked out. Columnist Drew Pearson reported that the department was about to submit bills to the Congress asserting federal authority in state and local elections. A week later, the Washington *Daily News* stated that the administration planned to give the attorney general a stronger hand in voting rights through the establishment of a fact-finding commission, a new Civil Rights Division, and increased civil injunction powers. The reports were accurate, for on March 5 the attorney general gave his approval to the final version of the four-part civil rights bill prepared by his department. On March 7, during discussions with New Jersey senators H. Alexander Smith and Clifford Case, Brownell gave the legislators permission to announce that the administration bill would reach the capital in a few days.

By early March 1956, even before the legislation's public release, both the Justice Department's internal discussions and press and congressional speculation had affixed to it the clear label of a "voting-rights bill." Because the bill emphasized voting protections, Brownell himself did not see it as unduly provocative to the South. His willingness to support increased civil suit authority, in fact, was predicated on the belief that it offered a means to assist black vote seekers without provoking Southern hostility by sole resort to dramatic criminal prosecutions. Department reliance on criminal sanctions instead of "preventive" civil injunction authority, the attorney general privately warned, would only "stir up an immense amount of ill-feeling in the community and inevitably tend to cause very bad relationships between state and local officials on the one hand and the federal officials responsible for the investigation and prosecution on the other."[13]

12. Anderson, *Eisenhower*, 19–20; Lawson, *Black Ballots*, 153.
13. Anderson, *Eisenhower*, 26–28; Lawson, *Black Ballots*, 153.

The attorney general, however, had not counted upon concerted opposition to administration civil rights legislation from other cabinet members and White House staffers. Brownell resubmitted his package to the cabinet on March 9, but J. Edgar Hoover's ominous briefing on Southern racial tensions effectively undercut the attorney general's arguments. Admitting that the Till murder had been a great boon to the Communist party in the South, the FBI director nevertheless maintained that any additional administration activity at the time to counter violent white resistance could be detrimental to social peace. Brownell, first defending his commission proposal, responded by claiming that the new body would merely "investigate allegations of deprivations of voting rights" and would neither "engage in witchhunts" nor "become the tool of any private pressure group." Brownell then added that the entire legislative package did not anticipate that "extensive use of civil remedies by the Department of Justice will be made in civil areas other than voting." With general cabinet support evidenced for the creation of the new commission and the Civil Rights Division, but not for parts III and IV, the President ordered a delay in transmission of the bill to Congress pending a final review and additional White House staff conferences with the attorney general.[14]

Following the March 9 cabinet session, Justice Department representatives began consultations with White House legal counsel Gerald Morgan, who recommended further narrowing of the bill to emphasize voting-rights protections. Upon Morgan's instructions, Section 594 corrupt-practices provisions were eliminated, as was Title 28 language for direct federal court jurisdiction in voting cases. As amended by the White House, the bill was resubmitted on March 20 to Republican legislative leaders, but Senate Minority Leader William Knowland repeated his assertion that there was "little prospect" of congressional approval for any proposals beyond those of the commission and the Civil Rights Division. On the twenty-third, the cabinet resumed deliberations on the bill, but the meeting quickly demonstrated that the Justice Department's modifications still had not bridged the differences between members. Lacking an administration consensus in favor of the entire package, Eisenhower again ordered the attorney general to delay the bill's submission to Congress.[15]

14. Personal and Confidential Memorandum for the Attorney General," March 9, 1956, Whiteman File, Cabinet Series, Box 6, DDEL.
15. Adams, *Firsthand Report*, 337–38; Anderson, *Eisenhower*, 36–37; "Pre-

On the day after the cabinet discussions, a skeptical Eisenhower, joined by Adams and Morgan, reviewed the entire civil rights package with the attorney general. Fearing that the South would see the bill as an unwarranted extension of federal power, the President warned Brownell not to appear as "another [Charles] Sumner," but after hearing the attorney general's arguments he issued a weak approval for Brownell to "go ahead with it if he wishes." Adams and Morgan cautioned Eisenhower, however, that he should not authorize a civil rights statement to Congress unless he felt greater conviction of its wisdom. Seeking to ease his worries, Eisenhower conferred privately with Brownell after Adams and Morgan departed, and the attorney general emerged from the private session indicating that he had gotten the President's "complete okay." Although no record of the private meeting surfaced, it is likely that Eisenhower gave Brownell permission to submit the entire package to Congress, but only with restrictions on its presentation that resembled those placed on the first *Brown* school integration brief. Parts I and II — the civil rights commission and the Civil Rights Division — could be presented by Brownell under clear administration sponsorship. Parts III and IV, however, would be identified not as administration proposals, but merely as "suggestions" offered by the attorney general in his capacity as a legal expert.[16]

With the administration's civil rights program shelved by executive branch disagreements until after the Easter recess, the House of Representatives began consideration of its own bills. A subcommittee of the House Judiciary Committee approved a bill authored by Congressman Emanuel Celler of New York, and Celler scheduled full committee hearings on civil rights legislation for April 10. Although invited to testify, as late as April 6 the attorney general still had not indicated whether or not he would appear at the hearing. On April 9, Brownell finally transmitted administration drafts of civil rights commission and Civil Rights Division proposals to both houses of Congress, and he added an accompanying statement urging consideration of the Part III and Part IV provisions. In a memorandum on the legislation sent to White House congressional liaison Bryce Harlow, the attorney

Legislative Meeting," March 20, 1956, Whitman File, Legislative Meetings Series, Box 2; "Memorandum for the Record," March 23, 1956, Whitman File, Cabinet Series, Box 7; Folsom to Brownell, March 19, 1956, Gerald Morgan Records, Box 6, DDEL.

16. Richardson, *Eisenhower*, 112; "Memorandum for Ann Whitman," Whitman File, Subject Series, Box 61, DDEL.

general explained his reasons for submitting all four parts. Denying that "any vast expansion of personnel will be needed," Brownell emphasized the need for preventive civil suit powers "to permit litigation at an early-enough stage to prevent violations of the federal law and hence to make unnecessary federal criminal prosecutions." Asserting that the primary function of the package was to uphold the Fifteenth Amendment, he added: "It is not contemplated that extensive use of civil remedies by the Department of Justice will be made in civil rights areas other than voting."[17]

On April 10, the attorney general testified before the House Judiciary Committee. Stating that "it is essential to prevent extremists from causing irreparable harm," Brownell stretched his understanding with the President to the maximum and spoke in support of both the administration's proposals and his department's "suggestions." As finally delivered to Capitol Hill, Part I of the administration's package called upon Congress to create a six-member civil rights commission. The new commission, with no more than three members from either major party, would have the authority to issue subpoenas and take testimony, and would deliver a final report within two years, the time of its expiration. Part II of the bill provided for the elevation of the Civil Rights Section of the Criminal Division to divisional status, with its own assistant attorney general. Part II was a logical corollary to the rest of the Justice Department package, for by broadening the scope of activity beyond criminal law alone, it clearly anticipated a civil rights enforcement role in the field of civil actions. Separately from the rest of the package, the attorney general submitted his department's modified parts III and IV. The pared-down Part III now only contained amendments to Section 241 of the U.S. Code, Title 18 extending the conspiracy statute to the acts of individuals, and changes to Section 1985 of Title 42 authorizing the Justice Department to initiate civil suits for injunctive relief of private persons. Amendments in Part IV called for changes in Section 1971 of Title 42 to permit individuals to sue for civil redress of voting-rights denials and to give the attorney general authority to seek injunctive relief in voting cases.[18]

In his responses to committee members' questions about the

17. Anderson, *Eisenhower*, 37–38; Sundquist, *Politics and Policy*, 227; Brownell to Harlow, Apr. 10, 1956, Harlow Records, Box 8, DDEL.

18. "Proposed Statement of the Attorney General," Apr. 10, 1956, Harlow Records, Box 8, DDEL.

legislation, Brownell urged Congress to act on all four sections of the civil rights bill. When asked if all four parts carried administration support, he replied, "Yes, I think I am authorized to say, as the letter in fact points out, that these are submitted for the consideration of the Congress. I also say that if the Congress doesn't pass them at this session, important as we think they are, then we certainly want them considered by the Commission." In an exchange that to observers had the sound of a rehearsed dialogue, Republican Kenneth Keating of New York requested Justice Department "assistance" in putting parts III and IV into legislative form, and Brownell responded, "We could do that very easily, Mr. Congressman, and we would be very happy to do that." Keating's arrangement with the attorney general for departmental "assistance" thereby enabled parts III and IV to be "bootlegged" up the Hill without direct administration sponsorship.[19]

On the Senate side of the Capitol, Senator Everett M. Dirksen and seventeen other legislators immediately introduced the first two parts of the civil rights bill. As in the House, the remaining two sections were separated from the rest of the legislation, and then were submitted later after "laundering" by Dirksen, Clifford Case, and thirteen other senators on April 24. Attempting to rally support for the administration package in public speaking appearances, on May 6 Brownell declared in a speech before the Ohio Junior Chamber of Commerce, "At the core of freedom is the right to vote." Before a Senate judiciary subcommittee, however, he was forced to confess that his department actually had drafted all four parts of the civil rights bill all along, and subcommittee chairman Thomas Hennings, angry because of Brownell's previous unwillingness to testify at congressional hearings, engaged him in a series of heated exchanges. Although the full Judiciary Committee later approved all four bills, none were reported to the Senate floor in 1956. Upon the advice of Senate Majority Leader Lyndon Johnson, the legislation remained bottled up in committee in order to avoid an embarrassing filibuster by Southern Democrats before the scheduled adjournment.[20]

In the House of Representatives, civil rights supporters lobbied the White House for additional assurances of administration backing for the entire package. On May 3, Bryce Harlow transmitted a

19. Sundquist, *Politics and Policy*, 228; Anderson, *Eisenhower*, 40–41; Lawson, *Black Ballots*, 156.
20. Anderson, *Eisenhower*, 41–42; "Address of the Attorney General Before the State Convention of the Ohio Junior Chamber of Commerce," May 6, 1956, ADA Papers, Administrative File, Box 8, SHSW.

letter to Congressman James Roosevelt stating that "the President has asked me to assure you" that Eisenhower had approved the various bills before their submission to Congress. But after the approval of the entire administration package by the House Judiciary Committee, a White House "must list" of pending legislation issued on May 24 included only the first two parts of the bill. Assistant Press Secretary Murray Snyder left little doubt but that the omissions were intentional. Although Harlow and Rabb, eyeing the upcoming election, sought an open presidential declaration of support for all four parts of the bill, Eisenhower insisted that "there were only two I ever did send down as recommendations for legislation." On June 27, the House Rules Committee adopted an open debate rule for floor consideration of the bill. With White House staff pressure exerted to line up Republican congressmen in support of reporting the bill out of committee, the package did reach the House floor. After continued wrangling about whether the entire bill carried administration endorsement, however, Republican congressional leaders drafted a legislative agenda for the final few weeks of the session that included only the commission and Civil Rights Division proposals among its fourteen priority measures. The full House of Representatives managed to pass all four parts of the administration bill before adjournment by a vote of 279 to 126, but the Senate's inaction resulted in stalemate.[21] Congress adjourned in 1956 without passage of any civil rights legislation.

Outside critics blamed Southern Democrats for blocking Senate floor action, but they also charged the White House with placing politics above legislative accomplishment by submitting the civil rights bill late and waffling on support for it. "If the Eisenhower Administration had had the faintest serious desire to pass a civil rights bill, the bill would have been introduced at the beginning of the session and pushed with maximum power thereafter," columnist Joseph Alsop charged. "The sole intention . . . was to encourage the Democrats to stage an intraparty Donnybrook Fair." However transparent the motivation of political expediency, the administration's authorship of civil rights proposals did serve the purpose of damaging the Democrats' standing with Northern black voters. The Pittsburgh *Courier*, already an administration supporter, carried the headline, "Dixie Democrats Kill

21. Parmet, *Eisenhower*, 448; Harlow to Diggs, June 7, 1956, Official File, Box 282; Keating to Harlow, July 17, 1956, Harlow Records, Box 8, DDEL; Sundquist, *Politics and Policy*, 228–29; Anderson, *Eisenhower*, 61.

Negro Vote." White House backers of the entire civil rights package also used the political opportunity presented by Southern Democratic intransigence to urge the President to issue a more enthusiastic endorsement. Maxwell Rabb counseled Eisenhower that a presidential indication of support for civil rights legislation would provide greater "operating depth" to "strengthen our political position vis-à-vis the coming election." The minorities adviser and his colleagues eventually got their wish, for on October 15 Eisenhower belatedly endorsed all four parts of the civil rights bill in a statement issued to the American Civil Liberties Union. The presidential voting returns on election day vindicated the advice of Eisenhower's civil rights advocates, for the President compiled impressive gains among urban and middle-class blacks without sacrificing significant numbers of white votes.[22]

Although the attention of the White House was fixed upon the election and upon the international crises of Hungary and Suez in the summer and fall of 1956, the Justice Department was at the same time receiving new evidence of massive Southern resistance to black voting. In May, the department gathered complaints against a Louisiana voter registration "purge," and the Criminal Division ordered an FBI preliminary investigation of ten of the state's parishes. Although a request of the Civil Rights Section for immediate suit action in the absence of congressional action on the civil rights bill was rejected at higher levels, Criminal Division chief Olney reported on the charges against Ouachita Parish to the Senate Judiciary Subcommittee on Privileges and Elections. The Civil Rights Section sought additional voting information from six Southern states, and Arthur Caldwell requested FBI assistance in seeking data from state election officials. However, J. Edgar Hoover declined to help, claiming that the request did not concern "a violation of any federal statute within our jurisdiction." Hoover persisted in his refusal to authorize an FBI role in Justice Department information-gathering activities, for he viewed such actions as placing the bureau in an advocacy position toward pending civil rights legislation.[23]

In response to filed sworn complaints from black vote seekers, the FBI did conduct an investigation of election law violations in the ten Louisiana parishes, and its report documented that black

22. Sundquist, *Politics and Policy*, 229–30; Lawson, *Black Ballots* 157, 162; Eisenhower, *Waging Peace*, 154.
23. Lawson, *Black Ballots*, 161; Elliff, "Aspects of Federal Civil Rights Enforcement" 648–51; John V. Lindsay to Jack Toner, Nov. 28, 1956, Persons Records, Box 12, DDEL.

registration levels had been slashed drastically. Justice Department attorneys presented their evidence to a federal grand jury assembled on December 4, but although the panel remained in session for thirteen days, it issued no indictments. A second grand jury session, meeting sporadically from January 29 to February 12, also produced no indictments. On February 12 alone, despite the clear demonstration of voting discrimination in Bienville, Jackson, and Ouachita parishes, the grand jury refused even to call any witnesses. Louisiana's actions against black registrants were representative of those in other Deep South states in 1956, for in Mississippi only 20,000 of 497,350 voting age blacks were registered, in Alabama only 53,336 of 516,245, and in Georgia only 163,380 of 633,390.[24]

With both Eisenhower's November election gains and the evidence of continuing discrimination in the South providing renewed justification for administration legislative activity, Brownell notified Republican leaders in December of his intention to resubmit the civil rights package to Congress early in 1957. The President himself, although still reluctant to deliver a public civil rights message, also indicated his support for congressional reconsideration of "moderate" proposals. From within the Justice Department, Warren Olney added the endorsement of the Criminal Division, proclaiming that "the key civil right is the right to vote. Wholesale discrimination against substantial groups in a community cannot exist under our democratic system unless those groups are also deprived of an effective voice at the polls." On January 10, President Eisenhower delivered his State of the Union message, and the address included administration endorsement of all four parts of the civil rights package.[25]

The Justice Department's urgency in obtaining protective legislation was heightened by continued Southern violence in the early months of 1957, although black calls for immediate federal intervention still fell on deaf ears. On the same day as the President's message to the Congress, a black church was bombed in Montgomery, Alabama, and the Reverend Martin Luther King, Jr., called upon Eisenhower to leave the capital and issue "wise counsel" in a chosen Southern city. Upon the advice of Sherman Adams and Brownell that a presidential declaration in the South

24. Javits, *Discrimination—USA*, 121–24.

25. Lawson, *Black Ballots*, 165; "Notes on Legislative Leaders Meeting," Dec. 31, 1956, Whitman File, Legislative Meetings Series, Box 2, DDEL; Warren Olney, "The Government's Role in Defending Civil Rights," Apr. 5, 1957, ADA Papers, Administrative File, Box 9, SHSW.

"could not possibly bring any constructive results," Eisenhower rejected King's suggestion and also a proposal of Adam Clayton Powell that the President issue a statement from the capital. By January 25, correspondence between Alabama Governor James Folsom, Attorney General Brownell, and Eisenhower revealed that federal officials saw no legal basis for intervention. Renewed calls from King and other black leaders for a private meeting with Eisenhower received the President's reply on February 6: "I have a pretty good and sizable agenda." Two days later, however, Eisenhower departed on a twelve-day vacation to Thomasville, Georgia. The Justice Department proved scarcely more receptive, responding to a second plea for protection by Clarence Jordan of the Koinonia Community in Americus, Georgia on January 22 with the disclaimer that the department lacked jurisdiction.[26]

In the absence of public presidential declarations on civil rights or direct Justice Department interventions to investigate racial violence, civil rights leaders sought to rally public attention to the crisis in the South through organizing a massive demonstration in Washington, D.C.. Led by Martin Luther King, Jr., the conferees planned a "Prayer Pilgrimage for Freedom" to coincide with the third anniversary of the *Brown* decision. However, acting as a White House "mole" in the planning sessions was Adam Clayton Powell, who kept administration officials briefed on the group's plans. In addition to advocating restraint to his fellow conferees in order to insure that nothing in the rally would embarrass the President, Powell also relayed all details of the discussions to the White House. To the clear relief of administration officials, the May 17 ceremonies at the Lincoln Memorial drew far fewer than the fifty thousand participants first predicted by the organizers, and the national press gave the rally only limited attention.[27]

While the administration carefully evaded attempts by civil rights leaders to push it toward a public stance on the South's racial turmoil, its civil rights proposals continued their tortuous path through the Congress. On February 4, 1957, a subcommittee of the House Judiciary Committee called new hearings on the administration bill that lasted nearly a month. In the Senate, Brownell appeared before the Judiciary Committee and denied the accusation of North Carolina Senator Sam Ervin that the ad-

26. Parmet, *Eisenhower*, 504; Lyon, *Eisenhower*, 731–32; Brownell to Eisenhower, Jan. 25, 1957, Persons Records, Box 12; Clarence L. Jordan to Eisenhower, Jan. 22, 1957; Morrow Records, Box 11; Governor Marvin Griffin to Brownell, March 5, 1957, Persons Records, Box 12, DDEL.
27. Parmet, *Eisenhower*, 505–8.

ministration envisioned the use of federal troops to enforce injunction orders. In a revelation with later ramifications in the Senate floor debate, however, Brownell admitted that Justice Department requests for injunction suit powers could apply not only in the voting rights field but also in school integration cases. Following the attorney general's testimony, Senate Minority Leader William Knowland warned the White House privately that Southern Democrats planned to use the fear of federal intervention in integration issues as a ploy to sabotage the bill. Knowland also informed the President that Senate opponents were determined to keep civil rights legislation off the Senate floor until the middle of May.[28]

In committee markups of the bill in both the House and Senate, Southern amendments surfaced calling for a jury trial requirement in any contempt cases spawned by Justice Department civil suits. Viewing the clear focus of the bill as the defense of black access to the ballot, on April 17 the President stated his opposition to mandatory jury trials. Calling a contempt case a "matter of fact" rather than a "matter of law," Eisenhower asserted that it would be wrong to "put it in the hands of a jury." Warren Olney labeled the jury trial amendment a "clever device to nullify the civil rights bill." The Criminal Division chief added, "If enacted with this amendment the new law would be no more effective than present laws in protecting the constitutional right to vote." Responding to an additional attempt in committee to water down the bill through a "right-to-work" amendment, press secretary James Hagerty advised the President to simply assert that right-to-work legislation was matter best left to the states. Although the House Judiciary Committee responded by approving a slightly modified version of the administration's bill, continuing Senate discussion of amendments to the legislation prompted Eisenhower to issue a second repudiation of any jury-trial provision as "welcoming anarchy" in the legal process.[29]

On June 18, the full House of Representatives passed the administration's civil rights bill by a vote of 286 to 126. With full attention now directed upon the Senate's deliberations, Minority Leader Knowland attempted to speed floor consideration by raising objections to the routine referral of the bill to the Rules Committee. Knowland's efforts were aided by Nixon, who as

28. Lawson, *Black Ballots*, 169.
29. "Pre-Press Conference Briefing," Apr. 17, 1957, Whitman File, Diary Series, Box 23; "Pre-Press Conference Briefing," May 15, 1957, Whitman File, Diary Series, Box 24, DDEL; Lawson, *Black Ballots*, 172–73.

Senate presiding officer upheld the minority leader's request over the objections of Senator Richard Russell of Georgia. The Senate rejected a point of order offered by Russell on a 45 to 39 vote, and the leadership scheduled debate on the motion to begin floor consideration for July 8, immediately following the holiday recess. Despite Knowland's successful maneuver, however, all was not rosy for the fate of the administration bill. The minority leader warned the President on July 2 that although the Senate would likely approve bringing the bill to the floor, a motion to strike Part III from the legislation could prevail.[30]

Knowland's warnings were borne out the next day when Senator Russell delivered a stinging attack upon the administration package on the Senate floor. Denying that the intent of the bill was "moderate," Russell claimed that the Justice Department had sought civil suit authority as a pretext for reviving Reconstruction "force bill" use of federal troops to uphold desegregation orders, and he called for a "national referendum" on civil rights legislation before its full consideration by the Senate. Although the President quickly rejected Russell's call for a referendum, privately he was alarmed at the senator's description of the legislation's intent. Eisenhower had based his support of the bill upon the belief that it specifically protected voting, not "any civil right," and his conviction had been reinforced by information provided to him by the attorney general on the extent of Mississippi voting-rights denials in the 1956 election.[31]

On July 4, Eisenhower publicly voiced his concern over the implication of Russell's remarks. Referring to the administration bill's Part III powers, he admitted, "I was reading parts of that bill this morning and I — there were certain phrases I didn't completely understand." The President requested clarification from the Justice Department, and Warren Olney prepared a memorandum on the "Authority of the President to Use the Armed Forces to Enforce Civil Rights Decrees." Olney repeated his department's reassurances that voting rights remained the primary focus of the legislation, but he admitted that under existing authority federal troops could be used to uphold court orders. In a meeting with Republican leaders Knowland and Charles Halleck, Brow-

30. Eisenhower, *Waging Peace*, 154–55, "Legislative Leaders Meeting," July 2, 1957, Whitman File, Legislative Meetings Series, Box 2, DDEL.

31. "Pre-Press Conference Briefing" and telephone call, July 3, 1957, Whitman File, Diary Series, Box 24; "Supplemental Notes," July 9, 1957, Whitman File, Legislative Meetings Series, Box 2, DDEL.

nell also conceded that Part III provisions did permit injunctive action in areas other than voting-rights matters. The two legislators replied that modifications of the bill would be necessary to ensure Senate passage.[32]

Troubled by the specter of federal troop intervention in desegregation cases, the President on July 10 conferred privately with Senator Russell. Although Eisenhower was unable to shake Russell's conviction that Part III would produce military intervention in the South, he reassured the Senator that in his view the "overriding provision" of the bill was the "citizen's right to vote." Russell in turn gave his "private" assurance that "in the matter of voting rights they agreed on the justice and need for his [Eisenhower's] stand." With the President's approval, senators Knowland and Hubert Humphrey sought to assuage Russell's concerns by offering an amendment to Part III repealing the applicability of the 1866 troop authority. The amendment quickly passed by a vote of 90 to 0. On July 16, the President reissued a routine endorsement of the administration civil rights bill, but his lukewarm support for Part III now had disappeared entirely. When asked at a press conference whether the administration intended to expand the attorney general's powers to impel school integration, Eisenhower replied hesitantly, "Well, no ... I think the voting right is something that should be emphasized." He went on, "If in every locality every person ... is permitted to vote ... he has got a means of getting what he wants in democratic government, and that is the one [right] on which I place the greatest emphasis." Attorney General Brownell quickly followed Eisenhower's lead, denying on a television interview program that his department had any intention of taking over the responsibility for initiating school integration suits from local school boards.[33]

The President's retreat from a major section of the civil rights package alarmed black officials within the administration. On July 12, E. Frederic Morrow delivered a warning to Sherman Adams of the consequences of an emasculated bill among black voters. On July 18, an outraged Val Washington wrote an angry letter to the President, which colleagues managed to prevent from being delivered. In his draft letter Washington bitterly proclaimed, "I refuse to believe that you would ever compromise any basic right because of pressures from those so prejudiced that they

32. Hughes, *The Ordeal of Power*, 242; Adams, *First Hand Report*, 341.
33. Lawson, *Black Ballots*, 179–83.

wish to continue humiliating loyal citizens." He concluded, "We have a right to share the American way of life — the sweet as well as the bitter." Such complaints received little attention, however, and without serious administration objections the Senate on July 24 adopted an amendment by a 52–38 vote striking Part III from the bill.[34]

Not content with the elimination of Part III, Senate opponents of the civil rights bill sought the attachment of a jury trial amendment that would apply to all federal contempt cases. Warned of the strategem by Senator Everett Dirksen, Eisenhower this time held firm behind the administration position. Replying to an attack on the civil rights bill from former governor James Byrnes of South Carolina, the President wrote: "It seems to me that the public interest in protection of voting rights is at least as great as public interest in maintenance of minimum wages, etc." (the enforcement of which did not require jury trials). On July 27, eleven law-school deans and thirty-four professors added their disapproval of the jury-trial amendment. In a White House staff meeting three days later, Deputy Attorney General Rogers belittled the South's charge that in the absence of jury trials the Justice Department might seek to become a "Gestapo," pointing out that Southern courts and Southern judges would still be responsible for overhearing civil rights litigation. Although the President refused to follow the advice of press secretary Hagerty to deliver an additional public statement on the bill, he maintained his opposition to the jury-trial amendment and ordered Vice President Nixon to lobby wavering Republican senators. Nevertheless, by garnering the support of Western Democrats through Southern appeals to "fairness" and by vote tradeoffs on water project legislation, the jury-trial amendment passed in the Senate by a 51–42 vote on August 1.[35]

Having committed himself to supporting enhanced voting-rights protections, Eisenhower was genuinely disappointed by the Senate's jury-trial vote, which he categorized to the cabinet as a "serious political defeat." Subsequent administration efforts therefore were directed at the restoration of voting-rights provisions without the millstone of the jury trial requirement. Deputy Attorney General Rogers labeled the amended Senate bill a "gun without bullets," and Nixon advocated tabling the entire civil

34. Morrow to Adams, July 12, 1957; draft letter, Washington to Eisenhower, July 18, 1957, Morrow Records, Box 6, DDEL; Eisenhower, *Waging Peace*, 157.
35. "Supplemental Notes," July 23, 1957, and "Pre-Press Conference Briefing," July 31, 1957, Whitman File, Diary Series, Box 24, DDEL.

rights package if doing otherwise meant accepting the Senate's version. The President delivered his own assessment of the Senate bill in a private letter to Georgia native Robert Woodruff. Admitting that "in the interests of gradual education and progress, I had no objection to the elimination of Section III from the bill," Eisenhower still expressed his deep regret at the jury-trial modification to Part IV. Despite the administration's disapproval of the amended civil rights bill, the Senate on August 7 passed it 72 to 18. Motions for a formal conference of House and Senate representatives to iron out differences were defeated, and the President indicated his willingness to veto any final version of the legislation resembling the Senate bill.[36]

Despite the President's hope of claiming administration credit for the passage of voting-rights legislation, the fate of the bill now rested with the Democratic congressional leadership, particularly Senate Majority Leader Lyndon Johnson. Val Washington bitterly attacked Johnson for his previous role in watering down the administration bill: "If a Southern jury would not convict confessed kidnappers of Emmett Till after he was found murdered, why would they convict an election official for refusing to give a Negro his right of suffrage?" Despite his support of the Senate amendments, however, Johnson had his own reasons for wanting the enactment of civil rights legislation in some form. The Democratic party, including congressional Democrats, had suffered in 1956 from its public identification as the haven of Southern civil rights obstructionism, and Johnson himself harbored presidential ambitions for 1960. Johnson also was receiving political counsel from his aides to develop a compromise bill acceptable to the White House. Adviser George Reedy later recalled, "I convinced Johnson that it would be possible to pass a civil rights bill if you limited it to voting rights. Because I had a sense that the Southerners felt guilty about depriving the Negroes of voting. They didn't feel guilty about depriving them of jobs, they didn't feel sensitive about housing, but they were defensive about the vote thing. That they couldn't justify."[37]

As Johnson began work on a compromise formula, Senator Knowland notified the White House of his belief that a bill could be attained that combined parts I and II and Part IV with a narrowed jury-trial provision. On August 16, Gerald Morgan and

36. "Notes of Cabinet Meeting," Aug. 2, 1957, Whitman File, Cabinet Series, Box 9, DDEL; Eisenhower, *Waging Peace*, 159–60.
37. Washington to Lyndon B. Johnson, Aug. 7, 1957, Morrow Records, Box 6, DDEL; Merle Miller, *Lyndon* (New York, 1980), 210–11.

the Justice Department drafted and presented an alternative package to Senate conferees. The new proposal called for the utilization of Part III suit powers upon the written request of local authorities and the removal of jury trials in contempt cases in which the statutory penalties assessed were no more than ninety days in jail or $300. A week later, Johnson offered his own package, which removed Part III but limited the jury-trial amendment to voting-rights cases alone and reduced the maximum statutory penalties for contempt convictions to $300 or a forty-five-day imprisonment. Although many black spokesmen, including Ralph Bunche, Jackie Robinson, and A. Philip Randolph, urged the President to reject the compromise, Republican leaders Knowland and Joseph Martin counseled Eisenhower to accept Johnson's offer. With congressional soundings indicating likely approval of the compromise, the administration gave its go-ahead and the House of Representatives adopted the Johnson modifications by a 279 to 97 vote. After a brief filibuster by Senator Strom Thurmond, the Senate followed suit on August 29 by a 60–15 margin.[38]

Although decidedly weaker than the administration's original bill, the compromise civil rights package gave the President his opportunity to claim a Republican civil rights victory. As a result, on September 9, 1957, Eisenhower signed the 1957 Civil Rights Act into law. In a letter thanking Vice President Nixon for his assistance during the Senate fight, the Reverend Martin Luther King, Jr., issued his personal approval of the final version of the bill, but cautioned: "It is also my conviction that the full effect of the civil rights bill will depend in large degree upon the progress of a sustained mass movement on the part of Negroes."[39] King's words pointed at the uncertain impact of the administration's hard-won voting-rights authority on Southern white resistance. It still remained for Southern officials and private citizens to demonstrate whether they now would honor the black demand for equal participation in the electoral process, underscored by the new Civil Rights Act, or whether they would persist in a course of violent obstruction that would continue to frustrate the administration's hopes of nonintervention.

38. "Supplemental Notes," Aug. 6, 20, 1957, Whitman File, Legislative Meetings Series, Box 2; "Memorandum," Aug. 16, 1957, Morgan Records, Box 6; Powell to Eisenhower, Aug. 30, 1957, Morrow Records, Box 9; telephone calls, Aug. 23, 30, 1957, Whitman File, Diary Series, Box 24, DDEL; Eisenhower, *Waging Peace*, 160–61.
39. King to Nixon, Aug. 30, 1957, Rogers Papers, Box 50, DDEL.

U.S. Naval Photographic Center/Dwight D. Eisenhower Library
President Eisenhower signs the Civil Rights Act of 1957 into law at his
Newport, R.I. vacation residence, September 9, 1957.

11.

The Most Effective and Bloodless Way

The two institutional outgrowths of the 1957 Civil Rights Act—the U.S. Commission on Civil Rights and the Civil Rights Division of the Justice Department—were intended by the Eisenhower administration to operate in a complementary manner to promote black self-protection through the exercise of the ballot. Although the Civil Rights Commission carried the official label of a "fact-finding body," its unstated mission was to provide a bipartisan forum through which Southern discrimination, particularly the denial of the franchise, could be exposed to the public. Administration officials hoped desperately that the exposure of shameful discrimination in itself would help to unite "responsible people . . . in common effort to solve these problems," and would minimize the need for federal intervention to protect black citizens. With the Civil Rights Commission then having provided legitimacy for legal actions by its public exposure of continuing racism, the newly created Civil Rights Division could move selectively to challenge obvious denials of the franchise.

228

The Civil Rights Commission served a useful purpose for the administration both by paving the way for later voting-rights action and by deflecting immediate Southern white discontent away from the Justice Department. The alliance between the CRC and the Civil Rights Division, however, proved an uneasy one at best. The Civil Rights Division needed the commission's fact-finding public activity as a means of exposing discrimination in a way less likely to subject the administration to charges of political motivation or anti-Southern bias. Yet ensuring the CRC's image of bipartisan independence meant that the division had to shy away from hints of direct orchestration of the CRC's fact-finding efforts. The Civil Rights Division's reluctance to assist the CRC's investigations openly in turn frustrated the commission's members on more than one occasion. For given the understandable hesitancy of Southern voting officials to incriminate themselves by turning over their records, the CRC required the active cooperation of the Justice Department in forcing access to evidence. If it cooperated, the Justice Department then risked jeopardizing its dearly sought obscurity in the voting-rights field and in civil rights generally.

As established by the 1957 Civil Rights Act, the U.S. Commission on Civil Rights was a bipartisan, six-member body with a two-year lifespan, possessing the authority to issue subpoenas, call witnesses, consult with local officials, and set up state advisory committees. The members, of whom no more than three could come from a single political party, served without pay except for per diem expenses, but retained a paid staff director and assistants. Although Congress mandated a final report from the commission by September 9, 1959, it took a full ten months for the group simply to gear up for its fact-finding efforts. Part of the delay stemmed from the insistence of the President upon appointing members who would provide an "ameliorating effect" upon the South, represent the "spectrum of America," and also cooperate with the administration's wishes for a low civil rights profile. Finding the "right people" to serve on the CRC, as well as the delays in congressional approval of the nominees, delayed the adoption of a guiding program by the commission for nearly a year.[1]

In an elaborate screening process, White House staffers prepared lists of candidates for possible selection to the CRC. Among those whom staffers suggested to the President were Governor Allan Shivers of Texas, former presidential candidates Adlai

1. Rabb to Adams, Nov. 12, 1957, Morgan Records, Box 6, DDEL; Dulles, *The Civil Rights Commission*, 15–18.

Stevenson and Thomas E. Dewey, industrialist Henry Ford II, former administration officials Oveta Culp Hobby and Charles E. Wilson, and Republican activist Claire Boothe Luce. E. Frederic Morrow and Val Washington, informed that one position on the commission would be reserved for a black representative, submitted separate names for the post. Many of the individuals slated for possible nomination either removed their names from consideration or were rejected during White House scrutiny, and Eisenhower publicly admitted in the fall of 1957 that it was proving "difficult to get exactly what you want."[2] On November 7, the President finally released his initial list of candidates for the CRC. Former Supreme Court justice Stanley Reed, tabbed to head the commission, withdrew his name a month later, and was replaced by Michigan State University president John A. Hannah, former assistant secretary of defense. The remaining five slots on the commission were occupied by Robert G. Storey, dean of Southern Methodist University Law School; former governor of Virginia John S. Battle; Father Theodore Hesburgh, president of Notre Dame University; former Florida governor Doyle Carleton; and Assistant Secretary of Labor J. Ernest Wilkins, a black. The group represented the balance that the President had sought, for the six members were equally divided between North and South and included three Democrats, two Republicans, and one independent.[3]

The guiding philosophy espoused by the new commission's leadership also reflected the President's ultimate success in finding men of moderate persuasion who shared his allegiance to symbolic racial democracy. Hannah, whose exposure to civil rights issues had been limited until confronted with desegregation problems in the Defense Department, viewed the commission's mission as the promotion of domestic peace and a democratic national image abroad. Hannah described civil rights as "the most important single problem facing this country from the standpoint of our domestic tranquility and from the standpoint of long-term relationships with the uncommitted areas of the world that are so vital to the long-time well-being of the country." The President's choice for CRC vice-chairman, Robert Storey, also was well aware of the need to cleanse the American image of the stain of official racism, for he had served as an assistant to Justice

2. Dulles, *The Civil Rights Commission*, 18; telephone call, Sept. 11, 1957, Whitman File, Diary Series, Box 27; "Adams Recommendations for CRC," Morrow Records, Box 10, DDEL.
    3. Eisenhower, *Waging Peace*, 161.

Robert Jackson during the Nuremburg Nazi war crimes trials. Storey later observed: "Today we are caught up in a dynamic challenge to our own democratic ideology—an ideology which revolves about the basic Christian concept of the essential dignity, rights, and responsibilities of the individual person in an organized society."[4]

Because of delaying actions staged by Senator Eastland of Mississippi, the Senate Judiciary Committee did not begin its confirmation hearings on the commission nominees until late February 1958. Responding to Eastland's public outrage at reports of collusion between the CRC and the Justice Department, chairman-designate Hannah reassured the Senate panel that his body would operate independently from the administration. Within two weeks after Hannah issued his public assurance, the full Senate confirmed all the nominees. The commissioners' assumption of their duties, however, was delayed even longer by the Senate's refusal to grant quick confirmation of Gordon Tiffany as the CRC's staff director. Tiffany, an associate of White House chief of staff Sherman Adams and a former attorney general of New Hampshire, received a severe grilling from Southern senators until early April. Denying in testimony before the Judiciary Committee any particular expertise in civil rights, Tiffany promised to follow a course of "moderation" in the performance of his duties and described his role as providing an efficient organizational structure for the CRC. Despite persistent Southern skepticism, the Senate approved Tiffany's nomination on May 15, and he was sworn in on June 9, 1958.[5]

Prompted by the delaying tactics of the CRC's Southern critics in the Congress, funding for the new commission also was delayed. Responding to the need for start-up money, President Eisenhower authorized an allocation of $200,000 from executive emergency funds and requested an additional $750,000 from Congress for the commission's work. Well aware of Southern concern over the intentions of the CRC, Eisenhower asserted that although the commission "has had a hard time getting off the ground," it would nevertheless perform a needed function in the "educational" and "spiritual field." After belated congressional approval of the administration's funding request for the CRC in early summer, Eisenhower signed the authorization on June 25. With financial support finally available, the CRC began to organ-

4. Dulles, *The Civil Rights Commission*, 19–22; Robert G. Storey, "The Report of the Civil Rights Commission," *ABA Journal*, 46 (Jan. 1960), 39.
5. Dulles, The Civil Rights Commission, 23–25.

ize its activities, with staff director Tiffany and his subordinates performing most of the legwork. Each commission member appointed a legal adviser to serve on the staff, and subcommittees were formed to handle diverse functions. The commission also began the process of establishing state advisory committees, and although the selection of individuals willing to serve on the state bodies proved difficult, by August a sufficient number of persons had been chosen to serve in all states except Mississippi and South Carolina.[6]

In setting out a common agenda, members singled out three principal areas for investigation — voting rights, educational desegregation, and housing policy. Of the three, however, voting rights clearly held top priority. Conscious of the need to "avoid irritating Senator Eastland's colleagues" and reduce the risk of further federal–state confrontations in the Deep South, the CRC limited its inquiry into school integration to a single conference in Nashville, Tennessee on March 5–6, 1959, which dealt with the experiences of schools already beginning desegregation. Agreement among members on an agenda for housing hearings was reached only in September 1958, a year before the commission's scheduled expiration, and the public sessions held in New York, Chicago, and Atlanta received far less attention than the CRC's voting rights inquiries.[7]

Commission members themselves expressed a number of reasons for emphasizing the primacy of voting-rights investigations. First, as a matter of internal harmony, voting rights constituted the single civil rights issue upon which members could reach a clear consensus, in sharp contrast to integration issues. In addition, the CRC's political contacts, both within the administration and in the Congress, favored concentration on the ballot. Senator Estes Kefaufer of Tennessee, for example, advised Chairman Hannah, "I hope the Commission will concentrate on this subject [voting], and not wander afield where the result will do nothing but muddy the waters of progress." As the Kefaufer remarks also implied, voting-rights deprivation was the area of discrimination least defensible by white Southerners on moral or legal grounds — a fact recognized by the defenders of segregation and CRC staffers alike.[8]

In the voting rights field the Congress had empowered the CRC to investigate "allegations in writing under oath or affirmation." Upon receiving their initial voting rights complaints in August,

6. Ibid., 25–30; *Public Papers of the Presidents, 1958*, 239.
7. Dulles, The Civil Rights Commission, 28, 30–31.
8. Lawson, *Black Ballots*, 230.

Presidential assistant Sherman Adams swears in the members of the newly created U.S. Commission on Civil Rights. From left: J. Ernest Wilkins, Rev. Theodore M. Hesburgh, John S. Battle, Doyle E. Carlton, Vice-chairman Robert G. Story, Chairman John Hannah, Eisenhower, and Adams.

therefore, CRC staffers began investigations in Alabama and Mississippi, followed by others in Florida, Tennessee, and Louisiana. Field investigators examined ninety-one complaints, interviewed black vote seekers, subpoenaed witnesses, and scheduled public hearings in Montgomery, Alabama for December 1958. The evidence received by the CRC was not wholly spontaneous, for legal adviser Harris Wofford privately solicited voting-rights complaints from Martin Luther King, and the Tuskegee Civic Association sponsored the initial round of Alabama testimony and coached some witnesses. After acquiring black testimony of voting discrimination in Alabama, the CRC sought the records of county voting registrars, but its requests were rebuffed. Attorney General and Governor-elect John Patterson personally denied the CRC access to the records of Macon County, Alabama, and State Circuit Court Judge George C. Wallace impounded the files of Barbour and Bullock counties, threatening to jail CRC investigators if they attempted to gain access.[9]

Despite being frustrated in their efforts to obtain Alabama records, the commissioners decided to go ahead with the Montgomery hearing. To assure an image of regional fairness, Vice-chairman Storey, a Southerner, was selected to preside at the session and lead the questioning. Upon opening the hearing on December 9, Chairman Hannah also emphasized the commission's neutrality as a "fact-finding body." Testimony from twenty-seven black residents, however, soon established the existence of a system of voting discrimination practiced by state officials. The county board of registrars held sessions infrequently, did not publicize them, and held them in a room so small that only two applicants could be received at any time. Blacks seeking registration were subjected to endless waits and were expected to complete complicated forms and copy an article of the state constitution, with a single error or omission grounds for disqualification.[10]

When Macon County officials appeared on the afternoon of the ninth, they persisted in refusing to release their records or to give testimony. One county probate judge admitted under questioning, however, that the absence of fourteen thousand blacks from the voter registration rolls of a county "might be unusual, peculiar

9. Dulles, *The Civil Rights Commission*, 31–33; Garrow, *The FBI and Martin Luther King, Jr.*, 27.
10. CRC, *Hearings . . . Voting: Montgomery, Alabama, Dec. 8–9, 1958, Jan. 9, 1959*, 4, 53–54.

in some places." The obstructionism practiced by the voting officials exasperated even Governor Battle, the South's most fervent defender on the CRC, and he decried the "error" of state officials in denying the franchise to "some people who may be entitled thereto." Attorney General Patterson replied with a heated denial that Alabama had "anything to hide," and he defiantly added, "The time for retreating has come to an end." But although Patterson succeeded temporarily in thwarting the CRC's search for evidence, his actions and those of county registrars helped the commission bring the existence of official deprivations of voting rights to popular notice. Even some Southern newspapers criticized Alabama's actions, and the President felt secure enough of public reaction to issue a statement calling the state's conduct "reprehensible."[11]

Following an anticlimatic second session of hearings, Hannah turned over the Montgomery transcripts to the Justice Department "for such action as he deems appropriate to the end that will assist this Commission to have made available to it the information that is required." Hannah's search for legal help from the department against Alabama officials had been approved by the full commission on a 4 to 2 vote, with Wilkins insisting on a sterner motion and Battle asking for no motion at all. Responding to the CRC request, the Civil Rights Division filed suit in federal district court to force the release of voting data from the three Alabama counties, and District Judge Frank Johnson ordered county officials to provide the registration information to the CRC before January 9, 1959. In spite of the order, however, continued obstruction ensured that only a cursory sampling of the files was accomplished by four commission staffers. Even so, the sample upheld the hearing testimony indicating racial discrimination, for one batch of rejected applications included the forms of 73 blacks and only 11 whites, and another group of 17 accepted applications contained only 1 from a black registrant. The commissioners in executive session unanimously judged that official compliance by the state of Alabama had been unsatisfactory, and they issued a request for additional legal action. But the Alabama state legislature, defying the CRC, responded by enacting bills that authorized the destruction of rejected voter registration applications.[12]

Despite the Justice Department's assistance in bringing suit to

11. Ibid., 131–32, 143, 147, 150–62, 206–7; *New York Times*, Dec. 11, 1958.
12. Dulles, *The Civil Rights Commission*, 39–41.

free Alabama voting records, several CRC members and staffers were dissatisfied at the limited cooperation extended by the administration. Seeking better coordination of commission investigations with White House civil rights policies, Hannah sought to arrange a CRC presentation before the cabinet. Hannah's plans, however, were temporarily frustrated by the new White House chief of staff, Alabama native Wilton B. Persons, who mysteriously "forgot" to schedule the session. In a letter to presidential legal adviser Gerald Morgan, staff director Tiffany added his voice to the calls for greater administration backing for the CRC's efforts, citing the political benefits among black voters and noting that the states refusing CRC requests were controlled by the Democrats. Morgan's reply contained a qualified endorsement for greater coordination of CRC and White House policy statements. In late February of 1959, the President himself pledged the administration's cooperation to chairman Hannah, but a memorandum drafted by White House staffers reiterated the assertion that the commission was "*not* a police agency, *not* an enforcement unit, *not* a pressure group, *not* an action body."[13]

In the aftermath of the Alabama hearings, the CRC scheduled a second set of public sessions on voting rights for July 13, 1959, in Shreveport, Louisiana. But, Louisiana officials, attempting to force the commission to release the names of its complainants, filed a court suit challenging the 1957 Civil Rights Act on he grounds that CRC hearings denied them the opportunity to "confront their accusers." State appeals to a federal district court for a restraining order against the hearings was granted by Judge Benjamin Dawkins just sixteen hours before their scheduled opening. Basing his ruling on the argument that Louisiana officials were not permitted to cross-examine CRC witnesses, Dawkins openly admitted that his order was of dubious constitutionality, but commented, "It is all part of the game." Although the CRC suspended the hearings, preliminary staff investigations had already uncovered strong evidence of an organized campaign to prevent black registration and to purge black names from the rolls. A state joint legislative committee had declared the disfranchisement of blacks as its goal and had distributed a manual to county election officials on ways to maintain the "purity" of the ballot. County

13. "Memorandum for the Files," Dec. 4, 1958, and "Notes," Robert Gray, Dec. 10, 1958, White House Office, Cabinet Secretariat, Box 2; Tiffany to Morrow, July 22, 1959, and "Executive Branch Cooperation with the Commission on Civil Rights," Feb. 27, 1959, Morgan Records, Box 6, DDEL.

registrars had unfairly applied literacy tests in order to remove blacks from voting lists, and two counties had blocked black registration by a rule requiring new voting applicants to be endorsed by two previously registered voters. Other black registrations had been challenged by White Citizens' Council petitions, including one that charged applicants with "errors in spilling [sic]."[14]

The CRC's Louisiana findings, although not brought to public attention through hearings, were included in its report of September 1959 to Congress. The complete report illustrated both the persistent sectional divisions among members on other civil rights issues and the commission's fundamental agreement on the sanctity of voting rights. The commissioners issued "recommendations" on positions with majority support, and offered "proposals" in cases of tie votes. Only Governor Battle objected to the entire report, labeling it "an argument in advocacy of preconceived ideas" rather than an "impartial factual statement." The overall tone of the study was moderate and hopeful, and members reiterated Lincoln's wish that the nation's citizens be touched "by the better angels of our nature."[15]

The voting-rights section of the CRC report recounted the techniques of discrimination practiced in the South, and it revealed that although the number of registered black voters had risen from 595,000 in 1947 to 1 million in 1956, the figure still represented only 25 percent of eligible blacks. In Alabama, although blacks made up nearly 33.3 percent of the voting age population, they constituted only 8.1 percent of the state's registered voters. In Mississippi, the figures were 41 percent and 3.9 percent. In forty-nine Southern counties with black majorities, fewer than 5 percent of blacks were registered, and sixteen Black Belt counties listed no black registrants at all. Among its remedial recommendations the CRC unanimously advocated federal census compilation of voting statistics, congressional action to preserve voter registration records for a minimum of five years, amendments to the civil rights laws prohibiting deprivations of the right to register and vote, and authority for the CRC to appeal directly to federal courts to enforce its subpoenas. An additional recommendation, opposed by Battle, called for the appointment by the President of temporary federal registrars to administer registration in counties the CRC identified as discriminatory, based upon verified com-

14. CRC, *Report (1959)*, 98–106.
15. Ibid., 17, 551.

plaints from nine or more individuals. Commission "proposals" included a constitutional amendment removing remaining constraints on voting. Southerners Carleton and Storey joined Battle in opposing a constitutional amendment on the grounds that the federal government should first have to demonstrate the insufficiency of its existing powers to protect the ballot.[16]

The activity of the CRC in its first two years helped free the administration from the necessity of issuing its own public pronouncements against Southern discrimination. The President's subsequent caution, however, produced its own kind of controversy when, before the black National Newspaper Publishers' Association in May 1958, Eisenhower untactfully advised, "No one is more anxious than I am to see Negroes receive first-class citizenship in this country . . . but you must be patient." Forced to respond to black furor over his call for "patience" and to continuing requests from civil rights leaders for a direct meeting, Eisenhower consented for the only time in his presidency to a private conference with Martin Luther King, Lester Granger, A. Philip Randolph, and Roy Wilkins on July 23, 1958. In the White House session, Wilkins called upon the administration to "protect the rights of citizens to register and vote," asserting, "The right to vote is the most effective and bloodless way to solve the whole problem." The President, however, gave no firm assurances of additional administration activity to protect black access to the vote.[17]

Without White House enthusiasm for greater involvement, the Justice Department and its Civil Rights Division acted with extreme caution in applying its new powers against the voting-rights deprivations revealed by the CRC. Civil Rights Division activity was slowed initially by Senate footdragging on W. Wilson White's confirmation as assistant attorney general because of his role as head of the Office of Legal Counsel during Little Rock. Even after White's confirmation, however, the division followed a restrictive policy of turning over only sworn written complaints to the FBI for preliminary investigations. The FBI, lacking informational contacts with black leaders, being untrained in voting-rights cases, and having a "lily-white" membership, preferred to seek cooperation with local authorities and did not pursue its investigations with great enthusiasm. As for the Civil Rights Division itself,

16. Ibid., 40–54, 136–45.
17. Morrow, *Black Man in the White House*, 218; Parmet, *Eisenhower*, 553; "Memorandum for the Files," June 24, 1958, Official File, Box 737, DDEL.

most of its staff of attorneys were transfers from other sections of the Justice Department, and therefore were untrained in civil rights matters. Because of the division's own limitations and the desire not to offend FBI Director Hoover and Southern congressional leaders, Attorney General William Rogers insisted upon department legal action only in "airtight" cases.[18]

Under White, a former U.S. attorney for the Eastern district of Pennsylvania, the Justice Department's Civil Rights Division filed only four voter discrimination suits under the 1957 Civil Rights Act in two years. In September 1958, Attorney General Rogers obtained the President's approval of the division's request to initiate a suit against officials in Terrell County, Georgia. Rogers explained the year-long delay in filing the suit by claiming that the Terrell County case was the "first time we have felt that the evidence was strong enough to proceed in court." Charging an "arbitrary refusal to register Negroes," the Civil Rights Division presented evidence in state superior court indicating that five black applicants, four of them college graduates, had been denied registration on the grounds of inability to read or write. Judge Walter Gear, condemning the Justice Department's suit as "arrogant and unwarranted," charged that "radical Republican leaders" sought to "intimidate the people of Terrell County." Declaring his "utmost confidence" in the county's board of registrars, Gear ordered the county to withhold its voting records from federal authorities and threatened to jail FBI agents if they interfered with his order. The Civil Rights Division carried its request for an injunction against county officials to federal district court, but on April 16, 1959, Judge T. Hoyt Davis denied the request and ruled the 1957 Civil Rights Act unconstitutional. Final determination of the suit only came in the U.S. Supreme Court on February 29, 1960, when the high court in *United States v. Raines* sided with the Justice Department and upheld the 1957 Civil Rights Act.[19]

Six months after the initiation of litigation in the Terrell County suit, the Civil Rights Division filed a second action against Ala-

18. Arthur B. Caldwell, "Federal Enforcement of Civil Rights," Nov. 13, 1957, Morrow Records, Box 10, DDEL; Allan J. Lichtman, "The Federal Assault Against Voting Discrimination in the Deep South, 1957–1967," *Journal of Negro History* 54 (1960): 347–50.

19. Rogers to Eisenhower, Sept. 1, 1958, Whitman File, Administrative Series, Box 35; telephone call, Sept. 4, 1958, Whitman File, Diary Series, Box 35, DDEL; Peters, *The Southern Temper* 161–162; Garrow, *Protest at Selma*, 12–13; Lawson, *Black Ballots*, 208.

bama officials for their refusal to make available the records of Macon County. In *U.S.* v. *Alabama,* the state's registrars argued that under the 1957 Civil Rights Act only "persons," and not the state itself, could be sued, and they resigned their official posts in order to frustrate attempts to obtain the records. On February 5, 1959, Federal District Judge Frank Johnson denied the Justice Department's injunction petition against state officials, concluding that the Civil Rights Act did not provide for the suing of the state but only of individual officeholders. Two other voter discrimination suits filed in 1959, against officials of Washington Parish, Louisiana, and Fayette County, Arkansas, experienced other roadblocks. In the Louisiana case, registrars were accused of purging black names from voting rolls, and on January 11, 1960 federal judge J. Skelly Wright ordered the restoration of 1,377 names. Ten days later, however, Wright was overruled by a Fifth Circuit Court of Appeals panel. Once again, it fell to the U.S. Supreme Court to reverse the appeals court ruling and uphold Wright's previous order. In the Fayette County case, brought against the Democratic Executive Committee for maintaining a "white primary," litigation began in November 1959, and resolution of the dispute was reached the following April through a consent agreement to end black restrictions.[20]

With the Justice Department's meager legal efforts to provide protection through the ballot subjected to delay and obstruction, acts of terrorism in the Deep South against blacks and their white sympathizers continued. Explosions rocked the meetinghouse of the Hebrew Benevolent Congregation in Atlanta, and Hoover reported to the President on October 14, 1958 that a terrorist group calling itself the "Confederate Underground" had claimed responsibility for the bombing. By the end of 1958, Justice Department officials in the first four years of the administration had recorded six racially motivated killings in the South; twenty-nine other shootings; forty-four beatings; five stabbings; forty-one bombings of homes, churches, and schools; and seven burnings of similar buildings. The lynching of Mack Charles Parker in Mississippi in April 1959 added yet another victim's name to the list. Although the FBI submitted a 378-page report on the Parker murder to the governor of Mississippi, a grand jury refused to issue any indictments.[21]

20. Garrow, *Protest at Selma,* 13–14; Lawson, *Black Ballots,* 209–11.

21. "Pre-Press Conference Briefing," Apr. 30, 1958, Whitman File, Diary Series, Box 32; Hoover to Eisenhower, Oct. 14, 1958, Official File, Box 732, DDEL; Sundquist, *Politics and Policy,* 238–39; Javits, *Discrimination — USA,* 224.

With the continuing violence in the South in mind, the administration sought limited additional legislation in civil rights in early 1959. At a legislative leaders' meeting of December 15, 1958, Attorney General Rogers revealed that his department intended to seek extension of the life of the Civil Rights Commission, subpoena power in voting-rights suits, and additional FBI jurisdiction in bombing cases. After the delivery of his State of the Union message for 1959, the President rededicated himself to efforts "to see this problem of voting solved," for it represented the key, in his view, to "the proper observation of the other rights." On January 28, Labor Secretary Mitchell, HEW Secretary Flemming, Defense Secretary Robert Anderson, and White House staffers reviewed an eight-part legislative program prepared by the cabinet departments. The administration package included a two-year extension for the CRC; imposition of criminal penalties of $10,000 and/or ten years' imprisonment for flight to avoid testimony in bombing cases; similar penalties for impeding federal court orders by force or its threat; preservation of voter registration records for three years, with Justice Department access guaranteed; authority for Part III suit actions; federal aid and technical advice to desegregating schools; jurisdiction for the commissioner of education to ensure desegregated education for military dependents; and the creation of a permanent committee on equal job opportunity.[22]

The administration submitted all of the proposals except the Part III suggestions to the Congress, but officials soon found their package in competition with a bill advocated by Lyndon B. Johnson and another by a group of congressional liberals. The majority leader's proposals included the creation of a community relations service to mediate desegregation disputes, the extension of the Civil Rights Commission, criminal penalties for transportation of explosives across state lines, and Justice Department subpoena power in voting rights suits. Absent from the package were any proposals that might require the Congress to "take sides" in the South's school integration controversies. The liberal program, guided by Senator Paul Douglas of Illinois and Representative Emanuel Celler of New York, included all of the proposals contemplated by the administration plus a renewed request for Justice Department civil suit authority. In the House of Repre-

22. "Notes," Dec. 15, 1958, Whitman File, Legislative Meetings Series, Box 3; Bureau of the Budget to Persons, Jan. 28, 1959, Morgan Records, Box 6; "Memorandum for the President," McPhee Records, Box 3, DDEL; Daniel M. Berman, *A Bill Becomes a Law: The Civil Rights Act of 1960* (New York, 1962), 7–8; Lawson, *Black Ballots*, 221.

sentatives, the Judiciary Committee reported a bill lacking the administration's proposals for school desegregation assistance or an employment committee, and although Celler filed a discharge petition to force the release of the bill from the Rules Committee, he had not gathered the requisite number of signatures at the time of adjournment in September. In the Senate's deliberations, after two and a half months of hearings a judiciary subcommittee reported a clean bill on July 15, but the full committee watered down the proposals and filibustered them to a stalemate.[23]

The only part of the administration's civil rights package to gain congressional approval in 1959 was the two-year extension of the Civil Rights Commission. Before a June 9, 1959 conference of the CRC with state advisory committees, President Eisenhower had endorsed its retention, stating that "at times, I think it holds up before us a mirror so that we may see ourselves, what we are doing, and what we are not doing, and therefore makes it easier for us to correct our omissions." A number of Southern legislators, however, openly wished for the extinction of the CRC, claiming that its upcoming September report would be nothing but a veiled attack upon the region's racial practices. Internal CRC disputes between Battle and J. Ernest Wilkins added fresh ammunition to the Southern claims of sectional bias. Following release of the report, Senator Olin Johnston of South Carolina gleefully pointed out its factual errors, including the attribution of an additional county to his state. Nevertheless, the CRC's Southern opponents had neither the votes nor the public sentiment to force the commission out of business. As CRC legal assistant Harris Wofford observed, the Southern press itself, although criticizing the commission's recommendations, generally joined in the condemnation of the voting discrimination practices cited in the report. Wofford added, "Here, it seems to me, is the open door. The solid South is split on this issue [voting rights]." Wofford's point was illustrated in the Senate, where Majority Leader Johnson obtained a suspension of the rules enabling the renewal of the CRC on the Senate's final day in session. House passage immediately followed by a 227 to 81 vote.[24]

Reminded once again in the 1959 session of the lack of congressional interest in assisting school integration, the administration

23. Berman, *A Bill Becomes Law*, 13–16; Sundquist, *Politics and Policy* 240–44.
24. Berman, *A Bill Becomes Law*, 33–34; *Public Papers of the Presidents, 1959*, 448; Dulles, *The Civil Rights Commission*, 70, 82–85.

narrowed its legislative program for 1960 even more exclusively to the protection of the vote. Harris Wofford noted that the administration clearly had decided to shift from the "frustratingly slow and complex problem of school desegregation to this clearcut issue of voting rights [that] is politically right and psychologically healthy." In addition, the CRC's 1959 recommendation of federal voting registrars impelled new administration legislative initiatives in the voting-rights field. Under the CRC's registrar recommendation contained in its first report, complainants would transmit sworn affidavits directly to the President alleging voting discrimination, and if the President received nine or more complaints from any county, parish, or district, he would be required to refer them to the CRC for verification. If in the CRC's view a pattern of discrimination then was demonstrated, the President would designate a federal representative to act as a temporary registrar until he deemed the registrar's services unnecessary. The CRC's advocacy of federal registrars in the South garnered much favorable comment among civil rights advocates, and the popularity of the CRC's plan mandated the administration's drafting of a comparable alternative.[25]

In response to the registrar idea, the Justice Department in the fall of 1959 drafted its own scheme for the creation of federal "referees." Under the administration plan, the attorney general first was required to file a suit under the 1957 Civil Rights Act seeking an injunction against obstructions of the vote. If the court order was obtained, the department then could request the court to rule additionally that a "pattern or practice" of discrimination existed. If the judge agreed, he could appoint "referees" to receive applications from prospective voters, take evidence, and report their concusions to the court. Unless judged "clearly erroneous," the referees' findings would be accepted, a judicial decree would list the individuals whose qualifications had been substantiated, and the referees would insure that all qualified voters were permitted to vote. Any additional interference could then result in the issuance of a contempt-of-court citation.[26]

Among the advantages Justice Department spokesmen cited for their plan was that offenders would not be guaranteed a jury trial, as they would under the provisions of the CRC proposal. In addition, department attorneys stressed that their approach cov-

25. Lawson, *Black Ballots*, 231; Berman, *A Bill Becomes Law*, 36.
26. Berman, *A Bill Becomes Law*, 44–45.

ered both state and federal elections because it relied upon the Fifteenth Amendment as its legal basis. The CRC's recommendation, they argued, might produce a "separate and unequal" voting system because it relied upon Article I, Section 4 of the Constitution (providing for the control of Congress over federal elections) as its statutory basis. Attorney General Rogers, in scorning the CRC plan, claimed: "When a federal registrar gives a Negro one of these [registration] certificates, it is going to be . . . worth about as much as a ticket to the Dempsey-Firpo fight." What Justice Department speakers did not mention publicly was another, less flattering, reason for their opposition to the CRC's approach. The CRC plan, unlike that of the administration, required the President to inject himself directly into voting rights protection activity. Given Eisenhower's aversion to direct involvement in civil rights enforcement and the administration's insistence that the federal judiciary bear the burden of implementation, it was not surprising that the Justice Department drafted an alternative that continued federal reliance upon the cumbersome processes of the judicial system.[27]

Wrangling between representatives of the CRC and the White House continued throughout the fall and winter of 1959, with each side defending the merits of its position. Harris Wofford transmitted a memorandum to presidential speech writer Malcolm Moos advocating administration acceptance of the commission's approach on the grounds that civil rights groups preferred it and, given CRC vice-chairman Storey's friendship with Lyndon Johnson, the majority leader also might support it. In December, the President did discuss the CRC's recommendations personally with chairman John Hannah. However, maintaining his distance from civil rights legislation generally, in his State of the Union address in January Eisenhower issued only a vague call to Congress to give consideration to both the Justice Department's and the CRC's recommendations.[28]

On February 8, 1960, Senator Dirksen resubmitted the administration's civil rights package of the previous year, as well as the Justice Department's new "referees" plan. Majority Leader Johnson had given his pledge to Dirksen that a bill would be reported

27. Ibid., 45–46; Lawson, *Black Ballots*, 233; Schlundt, "Civil Rights Policies," 217.

28. Dulles, *The Civil Rights Commission*, 89; Harris Wofford to Malcolm Moos, Dec. 22, 1959, Persons Records, Box 1; "Memorandum for Ann Whitman," Jan. 20, 1959, Whitman File, Diary Series, Box 47, DDEL; Berman, *A Bill Becomes Law*, 40.

to the Senate floor early in the session, and to ensure that result he arranged for its assignment to the Rules and Administration Committee instead of the Judiciary Committee. Dirksen in turn guided the legislation to the Senate floor by attaching it to a bill allowing a Missouri school district to replace its fire-gutted building with an army barracks. Once the bill reached the full Senate, however, a Southern filibuster delayed a final vote. From March 1 to March 5, amendments eliminated the administration's provisions for a permanent employment committee, but on March 10 senators rejected a cloture motion. The CRC, in the meantime, continued to advocate its own registrar plan, and staff director Tiffany attended a private New York conference of civil rights leaders in an "analysis and criticism of pending measures."[29]

In testimony in the House of Representatives, Deputy Attorney General Lawrence Walsh attempted to ease the concerns of House liberals on the Judiciary Committee that black voting petitioners would be vulnerable under the administration's referee plan to intimidating cross-examination in court hearings. Walsh informed his questioners that the Justice Department would not object to additional language ruling out the possibility of contested hearings before court-appointed referees. The Civil Rights Division itself then prepared the appropriate amending language to the proposal, stating that "the applicant shall be heard *ex parte*" with any rebuttals or objections to be received at a separate date. Despite Walsh's efforts, however, the administration's bill also floundered in the House, and supporters circulated a second discharge petition. Although under House rules the names of discharge signers were to remain secret, members of the liberal Democratic Study Group memorized the list and leaked the names to the press. With 145 Democrats and only 30 Republicans committed at the time of the press leaks to reporting out the civil rights bill, the partisan embarrassment created by the disclosures forced enough additional signatures to bring the bill to the House floor. On March 24, the full House passed a weakened version of the civil rights bill by a 311–109 vote after turning back efforts by Emanuel Celler to reattach provisions for a fair employment committee.[30]

With a bill acceptable to the administration having gained

29. Miller, *Lyndon*, 227; Berman, *A Bill Becomes Law*, 48; Sundquist, *Politics and Policy*, 246.

30. Berman, *A Bill Becomes Law*, 47; Sundquist, *Politics and Policy*, 247.

House approval, Attorney General Rogers lobbied for its adoption by the Senate as well as the reinstatement of the 1959 desegregation assistance proposals. Both Rogers and Deputy Attorney General Walsh rejected substitute bills offered by Senator Dirksen that called for the appointment of "enrollment officers" similar to the CRC's proposed "registrars." Working in private with Johnson, Rogers eventually gave the administration's consent to the elimination both of desegregation assistance and the federal employment committee from the Senate bill. The final version of the Senate bill, passed amid a flurry of election year rhetoric on April 18 by a 71 to 18 vote, provided for the court appointment of referees to supervise voting procedures and imposed stiffer fines and prison terms for voting-rights obstruction and interstate transportation of explosives. On April 21, the House of Representatives accepted the Senate's amendments to the bill. Determined to salvage Republican credit for the passage of the 1960 legislation, the President directed James Hagerty to prepare a statement of congratulations to congressional Republicans. However, with the actual passage of the watered-down legislation a political anticlimax, Eisenhower signed the 1960 Civil Rights Act in a May 6 ceremony attended only by Rogers and Walsh.[31]

Having already received a new lease on life from Congress in late 1959, the Civil Rights Commission had resumed its investigations in voting rights, education, and housing, and it added to its agenda the fields of minority employment and "administration of justice." With hearings still restricted in the other fields to the North and border South, however, voting rights remained the cutting edge of CRC activity in the Black Belt. In July 1960, the CRC's authority to hold hearings in Shreveport, Louisiana was upheld by the Supreme Court in *Hannah* v. *Laroche*. The high court, overturning the ruling of Judge Dawkins a year earlier, affirmed that the commission's procedures did not violate the requirements of due process. Nevertheless, the CRC was able to hold its Louisiana voting-rights hearings only in May 1961, after another year of delay. Despite harassment from a Senate subcommittee on investigations, led by Senator John McClellan of Arkansas, which scrutinized commission financial practices, in 1960 the CRC initiated a survey of discrimination in sixteen Black Belt counties of five Southern states. In addition, after the squabbling

31. Berman, *A Bill Becomes Law*, 99–112; Sundquist, *Politics and Policy* 249–50; telephone call, Eisenhower to Hagerty, Apr. 26, 1960, Whitman File, Diary Series, Box 49, DDEL; Eisenhower, *Waging Peace*, 162.

between the commission and administration officials over 1960 legislative proposals had subsided, the CRC gained closer cooperation with the White House with the creation of an administration "subcabinet" on civil rights that included a commission representative.[32]

For the Civil Rights Division of the Justice Department, the year 1960 also brought renewed activity. In January, W. Wilson White resigned as assistant attorney general in charge of the division. Under his successor, Harold Tyler, the Civil Rights Division eliminated its previous stipulation that voting-rights investigation only follow receipt of formal written complaints, and division field personnel supplemented the investigative resources of the FBI. Tyler also requested and received the transfer to his control of twenty additional attorneys from the Anti-Trust and Public Lands division. Tyler's efforts in voting-rights enforcement received an additional assist from the solicitor general's office, as J. Lee Rankin filed a memorandum in March with the Supreme Court opposing a Tuskegee, Alabama redistricting scheme that had disfranchised black city residents. On November 14, 1960, the high court sided with the solicitor general and overturned the Tuskegee plan. Following another Supreme Court ruling of May 16 that held that the 1960 Civil Rights Act provided for a state to be charged as a defendant in a voting rights suit, the Civil Rights Division geared itself for increased litigation. Rogers notified U.S. attorneys to prepare for accelerated activity and the Justice Department requested an additional $100,000 in supplemental appropriations for the Civil Rights Division. In July, Tyler named John Doar, a young Wisconsin attorney and Princeton University graduate, to head the division's renewed voting-rights effort.[33]

After the passage of the 1960 Civil Rights Act and the subsequent internal reorganization, the Civil Rights Division filed requests with twenty-three Southern counties for voting records and initiated six suits. Despite the division's new interest in voting litigation, however, a number of official restrictions stayed in place. Any important cases still required the approval of a department-wide oversight committee, and as a consequence, four of the six voting rights suits were delayed until after the November elections. Rogers still insisted upon evidence "beyond a reasonable doubt" before suit action was authorized, even

32. Dulles, *The Civil Rights Commission*, 86–91.
33. Lichtman, "Federal Assault" 351–52; Lawson, *Black Ballots*, 248–49.

though only a preponderance of evidence was required to initiate litigation. The employment of federal referees, made possible by the 1960 Civil Rights Act, was utilized only twice and resulted in the registration of fewer than one hundred additional black voters in the entire South. The Justice Department also refused to lift its unofficial ban on filing suits in Senator Eastland's home state of Mississippi. Although Harold Tyler attributed the absence of suit activity in Mississippi to the state's massive resistance to information gathering, data from the CRC's Black Belt study alone might have sufficed, for it showed that thirteen counties lacked a single black voter. The Civil Rights Division presumably also could have developed its own preliminary documentation, filed suit, and then demanded additional records under Rule 34 of the Federal Rules of Civil Procedure. However, the division not only failed to follow such a course, but it acted privately to discourage CRC consideration of additional public hearings in the state.[34]

Under Tyler the Civil Rights Division first demanded the voting records of eleven counties in Louisiana, Alabama, South Carolina, and Georgia in May 1960. On June 7, the Justice Department filed a civil complaint against election officials in Bienville Parish, Louisiana—the first case in which the department requested the appointment of a voting referee. In the Bienville suit, government attorneys sought the restoration of 560 black names removed from registration rolls. Ruling on the federal government's request for the registration records of Sumter County, Alabama, on August 11, 1960 federal judge Frank Johnson ordered release of the records within fifteen days and issued a similar ultimatum to officials of Macon county on November 17. Despite Johnson's orders, however, Alabama attorney general MacDonald Gallion refused on three separate occasions to honor Justice Department requests for information. On August 12, the Civil Rights Division issued additional requests for records to officials of Bolivar, Forrest, and Leflore counties in Mississippi. Although representatives of Leflore County allowed federal examination of their files in September, the other two counties barred access to Justice Department investigators. Nevertheless, the department declined to file suit in Mississippi until August 1962. In December, the Justice Department began a second suit against Fayette County, Arkansas, officials seeking the lifting of eviction notices issued to voting black sharecroppers. And on the last day of the adminis-

34. Lichtman, "Federal Assault," 352–55.

tration's tenure, U.S. attorneys filed suit in behalf of a Louisiana cotton farmer who had suffered economic retaliation for giving testimony to the CRC.[35]

Despite the Civil Rights Division's belated efforts to defend black voting rights through civil suits, by the end of the Eisenhower administration the promise of black self-protection through the exercise of the ballot clearly had not been realized. One example of official discrimination in 1960 alone illustrated the fact that, for those black citizens most vulnerable to economic deprivation and intimidation, the distant promise of the vote offered no immediate relief. In June 1960, the state of Louisiana cut off welfare assistance to all mothers of illegitimate children or anyone else declared an "unsuitable" recipient. With $21 million of the state's $28 million welfare budget provided by the federal government, representatives of the Urban League pleaded to the Department of Health, Education and Welfare for asssitance, but their pleas received an irritatingly slow response. After suspending payments for seven months, the city of New Orleans finally restored about 90 percent of its previous AFDC recipients to the welfare rolls, but longer delays continued in the rest of the state. Only in July 1961, over a year later, did HEW issue a requirement to the state to provide food or shelter in a foster home to those denied welfare assistance.[36]

If the faith placed in the statutory protections of voting rights had not been justified, especially in the absence of vigorous enforcement, the reliance on the doctrine of black self-protection through the vote had also insured that the federal government remained unprepared to act in other ways to defend the lives and property of minority citizens. From 1957 to 1960, the Justice Department brought only ten voting-rights suits, and by the end of the decade blacks still constituted just 3 percent of the voters in at least seventeen Black Belt counties. But making the lack of progress in voting rights even worse, only one civil rights prosecution of the Justice Department in all of 1960 resulted in a conviction, with penalties of two and a half months' imprisonment and a $500 fine imposed. Official acts of brutality by local law-enforcement personnel notably were undeterred by the unfulfilled promise of black political power. Although the Civil Rights Division re-

35. John F. Cushman to Goodpaster, June 6, 1960, Persons Records, Box 13, DDEL; Lichtman, "Federal Assault," 355–56; Anthony Lewis, *Portrait of a Decade* (New York, 1964), 113.
36. Parris and Brooks, 377–79.

ceived 1,328 complaints of police brutality in its first two and a half years, only forty-two civil suits followed, with *none* producing a verdict in favor of the plaintiff. Of fifty-two criminal prosecutions brought by the division in the field of police brutality, forty-six ended in acquittals.[37] Administration officials had succeeded in proclaiming their faith in democratic assumptions, and through their concentration on the ballot they had avoided additional major confrontations with Southern authorities over the more controversial issue of racial integration. But for black Americans themselves, the Eisenhower administration's promise of the vote had not proven itself yet the "most effective and bloodless way" to secure their rights and protections as equal citizens.

37. Dulles, *The Civil Rights Commission*, 134; Aptheker, *Soul of the Republic* 34, 42; U.S. Department of Justice, Annual *Report* (1960), 331, 339.

Epilogue

12.

A Legacy of Symbolism

The beginning of 1960 marked a new phase in the
civil rights movement in the South, one spurred by
the activity of a new generation of black activists. Increasingly
aware of the federal government's reluctance to intervene with
police power to protect citizenship rights, black college students
in the South turned to new strategies to force public confrontations with the practitioners of Jim Crow. Before 1960, civil rights
protest primarily had featured techniques, including court suits
and local black boycotts, that had not forced face-to-face confrontation between segregationists and their black victims. Only
on rare occasions, as with the successful sit-ins at Wichita, Kansas
and Oklahoma City, Oklahoma outlets of the Katz drugstore chain,
had the confrontational tactics of "direct action" been employed.
But on February 1, 1960, a new era began when Joseph McNeill, a
freshman at North Carolina Agricultural and Technical College,
started a student sit-in at a Woolworth variety store cafeteria in
Greensboro, North Carolina. Four days later, protests spread to
the city's S.H. Kress store. With community tensions rising and
members of the Ku Klux Klan offering assistance to segregationists, Greensboro black protestors assented to withdraw from the

stores for two weeks to allow local business leaders to reevaluate their service policies.[1]

Receiving aid and volunteers from the newly formed Student Nonviolent Coordinating Committee (SNCC), the sit-in movement soon extended to a host of other Upper South cities, including Richmond, Hampton, Portsmouth, Nashville, and Chattanooga. From his observation post in Washington, E. Frederic Morrow noted the importance of the emerging organized black activity. In his internal memorandum on the "Student Protest Movement in the South," Morrow described it as a "new trend . . . adding to legal suits economic pressures and direct action." President Eisenhower and his other advisers, however, were uncertain whether the rise of black civil disobedience and direct action was a positive development or not. Adoption by Southern blacks of nonviolent confrontation as a strategy to force negotiation with segregationists did represent a form of direct black resolution of racial disputes not reliant upon federal sponsorship. On the other hand, any official attempts by Southern governments through their police power vigorously to suppress the demonstrators opened up additional dangers of police brutality, civil rights violations, and federal-state confrontations.[2]

The administration's fears that the sit-in movement might not fail to release it from intervention but actually make involvement more likely were underlined in early March. Martin Luther King, Jr., and A. Philip Randolph issued calls to the White House for federal intervention to restrain Alabama police violence against demonstrators. A week later, on March 16, 1960, the President refused to offer any "sweeping" opinion on the merits of the sit-in movement. Although he expressed general sympathy with the aims of the protestors, Eisenhower suggested that the government's responsibility was limited to preventing discrimination in areas of "public charter," and he added that he was "not in a position to judge" the legitimacy of the lunch-counter protests. Acting separately, however, representatives of the Justice Department gave limited assistance to the direct-action movement. In response to black protests, the department filed suit in May against officials of Harrison County and the city of Biloxi, Missis-

1. For a fine treatment of the racial politics and confrontations in Greensboro during the sit-ins and later, see William H. Chafe, *Civilities and Civil Rights: Greensboro, North Carolina, and the Black Struggle for Freedom* (New York, 1980).

2. Morrow, "Student Protest Movement in the South," March 7, 1960, McPhee Records, Box 4, DDEL.

sippi for denying blacks access to beach facilities. Government lawyers claimed federal jurisdiction in the case because of the use of federal funding in the beach's antierosion project and seawall.[3]

In early June, the Justice Department also extended its good offices in an effort to resolve the drugstore segregation controversy. Attorney General Rogers invited representatives of the F.W. Woolworth's, S.H. Kress, and W.T. Grant chains to an informal meeting to discuss the possible desegregation of their lunch-counter facilities. Two months later, the variety-chain executives informed the attorney general of their willingness to desegregate lunch counters in sixty-nine Southern communities. Their action represented an important breakthrough, for 70 percent of the outlets affected had not yet witnessed sit-in protests. A delighted Rogers proclaimed that the outcome demonstrated the superiority of solutions obtained "when responsible local citizens take the first steps." Elsewhere, however, voluntary acceptance of integration by local entrepreneurs was not so easily achieved. In Jacksonville, Florida, sit-ins led to violence, and a petition by 1,400 blacks in late August for administration assistance went unheeded. Nevertheless, by the end of 1960, 50,000 blacks were engaged in direct-action campaigns in the South, including sit-ins, walk-ins, stand-ins, and pray-ins. Although approximately 3,600 protestors were arrested for violations of public order or segregation statutes, the demonstrations forced the integration of public facilities in 126 Southern cities, primarily in the Upper South.[4]

Despite the increase of direct action and the new law-enforcement challenges it produced, White House attention to civil rights in 1960 was diverted by the political concerns of the upcoming November presidential election. With Eisenhower not eligible to succeed himself, the job of carrying the administration's record to the public fell to the vice president. On the surface, it appeared that a Nixon candidacy signaled a greater Republican commitment to federal civil rights activism in the future. As a congressman, Nixon had voted against the poll tax and for a fair employment practices commission. In his vice-presidential duties as Senate presiding officer and as chairman of the President's Committee on Government Contracts, Nixon had gained

3. King to Eisenhower, March 9, 1960; Randolph to Eisenhower, March 10, 1960, Morrow Records, Box 10; James Reston, *Sketches in the Sand* (New York, 1967), 121; Justice Department Press Release, May 17, 1960, Persons Records, Box 13, DDEL.

4. Lester A. Sobel, ed., *Civil Rights, 1960–1963* (New York, 1964), 11–12; Alexander, *Holding the Line*, 120–21.

Greensboro News & Record
A new era begins: black students launch sit-ins at Woolworth's, Greensboro, North Carolina, February 2, 1960. From left: Joseph McNeil, Franklin McCain, Billy Smith, and Clarence Henderson.

additional notoriety within the administration as a civil rights advocate.[5]

The vice-president's support for black rights, however, rarely had advanced beyond the level of symbolic gestures, and his public utterances on civil rights usually had been shaped according to partisan needs. Nixon's actual philosophy of the role of the federal government in civil rights differed but marginally from Eisenhower's. He wrote in his campaign biography, *The Challenges We Face:* "In the world-wide struggle in which we are engaged, racial and religious prejudice is a gun we point at ourselves." But he also affirmed that administration policy "is not now, and should not be, immediate and total integration." Asked for a written interview by the Pittsburgh *Courier,* Nixon's answers (drafted primarily by campaign staffers) revealed the candidate's limited commitment to civil rights. Declaring "I am against *forced* segregation," the vice-president endorsed the administration's civil rights program and emphasized the importance of voting rights: "There is nothing more basic to progress in a democracy than for citizens to exercise their right to vote." Nixon's primary aim in the field of civil rights was the purification of the moral image of the United States abroad. "I believe that the civil rights issue is vitally important to our nation because it is basically a moral issue. Stated briefly, it is this: When we say we stand for equality under law, do we mean it or not?"[6]

Nixon did not seek to soften his public image as a civil rights supporter before the party's nominating convention, for his main challenge for the nomination came from Governor Nelson A. Rockefeller of New York. Entering the convention with an unshakable grip on the presidential nomination, the vice president still sought assurances of Rockefeller's active support in the general election. In addition, Nixon wished to avoid being outflanked on civil rights by a stronger Democratic platform plank. As a result, he engaged in three-way negotiations with Rockefeller and platform committee representative John Tower of Texas and lobbied platform committee delegates for a strong civil rights plank. The eventual Republican platform statement pledged the "full use of the power, resources, and leadership of the federal government" in combatting discrimination, recited the Eisenhower record of accomplishment, and even "affirmed" the

5. Richard M. Nixon, *The Challenges We Face* (New York, 1960), 184–86.
6. Ibid., 184–86; undated interview with Pittsburgh *Courier*, Rogers Papers, Box 50, DDEL.

right of "peaceable assembly" to protest private discrimination — a clear reference to the sit-in movement.[7]

Once the Nixon general election campaign began, however, the candidate immediately backtracked from his preconvention posture of civil rights advocacy. Warned of the displeasure of Southern Republicans with the party platform, Nixon aides issued letters to supporters in the region denying any Nixon connection or affiliation with the NAACP. In a speech on August 17 at Greensboro, North Carolina, the birthplace of the direct-action movement, Nixon issued a personal disclaimer from vigorous federal action in civil rights, asserting that "law alone . . . is not the answer" and "is only as good as the will of the people to obey it." The Nixon campaign, following the Eisenhower lead, also solicited and received the help of South Carolina's former governor and segregationist leader James F. Byrnes, who assiduously avoided Joseph P. Kennedy's courtings in behalf of his son. Dismaying Morrow and Val Washington by using only Jackie Robinson as a black campaign spokesman and by ignoring the black press, Nixon persisted in avoiding any unqualified declarations of support for civil rights. Asked for his position during a Southern swing in Jackson, Mississippi, on September 24, the vice-president replied only, "I know that you are aware of my deep convictions on this issue."[8]

Given his predecessor's success in employing a "Southern strategy" in winning the presidency, Nixon could be excused for attempting to duplicate it in 1960. But popular awareness of civil rights as a moral question was much greater in 1960 than in 1952 or even 1956. Eisenhower himself, despite his consistent sympathies for the white South, had demonstrated in 1956 his recognition of the political need to provide additional gestures of support for civil rights beyond those offered four years earlier. By 1960, rhetorical retreat on civil rights did not suit a Northern voting public growing more aware of Southern discrimination and measuring the moral fitness of presidential candidates in part on the basis of their public allegiance to the principle of equal opportunity. In its political task of providing a successful blend of

7. Sundquist, *Politics and Policy* 252–53; "Draft of 1960 Civil Rights Plank," Rogers Papers, Box 51, DDEL.
8. W.F. Parker to Rogers, July 18, 1960, Rogers Papers, Box 51, letter to Colonel Percy Thompson, Aug. 17, 1960, Whitman File, Name Series, Box 16; telephone call, Sept. 12, 1960, Whitman File, Diary Series, Box 52, DDEL; Nixon, *Six Crises* (Garden City, N.Y., 1962), 325; Lewis, *Portrait of a Decade*, 114.

rhetorical moral urgency and moderate policies, the Nixon campaign failed miserably. Breaking with the Eisenhower pattern, Nixon in 1960 did not even make a campaign appearance in Harlem. Running mate Henry Cabot Lodge, assuming the role of civil rights spokesman Nixon had once played, did promise the appointment of a black to the cabinet, only to have his "trial balloon" punctured by Nixon campaign aides. With the vice president's advisers insisting that all appointments would be made strictly on "merit," an embarrassed Lodge was forced to repudiate his statement during a Winston-Salem, North Carolina appearance.[9]

The Nixon campaign's biggest civil rights blunder, however, stemmed from the October 19 arrest of Martin Luther King by local police in Atlanta, Georgia for participation in a department store sit-in. Having been given a suspended sentence six months earlier for a traffic violation, the civil rights leader was sentenced by a DeKalb County judge to four months at hard labor for violating probation. Fearful for King's physical safety, his associates pleaded with the administration to intervene with the judge to reduce the sentence. Although the vice president, who had conferred with King on several previous occasions, agreed that the civil rights leader had received a "bum rap," he refused to act in his capacity as a lawyer to telephone his protests to the judge. Such an action would be "improper," Nixon felt, and he notified reporters through Press Secretary Herbert Klein that he would have "no comment" on the matter. The candidate believed that any obligation to take action on King's behalf lay with the President, for in his politically safe position as a "lame duck," Eisenhower could respond freely without fear of the electoral consequences.[10]

Upon the urgings of Attorney General William Rogers, a Nixon ally, Deputy Attorney General Walsh drafted a statement for delivery by James Hagerty, the presidential press secretary, protesting King's "fundamentally unjust arrest" and claiming that the President had directed the Justice Department "to take all proper steps to join with Dr. Martin Luther King in an appropriate application for his release." Eisenhower, however, never gave the necessary final approval for release of the statement. John F. Kennedy's campaign staff seized the opportunity to capitalize on

9. Carl M. Brauer, *John F. Kennedy and the Second Reconstruction* (New York, 1977), 42.
10. Nixon, *Six Crises*, 362–63.

the incident and secure the support of black voters and sympathetic whites. Following the advice of former CRC staffer and campaign aide Harris Wofford, Kennedy, not known as a forceful advocate of civil rights, transmitted a message of sympathy to Coretta Scott King. Campaign manager Robert Kennedy, although initially skeptical of the political benefits of intercession, had his own legal objections to the sentence relayed to the judge. The following day, in an action that apparently underlined the effectiveness of the Kennedy communications, King was released from jail.[11]

It was the supreme irony of the campaign that the Nixon candidacy stumbled because of the vice president's failure to capitalize upon the King arrest through a symbolic gesture of help. Nixon had been one of the most willing and able practitioners of racial symbolism in the Eisenhower administration. But his failure, in Eisenhower's words, to "make a couple of phone calls" led to a spurt in black Democratic support that boosted Kennedy's national lead in the campaign's final two weeks. Kennedy supporters encouraged the trend by distributing literature on the King incident to black churches the Sunday before the election. On Election Day, Kennedy won the White House by a slim national margin of only 120,000 popular votes and 84 electoral votes, despite a white voter majority of 52 percent for Nixon. Postelection polls of black voters showed that they had preferred the Democrat by better than a 2–1 margin, and perhaps as high as 3 to 1. The Kennedy advantage among blacks roughly held irrespective of differences in age, sex, region, or community size. Without his margin of black support, Kennedy could not have carried the key states of Illinois, Michigan, New Jersey, Texas, and South Carolina. In contrast, Nixon's level of black support represented a disappointing slippage of between 5 and 10 percent from the Republican figures of 1956.[12]

11. Draft statement by Lawrence Walsh, Oct. 31, 1960, Official File, Box 731, DDEL. For a description of the Kennedy decision to respond to the King arrest, see Arthur M. Schlesinger, Jr., *Robert Kennedy and His Times* (New York, 1978), 233–35.

12. Hughes, *The Ordeal of Power*, 323; NAACP, *The Crisis* 68 (1961): 5–14; Gallup, ed., *The Gallup Poll*, 1964. Estimates again vary for the breakdown of the 1960 black vote and its importance to the Kennedy victory. According to aides Theodore Sorenson and Arthur M. Schlesinger, Jr., poll estimates of the Kennedy percentages varied from 68 to 78 percent of the total black vote. In all probability, Kennedy gained around 7 percent more of the Negro vote in 1960 than Stevenson had in 1956, or seven of every ten black votes. See Theodore Sorenson, *Kennedy* (New York, 1965), 222; and Arthur M. Schlesinger, Jr., *A Thousand Days: John F. Kennedy, in the White House* (Boston, 1965), 930.

By electing John F. Kennedy, the American public had narrowly endorsed a change in party leadership in the White House.
With twinges of regret mixed with a considerable sense of relief,
officials of the Eisenhower administration prepared for the transition of power and for their departure from positions of official
responsibility. Although their control over racial issues was less
complete than they had hoped, Eisenhower and his advisers had
nevertheless helped shape a legacy of philosophical assumptions
and national policies that would continue to affect the national
political consideration of racial issues for years to come. Initially
the Republican administration had been content to issue executive orders continuing military desegregation, removing discriminatory sanctions from the nation's capital, appointing blacks to
visible but unimportant executive positions, and creating fact-
finding committees on minority employement. Dedicated to
slowing the onward march of centralized government power, they
had turned aside suggestions for a greater federal ehforcement
role in guaranteeing fair employment and housing. The times had
been kind to them in their effort to minimize federal intervention
in the private economy, for the general prosperity of the 1950s had
defused much of the political interest in additional government
economic activism, whether in the civil rights field or elsewhere.

If left to their own desires, Eisenhower and his subordinates
likely would not have ventured beyond the initial boundaries of
their policy of racial symbolism. But they had not been able to
seize sufficient control over the march of events to prevent additional entanglement in the legal and moral confrontations over
Jim Crow discrimination in the South. Forced by the Truman
administration into taking a stance on public school segregation,
the Eisenhower Justice Department reluctantly had filed briefs
upholding the right of the Supreme Court to employ the Fourteenth Amendment as a tool to strike down Jim Crow. Challenged
in the aftermath of the *Brown* decision by Southern "massive
resistance," the administration had taken the first halting steps
toward the enforcement of court-ordered desegregation decrees.
In their desperate search for ways to free themselves from further
involvement, administration officials had turned to the advocacy
of voting rights as a means of providing blacks with a tool for
self-protection, and the results were manifested in the civil rights
acts of 1957 and 1960. In addition, the creation of the U.S. Commission on Civil Rights had provided the administration a bipartisan forum from which to shame the South, and the rest of the

nation, into compliance with democratic ideals without itself becoming directly involved.

In explaining its approach to racial issues, the Eisenhower administration had given both voice and official sanction to a new and more respectable kind of civil rights conservatism, although the President himself had preferred the label "moderation." The Eisenhower doctrine of civil rights, which had supported the removal of official sanctions mandating discrimination but had preferred to leave additional progress to the private sector, represented a repudiation of the older white-supremacist tradition of conservative racial thought. At the same time, however, it was a rejection of the newer tradition of government fiscal and regulatory intervention in the private sector symbolized by the New Deal and the Fair Deal. The President's philosophy of civil rights did succeed in jettisoning the unpalatable overt racism of Jim Crow, allowed actions aimed at removing federal segregation and projecting an official image of racial democracy, and fused these elements within a general domestic program aimed at limiting governmental intrusions upon private freedom. By the 1970s, Eisenhower's antistatist doctrine, which declared support both for general civil rights principles and for limitations on federal enforcement powers, had become so popular among conservatives of both parties that even such former champions of white supremacy as Alabama's George Wallace and South Carolina's Strom Thurmond had incorporated it into their political rhetoric.

In spite of the Eisenhower administration's uneasiness with the exercise of federal power, the heightened focus upon black constitutional rights that was a byproduct of its confrontations with Jim Crow had meant that by the end of the decade Americans did possess a rudimentary "progress chart" of legal equality. By the time of the inauguration of John F. Kennedy, executive orders and regulatory judgments formally barred discrimination in the military services and in federal hiring. Federal rulings prohibited segregation in interstate transportation and public services in the District of Columbia. National legislation promised equal black access to the voting booth and set down limited criminal and civil sanctions for the protection of other minority citizenship rights. The federal courts banned officially mandated segregation in public schools, invalidated restrictive covenant enforcement and zoning for discriminatory purposes, and barred racial exclusion from jury service. Because of Eisenhower's decision, however uncharacteristic, to intervene at Little Rock, precedents existed even for the application of federal troops to enforce court-ordered school desegregation.

Nevertheless, given their philosophical and partisan objections to federal "coercion," Eisenhower and his subordinates had displayed a consistent pattern of hesitancy and extreme political caution in defending black legal rights. As black aide E. Frederic Morrow later observed, "Civil rights in the Eisenhower administration was handled like a bad dream, or like something that's not very nice, and you shield yourself from it as long as you possibly can, because it just shouldn't be." Much of the blame for the administration's excessive caution lay squarely with the President himself. In 1954, criticizing a group of senators for lacking backbone on another matter, Eisenhower had written: "They do not seem to realize when there arrives that moment at which soft speaking should be abandoned and a fight to the end undertaken. Any man who hopes to exercise leadership must be ready to meet the requirement face to face when it arises; unless he is ready to fight when necessary, people will finally begin to ignore him." Measured by his own standards, the President's leadership in the civil rights struggle had fallen short. His failure to commit himself unequivocally to racial justice, his willingness to settle for the political containment of racial problems rather than their solution, and his reluctance to intervene in matters of divided federal-state jurisdiction meant that white Southern resistance to black legal equality persisted as an immediate civil rights challenge to the Kennedy administration.[13]

In time Eisenhower's immediate successors demonstrated a greater willingness to use the enforcement machinery of the federal government to uphold black legal and political rights. But other aspects of the Eisenhower administration civil rights legacy helped frustrate black attempts to initiate an extended governmental response to the problems of material disadvantage that underlay continuing racial inequality. The optimistic rhetoric of symbolic equality employed by the Eisenhower administration in the 1950s had encouraged white Americans to believe that the attainment of racial democracy would require only the removal of the official buttresses of discrimination. The achievement of racial equality, official spokesmen had claimed, would be not only painless but actually therapeutic to white consciences and white

13. Konvitz, *A Century of Civil Rights* 255; Ferrell, ed., *The Eisenhower Diaries*, 270; Lyon, 781.

pocketbooks alike. Immersed in what historian Robert Wiebe has described as a "myth of middleclassness," the Eisenhower administration had never confronted the possibility that the realization of genuine racial equality might require white material sacrifices or the adoption of redistributionary fiscal policies.[14]

When the enactment of legal prescriptions for equality alone did not produce universal black social advance, many whites assumed that the blame lay with the disadvantaged themselves, rather than in the basic assumptions supporting federal racial policy. By 1963, although a vast majority of white Americans professed no longer to believe in black inferiority, fully two-thirds concluded that blacks were "less ambitious." At the same time, black leaders who had based their previous strategies upon non-violent moral protest and governmental legal response began to question the depth of the white commitment to racial equality. Writing from the Birmingham city jail, Martin Luther King observed, "Over the past few years I have been gravely disappointed with the white moderate. I have almost reached the regrettable conclusion that the Negro's great stumbling block in his stride toward freedom is not the White Citizen's Counciller or the Ku Klux Klanner, but the white moderate, who is more devoted to "order" than to justice; who prefers a negative peace which is the absence of tension to a positive peace which is the presence of justice."[15]

The major civil rights accomplishments of the Kennedy and Johnson administrations — the 1964 Civil Rights Act and the 1965 Voting Rights Act — were logical and essential extensions of federal power in the pursuit of black citizenship equality, a search that had been revived in the 1950s. The Civil Rights Act strengthened government suit powers in public facilities and public education cases, created the Equal Employment Opportunity Commission, and tightened federal prohibitions against employer and union discrimination. The Voting Rights Act assigned federal registrars to the South and created official machinery for screening changes in Southern electoral laws. By 1965, however, voices within the civil rights movement were calling for the government to move in new directions. Kenneth Clark's "Dark Ghetto," Bayard Rustin's "From Protest to Politics," and the calls of A.

14. Robert H. Wiebe, "White Attitudes and Black Rights from Brown to Bakke," in Michael U. Namorato, ed., *Have We Overcome?* (Jackson, Miss., 1979), 171.

15. William Brink and Louis Harris, *The Negro Revolution in America* (New York, 1964), 142; Martin Luther King, Jr., "Letter from Birmingham Jail," Apr. 16, 1963, in *Why We Can't Wait* (New York, 1963), 77–90.

Philip Randolph and other black spokesmen for a "freedom budget" all signaled the rising black demand for an all-out federal effort to eradicate the poverty that blocked the full attainment of equality. During the Johnson administration, new ventures were tried from 1964 to 1967 in community action, job training, educational "head starts," model cities, fair housing, and welfare assistance. But although the War on Poverty produced measurable advances in black living standards in its brief heyday, it neither overcame the heritage of white faith in solely legal solutions nor satisfied the escalating demands of militant young blacks for a greater share of the economic pie.

Black rage tragically erupted in urban rioting at the same time that whites increasingly questioned both the necessity and the legitimacy of "special help" for the minority poor. Many whites reacted to the escalating violence in American cities with puzzlement and anger, and their sentiments were shared by many former officials of the Eisenhower administration. From the seclusion of Gettysburg, the former president himself condemned the fact that "the United States has become atmosphered, you might say, in a policy of lawlessness. If we like a law, we obey it. If we don't we are told, 'You can disobey it,' " Former Secretary of Agriculture Ezra Taft Benson went further, claiming that the civil rights movement had become the willing instrument of communism. Even E. Frederic Morrow could only respond with a mixture of confusion and sadness at the burning and looting in Watts, Detroit, and other communities. In a marked contrast from his former image of civil rights advocacy in the 1950s, Richard M. Nixon, running once again for the presidency in 1968, capitalized on public concern over a controversial war abroad and white demands for domestic "law and order" and finally succeeded in winning the nation's highest office.[16]

In the 1970s, national administrations gradually whittled away at the programs of the Johnson years, and whites opposed to the redressing of past discrimination through legal "favoritism" employed the very rhetoric of the civil rights movement to block "reverse discrimination." Yet to many black observers in the late 1960s and the 1970s, the stillborn reforms of the Great Society, the murder of Martin Luther King, the diversion of national resources to the Vietnam War, and the continuing white resistance to redis-

16. Lyon, *Eisenhower*, 843; Ezra Taft Benson, "Our Immediate Responsibility," Oct. 25, 1966, in *Speeches of the Year* (Extension Publications, BYU Press, 1966), 6–7; Morrow, *Way Down South Up North*, 112.

tributionary policies, when taken together, represented nothing other than a triumph of tokenism. Describing at an early stage the depth of black frustration with the American political system, in 1966 Le Roi Jones issued a personal condemnation of the self-imposed limitations even of liberal politicians:

> Liberals are people with extremely heavy consciences and almost nonexistant courage. Too little is always enough. And it is always the *symbol* that appeals to them most. The single futile housing project in the jungle of slums and disease eases the liberals' consciences, so they are loudest in praising it — even though it might not solve any problems at all. The single black student in the Southern university, the promoted porter in Marietta, Georgia — all ease the liberal's conscience like a benevolent but highly addictive drug. And, for them, "moderation" is a kind of religious catch phrase.[17]

If the liberals of the 1960s were guilty of being satisfied with symbolic victories over racism, however, their limitations of vision and political courage were but a logical outgrowth of the racial politics of the Eisenhower years. It would remain for subsequent generations of black Americans to provide the definitive judgment as to whether the symbolic promise of equality contained in the rhetoric of official America — the dominant civil rights legacy of the Eisenhower administration — had ultimately borne the fruits of genuine racial progress or the bitter harvest of hypocritical national self-deception.

17. Le Roi Jones, "tokenism: 300 years for five cents," *Home* (New York, 1966).

Bibliographical Essay

The study of the development of civil rights policies during the Eisenhower administration requires the utilization of a large and constantly growing body of materials on recent American politics and race relations. This essay, accordingly, does not identify all of the sources cited in the footnotes or employed as background reading. Instead, its purpose is to highlight some of the major primary and secondary sources relating to the formulation and execution of executive branch racial policy in the 1950s.

Primary Sources: Manuscript Collections, Government Documents, Civil Rights Publications, and Newspapers

The starting point for the study of the Eisenhower administration's racial policies is the Eisenhower Library in Abilene, Kansas. For the student of civil rights a variety of materials is now available. The most important of these is the massive collection of President Eisenhower's official papers, also referred to as the Ann

Whitman File after the president's personal secretary. The Whitman File contains the Eisenhower "diaries," which are more accurately described as daily summary memoranda of the president's meetings and conversations. Also included are cabinet, legislative meeting, press conference, speech, and other series. Official White House memoranda and correspondence can also be found in the Eisenhower collection of Records as President, which contains an official file, a general file, a confidential file, and a personal file. Civil rights material in these records primarily consists either of correspondence with black spokesmen that reached the president's attention or of staff memoranda.

In addition to Eisenhower's papers, the files of a number of White House staffers and cabinet officials are important, particularly in view of the decentralized nature of the consideration of "non-crisis" civil rights issues. Of obvious value are the papers of black White House assistant E. Frederic Morrow. In addition, the papers of other officials illuminate the administration's civil rights deliberations. Press Secretary James C. Hagerty's records and diary passages reveal his role as an in-house advocate of civil rights. The papers of congressional liaison Bryce N. Harlow document the administration's tactics on the desegregation and school construction issues. Files for Henry R. McPhee and Gerald D. Morgan show their roles as legal advisers on civil rights and other matters. While not bearing directly on racial issues, the papers of Howard Pyle and Wilton B. Persons give insights into the chain of command in the White House. Among the cabinet officials whose collections are available at the Eisenhower Library are Attorney General William P. Rogers and Secretary of Health, Education and Welfare Oveta Culp Hobby. Most valuable to the civil rights scholar, given his involvement in fair employment issues and his general advocacy of civil rights, are the papers of Secretary of Labor James Mitchell. In contrast, one of the most disappointing gaps in the library holdings is the unavailability of the papers of Attorney General Herbert Brownell, although his oral history transcript is available under restrictions.

As a general rule, the oral history holdings at the Eisenhower Library do not add significantly to the documentary record on civil rights, although they do offer a source of biographical background on various administration officials. Two important exceptions to this rule exist. One of these is the series of interviews conducted by the Columbia University Oral History Project pertaining to the Little Rock school desegregation crisis. Virtually every participant, from Governor Orval E. Faubus to administration officials to NAACP leaders to school officials to segregationist organizers, was interviewed extensively about the events surrounding the crisis. Their recollections provide a comprehensive, if sometimes contradictory, account of the racial confrontations at Little Rock. The other exception is the series of interviews done with black staffer E. Frederic Morrow. Morrow's honest, sometimes painful recollection offers a vivid portrait of life in the Eisenhower White House from the perspective of a black man.

Consistently undervalued yet important sources of documentation on the justification for, and the impact of, government programs in civil rights are published government reports and documents. In addition to the best known of these, the *Congressional Record* and *The Public Papers of the Presidents* series, other agency reports, congressional hearings, and public information pamphlets supply much valuable information. Among the most useful documents for assessing the impact of federal government policies on black citizens are the annual and semiannual reports of the departments of Agriculture, Defense, HEW, Justice, and Labor; the District of Columbia Board of Commissioners, the Farm Credit Administration, the Federal Home Loan Bank Board, the Housing and Home Finance Agency, the Veterans Administration, and the President's committees on Government Employment Policy and Government Contracts. In the case of the presidential committees, public relations pamphlets state the administration's claims of success in the employment field and offer defenses of a limited federal enforcement role. Two other types of government records merit special attention. Because of their value in presenting the philosophical perspectives and policy preferences of executive appointees, congressional nomination hearings and legislative hearings are useful in tracing the evolution of executive branch racial policies. Finally, because of its unique position as an investigative body studying a range of civil rights problems, the conference reports, hearings, and biannual reports of the U.S. Commission on Civil Rights offer insights into the commission's own internal dynamics as well as the state of American race relations at regular intervals.

For evidence of the lobbying activities and legal pressures exerted by civil rights and liberal organizations and spokesmen upon the Eisenhower White House, the previously cited collections at the Eisenhower Library offer thorough testimony. For insights into liberal coalition-building on civil rights legislation, selected portions of the papers of the Americans for Democratic Action, located at the State Historical Society of Wisconsin, also were helpful. For a larger view of black political activism at the local, state, and national levels, however, it is valuable to consult the papers and publications of leading black organizations, including the NAACP, CORE, the National Urban League, and the Southern Christian Leadership Conference.

Of special value are the files of the national and branch offices of the NAACP, which are located at the Library of Congress. Additional collections documenting the activities of various Southern-based civil rights groups and leaders can be found at the Martin Luther King Center in Atlanta, Georgia, and the State Historical Society of Wisconsin. Major civil rights publications include the Congress of Racial Equality's *CORE-Later*, the Urban League's *Opportunity*, and the NAACP's *Crisis*. Annual reports of these organizations also provide evidence of their growth in numbers and finances and offer assessments of the state of American race relations for each year of the decade. Topical studies of specific racial problems commissioned by civil rights organizations also include *Civil Rights in the U.S.: A Balance Sheet of Group Relations* (New York, 1952–54), sponsored by the National Jewish Congress and the NAACP; The National Urban League's *The Racial Gap, 1955–1965; 1965–1975* (New York, 1967); and the Urban League of Greater New York, *Research Study: A Study of the Problem of Integration in New York City Public Schools Since 1955* (New York, 1963). Supplementing the organizational publications of civil rights groups are the accounts from the Afro-American press. Among the leading black newspapers consulted were the Chicago *Defender*, the Kansas City *Call*, the Pittsburgh *Courier*, the New York *Amsterdam News*, the Baltimore *Afro-American*, the Birmingham *World*, and the Norfolk *Journal and Guide*. For national and international coverage of racial issues and reaction to administration racial policies by the white press, as well as coverage of race relations in the nation's capital, the *New York Herald-Tribune*, the *New York Times*, the *Washington Post*, and the *Washington Star* proved most useful.

Published Memoirs and Secondary Sources

Literature on both the emergence of the modern civil rights movement and the history of the Eisenhower administration is expanding rapidly, making the task of keeping up with recent studies a difficult one in either field. Overviews of the civil rights revolution include Herbert Aptheker, *Soul of the Republic: The*

Negro Today (New York, 1964); Richard Bardolph, *The Civil Rights Record* (New York, 1970); Robert H. Brisbane, *Black Activism* (Valley Forge, Pa., 1974); Thomas R. Brooks, *Walls Come Tumbling Down* (Englewood Cliffs, N.J., 1974); Milton R. Konvitz, *A Century of Civil Rights* (New York, 1966); Anthony Lewis, *Portrait of a Decade: The Second American Revolution* (New York, 1964); Louis Lomax, *The Negro Revolt* (New York, 1962); Dorothy K. Newman, Nancy J. Amidei, Barbara L. Carter, Dawn Day, William J. Kruvant, and Jack S. Russell, *Protest, Politics, and Prosperity: Black Americans and White Institutions, 1940–1975* (New York, 1978); Richard Polenberg, *One Nation Divisible: Class, Race, and Ethnicity in the United States Since 1938* (New York, 1980); Harvard Sitkoff, *The Struggle for Black Equality* (New York, 1981); and Michael U. Namorato, ed., *Have We Overcome?* (Jackson, Miss., 1979).

Among the growing body of works focusing upon black mobilization and the contributions of civil rights organizations are Clayborne Carson, *In Struggle: SNCC and the Black Awakening of the 1960's* (Cambridge, Mass., 1981); Herbert Garfinkel, *When Negroes March: The March on Washington Movement in the Organizational Politics for FEPC* (Glencoe, Ill., 1959); David J. Garrow, *Protest at Selma* (New Haven, Ct. 1978); August Meier and Elliott Rudwick, *CORE: A Study in the Civil Rights Movement, 1942–1968* (New York, 1973); Robert L. Zangrando, *The NAACP Crusade Against Lynching, 1909–1950* (Philadelphia, 1980); and Howard Zinn, *SNCC: The New Abolitionists* (Boston, 1964). Biographies and personal accounts of civil rights leaders include Jervis Anderson, *A. Phillip Randolph: A Biographical Portrait* (New York, 1973); James Forman, *The Making of a Black Revolutionary* (New York, 1975); Neil Hickey and Ed Edwin, *Adam Clayton Powell and the Politics of Race* (New York, 1965); Adam Clayton Powell, Jr., *Adam by Adam* (New York, 1971); David L. Lewis, *King: A Critical Biography* (New York, 1970); Stephen B. Oates, *Let the Trumpet Sound: The Life of Martin Luther King, Jr.* (New York, 1982); and Roy Wilkins, *Standing Fast* (New York, 1982).

A distinct group of works attempts to trace the white adoption of civil rights as a moral cause and a policy field. General discussions of the symbolic role of racial policies for white Americans include Edwin Dorn, *Rules and Racial Equality* (New Haven, 1979); Thomas R. Dye, *The Politics of Equality* (Indianapolis, 1971); and Jacob Murray Edelman's *The Symbolic Uses of Politics* (Urbana, Ill. 1964) and *Politics as Symbolic Action* (Chicago, 1971). The concerns of race relations experts in the 1940s and early 1950s with preserving the American democratic identity are documented in the classic study of Gunnar Myrdal, *An American Dilemma: The Negro Problem and Modern Democracy*, 2 vols. (New York, 1944) and Gordon W. Allport, *The Nature of Prejudice* (Boston, 1954). Critiques of the Myrdal model of "cumulative causation" and its assertion of a dominant democratic ethos in American society include Ralph Ellison, *Shadow and Act* (New York, 1953); Raymond S. Franklin and Solomon Resnik, *The Political Economy of Racism* (New York, 1973); Louis L. Knowles and Kenneth Prewitt, eds., *Institutional Racism in America* (Englewood Cliffs, N.J., 1969) and Stanford M. Lyman, *The Black American in Sociological Thought* (New York, 1972). Analyses of national political involvement in racial issues from the New Deal to the 1950s are contained in John B. Kirby, *Black Americans in the Roosevelt Era: Liberalism and Race* (Knoxville, Tenn., 1982); Harvard Sitkoff, *A New Deal for Blacks* (New York, 1978); John M. Blum, *V Was for Victory: Politics and American Culture During World War II* (New York, 1976); Richard Polenberg,*War and Society: The United States, 1941–45* (Philadelphia, 1972); William C. Berman, *The Politics of Civil Rights in the Truman Administration* (Columbus, Ohio, 1970); Donald R. McCoy and Richard T. Ruetten, *Quest and Response: Minority Rights and the Truman Administration* (Lawrence, Kan., 1973); Alonzo L. Hamby, *Beyond the New Deal: Harry S. Truman and American Liberalism* (New York, 1973); Barton J. Bernstein, "American in War and Peace: The Test of Liberalism," in Bernstein, ed., *Towards a New Past: Dissenting Essays in American History* (New York, 1967), 289–321; and Peter J. Kellogg, "Civil Rights Consciousness in the 1940's," *The Historian* 42 (1979): 18–41, and "American Liberals and Black America: A Study of White Attitudes, 1936–1952," (unpublished Ph.D. diss., Northwestern University, 1971).

Works on the Eisenhower Administration include general overviews, background studies of Eisenhower himself, and contemporary accounts by administration officials, reporters, and observers. Among the many studies of the administration in recent years are Charles C. Alexander, *Holding the Line: The Eisenhower Era, 1952–1961* (Bloomington, Ind., 1975); Herbert S. Parmet, *Eisenhower and the American Crusades* (New York, 1972); Gary W. Reichard, *The Reaffirmation of Republicanism: Eisenhower and the Eighty-Third Congress* (Knoxville, Tenn., 1975); Elmo Richardson, *The Presidency of Dwight D. Eisenhower* (Lawrence, Kan., 1979); James L. Sundquist, *Politics and Poli-*

cy: *The Eisenhower, Kennedy, and Johnson Years* (Washington, D.C., 1968); Stephen E. Ambrose, "The Ike Age," *New Republic,* May 9, 1981, 26–34; and Robert Griffith, "Dwight D. Eisenhower and the Corporate Commonwealth," *American Historical Review* 87 (1982):87–122.

Among the published collections of administration documents are Robert L. Branyan and Lawrence H. Larson, eds., *The Eisenhower Administration, 1953–1961: A Documentary History,* 2 vols. (New York, 1971); and Robert H. Ferrell, *The Eisenhower Diaries* (New York, 1981) and *The Diary of James C. Hagerty: Eisenhower in Mid-Course, 1954–1955* (Bloomington, Ind., 1983). Eisenhower offers his own overview of the administration in his two-volume White House memoirs, *Mandate for Change* and *Waging Peace* (Garden City, N.Y., 1963). The chief insider accounts of the administration are Sherman Adams, *Firsthand Report* (New York, 1961); Robert J. Donovan, *Eisenhower: The Inside Story* (New York, 1956); William Bragg Ewald, *Eisenhower the President* (Englewood Cliffs, N.J. 1981); Emmet John Hughes, *The Ordeal of Power: A Political Memoir of the Eisenhower Years* (New York, 1963); Arthur Larson, *Eisenhower: The President Nobody Knew* (New York, 1968); E. Frederic Morrow, *Black Man in the White House* (New York, 1963), *Way Down South Up North* (Philadelphia, 1973), and *Forty Years a Guinea Pig* (New York, 1980); Richard M. Nixon, *Six Crises* (Garden City, N.Y., 1962), and Merlo J. Pusey, *Eisenhower the President* (New York, 1956). Assessments by outside observers include Jacob Javits, *Discrimination—USA* (New York, 1960); Walter Johnson, *1600 Pennsylvania Avenue* (Boston, 1960); Arthur Krock, *In the Nation* (New York, 1966); James Reston, *Sketches in the Sand* (New York 1967); and I.F. Stone, *The Haunted Fifties* (New York, 1963). Biographical information on Eisenhower can be gleaned from his own *At Ease: Stories I Tell to Friends* (Garden City, N.Y. 1967); John Gunther, *Eisenhower* (New York, 1951); Peter Lyon, *Eisenhower: Portrait of the Hero* (Boston, 1974); Kevin McCann, *Man From Abilene* (Garden City, N.Y., 1952); Kay Summersby, *Eisenhower Was My Boss* (New York, 1948); and Allen Taylor, *What Eisenhower Thinks* (New York, 1952).

No previously published work has provided a comprehensive overview of the Eisenhower administration's racial policies, although Ronald Alan Schlundt's "Civil Rights Policies in the Eisenhower Years" (Ph.D. dissertation, Rice University, 1973) does cover the major policy developments. Instead, a wide body of secondary literature has accumulated on a number of separate subjects within the civil rights field. On the subject of military desegregation, principal works include Richard M. Dalfiume, *Desegregation of the U.S. Armed Forces: Fighting on Two Fronts, 1939–1953* (Columbia, Mo., 1969); Jack D. Foner, *Blacks and the Military in U.S. History* (New York, 1974); Morris J. MacGregor and Bernard C. Nalty, *Blacks in the Armed Forces: Basic Documents, Vol. 12—Integration* (Wilmington, Del., 1977); Lee Nichols, *Breakthrough on the Color Front* (New York, 1954); and Richard J. Stillman II, *Integration of the Negro in the U.S. Armed Forces* (New York, 1968). Among studies of race relations and racial policy in the District of Columbia are Martha Derthick, *City Politics in Washington, D.C.* (Cambridge, MA, 1962); Constance M. Green, *The Secret City: A History of Race Relations in the Nation's Capital* (Princeton, N.J., 1967); Carl F. Hansen, *Danger in Washington: The Story of My Twenty Years in the Public Schools in the Nation's Capital* (West Nyack, N.Y., 1968); National Association of Intergroup Relations Officials, "Civil Rights in the Nation's Capital," (Washington, D.C. 1959); and Jeanne Rogers, "Nation's Showcase," in Don Shoemaker, ed., *With All Deliberate Speed* (Westport, Conn., 1970).

Other works touch upon the issues of black material disadvantage, unequal employment, and housing discrimination. Works on black employment and self-employment include Theodore L. Cross, *Black Capitalism* (New York, 1969); Steven M. Gelber, *Black Men and Businessmen* (Port Washington, N.Y., 1974); F. Ray Marshall, *The Negro and Organized Labor* (New York, 1965); and William Peters, *The Southern Temper* (Garden City, N.Y., 1959). Meriting special mention is the multivolume series compiled by the Wharton School of Finance, directed by Herbert R. Northrup, *The Racial Policies of American Industry*, 27 vols. (Philadelphia, 1968). On minority housing issues, see Alfred Avins, ed., *Open Occupancy vs. Forced Housing Under the 14th Amendment* (New York, 1963); Blake McKelvey, *The Emergence of Metropolitan America, 1915–1966* (New Brunswick, N.J., 1968); and Irving Berg, "Racial Discrimination in Housing: A Study in the Quest for Government Access by Minority Interest Groups, 1945–1962" (Ph.D. dissertation, University of Florida, 1967).

As might be expected, the largest single collection of works pertaining to civil rights in the 1950s deals with racial integration in the South, particularly the school desegregation issue. The most valuable work in the field is Richard Kluger's monumental study of the *Brown* decision, *Simple Justice* (New York, 1975). Other important studies on *Brown* include Daniel Berman, *It Is So Ordered* (New York, 1966); Albert P. Blaustein and Clarence Clyde Ferguson, Jr., *Desegregation and the Law* (New Brunswick, N.J., 1957); Leon Friedman, ed., *Argument* (New York, 1969); Stephen L. Wasby, Anthony H. D'Amato, and Rosemary Metraler, *Desegregation from Brown to Alexander* (Carbondale, Ill., 1977); and J. Harvie Wilkinson III, *From Brown to Bakke: The Supreme Court and School Integration, 1954–1978* (New York, 1979). The Eisenhower administration's responses to both the school integration and school construction issues are examined in James C. Duram, *A Moderate Among Extremists: Dwight D. Eisenhower and the School Desegregation Crisis* (Chicago, 1981). Earl Warren's appointment and role in the *Brown* decision are discussed in Leo Katchen, *Earl Warren* (New York, 1967); Jack Harrison Pollack, *Earl Warren* (Englewood Cliffs, N.J., 1979); John D. Weaver, *Warren* (Boston, 1967), and the Chief Justice's own *The Memoirs of Earl Warren* (Garden City, N.Y., 1977).

The Southern response to court-ordered desegregation is covered in a multitude of studies. Among the best of these are Harry Ashmore, *The Negro and the Schools* (Chapel Hill, 1954); William Bagwell, *School Desegregation in the Carolinas* (Columbia, SC, 1972); Numan V. Bartley, *The Rise of Massive Resistance: Race and Politics in the South during the 1950's* (Baton Rouge, 1969) and "Looking Back at Little Rock," *Arkansas Historical Quarterly* 25 (1966):101–116; Robbins L. Gates, *The Making of Massive Resistance* (Chapel Hill, 1962); Morton Inger, *Politics and Reality in an American City: The New Orleans School Crisis of 1960* (New York, 1969); Neil McMillen, *The Citizens' Council: Organized Resistance to the Second Reconstruction, 1954–64* (Urbana, Ill., 1981); Benjamin Muse, *Ten Years of Prelude: The Story of Integration since the Supreme Court's 1954 Decision* (New York, 1964); I.A. Newby, *Challenge to the Court* (Baton Rouge, La., 1967); Bob Smith, *They Closed Their Schools* (Chapel Hill, N.C., 1965); J. Harvie Wilkinson III, *Harry Byrd and the Changing Face of Virginia Politics, 1945–1966* (Charlottesville, 1968); and C. Vann Woodward, *The Strange Career of Jim Crow*, 3rd rev. ed. (New York, 1974). Personal accounts include Omer Carmichael and Weldon Jones, *The Louisville Story* (New York, 1957), Martin Luther King, Jr., *Stride Toward Freedom: The Montgomery Boycott* (New York, 1958); and, for the Little Rock crisis, Virgil T. Blossom, *It Has Happened Here* (New York, 1959); Orval Faubus,

Down From the Hills (Little Rock, 1980); and Brooks Hays, *A Southern Moderate Speaks* (Chapel Hill, N.C., 1959). For a comparison with school integration problems in the North, see Diane Ravitch, *The Great School Wars: New York City, 1805–1973* (New York, 1974). For the role of the Justice Department and the FBI in integration matters, see John T. Elliff, "Aspects of Federal Civil Rights Enforcement: The Justice Department and the FBI, 1939–1964," *Perspectives in American History* 5 (1971):605–673. Administration viewpoints are expressed in Herbert Brownell, Jr., "Protecting Civil Rights," *Chicago Bar Record* 39 (1957):55–59; and Warren Olney III, "A Government Lawyer Looks at Little Rock," *California Law Review* 45 (1957): 516–23. Major analyses of the impact of Southern federal judges, including Eisenhower appointees, on the integration movement are Jack Bass, *Unlikely Heroes* (New York, 1981); J.W. Peltason, *Fifty-Eight Lonely Men* (Urbana, Ill., 1961); and Frank T. Read and Lucy S. McGough, *Let Them Be Judged* (Metischen, N.Y., 1978).

A similarly growing literature is accumulating on the subjects of civil rights legislation, black voting rights, and the political impact of black voting. The best overview of the entire subject of federal voting rights legislation and its modern history is Stephen F. Lawson, *Black Ballots: Voting Rights in the South, 1944–1969* (New York, 1976). The relationship between black political power and Southern judicial behavior is examined in Charles V. Hamilton, *The Bench and the Ballot: Southern Federal Judges and Black Voters* (New York, 1973). An early skirmish in the Southern voting rights struggle is described in Darlene Clark Hine, *Black Victory: The Rise and Fall of the White Primary in Texas* (Milwood, N.Y., 1979). The major accounts of the development of federal legislation in the 1950s are J.W. Anderson, *Eisenhower, Brownell, and the Congress* (Birmingham, Ala., 1964), which recounts maneuvering on the civil rights bill in 1956; and Daniel M. Berman, *A Bill Becomes a Law: The Civil Rights Act of 1960* (New York, 1962). Lyndon Johnson's role in shaping the final version of the 1957 Civil Rights Act is discussed in Merle Miller, *Lyndon* (New York, 1980).

The violence against blacks which stimulated official interest in voting rights protections is recounted in Jack Mendelsohn, *The Martyrs* (New York, 1966). Accounts of federal enforcement of voting rights law are contained in Leon Friedman, ed., *Southern Justice* (New York, 1965); and Allan Lichtman, "The Federal Assault Against Voting Discrimination in the Deep South, 1957–1967," *Journal of Negro History* 54 (1969):346–67. For perspectives on the U.S. Commission on Civil Rights, see Foster Rhea Dulles, *The Civil Rights Commission, 1957–1965* (East Lansing, Mich., 1968); Wallace Mendelson, *Discrimination* (Englewood Cliffs, N.J., 1962); and Robert G. Storey, "The Report of the Commission on Civil Rights," *American Bar Association Journal* 46 (1960):39–42, 106–108. Statistics and interpretation of the impact of black voting in presidential elections in the late 1940s through the 1950s can be found in Henry Lee Moon, *Balance of Power: The Negro Vote* (Garden City, N.Y., 1948); George H. Gallup, ed., *The Gallup Poll: Public Opinion, 1935–1971,*3 vols. (New York, 1972); Everett Carll Ladd, Jr., and Charles D. Hadley, *Transformations of the American Party System: Political Coalitions from the New Deal to the 1970s* (New York, 1975); and Charles A.H. Thomson and Frances M. Shatuck, *The 1956 Presidential Campaign* (Washington, D.C., 1960). Also of value are Moon's post-election analyses in the NAACP's *The Crisis,* but his figures must be compared with more cautious estimates from the other sources listed.

The best monograph on the emergence of the Greensboro sit-in of 1960 and its influence on the Second Reconstruction is William H. Chafe, *Civilities and Civil Rights: Greensboro, North Carolina, and the Black Struggle for Freedom* (New York, 1980). Materials recounting the 1960 election and the role of race in it include Theodore C. Sorenson, *Kennedy* (New York, 1965) and "Election of 1960" in Arthur M. Schlesinger, Jr., and Fred L. Israel, eds., *The Coming to Power: Critical Presidential Elections in American History* (New York, 1972), 437–57; Schlesinger's own *A Thousand Days: John F. Kennedy in the White House* (Boston, 1965) and *Robert Kennedy and His Times* (New York, 1978); and Theodore H. White, *The Making of the President, 1960* (New York, 1961). Assessments of the impact of black political participation are Edward S. Greenberg, ed., *Black Politics* (New York, 1959); William R. Keech, *The Impact of Negro Voting* (Chicago, 1968); Pat Watters and Reese Cleghorn, *Climbing Jacobs Ladder: The Arrival of Negroes in Southern Politics* (New York, 1967); and Frederic M. Wirt, *Politics of Southern Equality* (Chicago, 1970).

Index

Twentieth-Century America Series
DEWEY W. GRANTHAM, GENERAL EDITOR

Each volume in this series focuses on some aspects of the politics of social change in recent American history, utlizing new approaches to clarify the response of Americans to the dislocating forces of our own day — economic, technological, racial, demographic, and administrative.

THE UNIVERSITY OF TENNESSEE PRESS: KNOXVILLE